Praise for Sta

This is the story of a daughte search for her ancestors while als being an account of her discoveries about this large enterprising immigrant Jewish family (milliners, jewelers, general store merchants) that helped to build the Seattle we know today. Karen I. Treiger enriches her pages by setting family members in the historical context of time and place (from Eastern Europe to Seattle and Portland). Her concern to learn from her forebears' difficulties and tragedies as well as from their business and personal successes and happiness make her family history an engaging and meaningful read.

— Priscilla Long, author of *Fire and Stone: Where Do We Come From? What Are We? Where Are We Going*

Karen Treiger has woven a rich Pacific Northwest tapestry of family memories-recalled, researched and reimagined. Writing this book leaves her mark on history and becomes a vital link between the past and the future. We all have roots, and her story will lead you to wonder about your own.

— Steve Steinberg, author of award-winning books on baseball history (great grandson of Chayim Leib and Chaya Tsivia Steinberg)

In this captivating relatable memoir, Treiger honors her father's memory through her deep research and vivid portraits of five ancestral families. As she describes their lives, she offers a unique and panoramic view of early Seattle and the growth of its Jewish community. Her voice as an explorer is what distinguishes these stories. She is wonderfully determined: She dives into archives, bikes to sites of past family businesses, and knocks on doors of houses where relatives lived. Her discoveries lead her to vulnerable and insightful inner work. As she looks through the window of past generations, she also sees a mirror –to view deeper truths and urgent questions about her own life. Readers of this memorable book will be moved to consider the lessons of the past in the way that she did."

— Barbara Mackoff, author *The Inner Work of Leaders and Growing a Girl.*

It's a rare combination when a thorough and thoughtful researcher is also a gifted writer. Karen Treiger expertly melds these two skills to create a compelling narrative, telling the story of the Pacific Northwest through the meticulously researched and lovingly rendered stories of her own family history. We are taken deep into the past of many well-known landmarks as this quintessential American success story plays out across the various members of Treiger's family. A fantastic read!

— David Naggar

Karen Treiger's breezy history of five branches of her family gives vivid insight into the building of Seattle and its Jewish history from the 1870s to the mid twentieth century. Treiger herself is a character, tracing her explorations and research and providing a how-to illustration for doing family history. The stories, both extraordinary and mundane, are told with an eye on the context of the times and places. This is no narrowly focused picture of one family's experiences, rather it is well worth reading for anyone interested in the bigger picture of Seattle's development.

— Howard Droker, Co-Author of *Family of Strangers: Building Jewish Communities in Washington State*

My cousin Karen Treiger has researched and written a wonderful history of our shared and extended family. I am moved as she shares the stories and challenges facing the wave of immigration in the 19th and early 20th centuries – a story so central to the American Dream. It is the story of hard-working immigrants seeking the opportunity for a better life in the new world; of overcoming obstacles, physical as well as societal, and leveraging their cultural strengths to succeed.

Not every story has a happy ending. Still, Karen highlights the accomplishments our ancestors provided to the city of Seattle. Each generation left the world better than they found it and instilled an amazing work ethic and desire to excel in their children – extending to the current sixth generation. An anecdote here, or a quote there, brings forth a flood of memories and emotion. On behalf of descendants across America, thank you for bringing forth this book.

— Steven Goldfarb, President, Alvin Goldfarb Jewelers and 5th generation descendant of Paul and Jenny Singerman

Although I knew several individuals from Karen's five families, my focus is on her father, Irwin. Irwin and I were classmates at Seattle's Garfield High School where I worked on the school newspaper, The Messenger, with Irwin as Editor. We later crossed paths at the Seattle Symphony; at the 1962 Seattle World's Fair (founded in part by my father when he was on the Seattle City Council and where I managed an exhibit for the imminent New York World's Fair 1964-1965); and Bogel and Gates where my boss, a senior member of that eminent law firm, later became president of MacMillan-Bloedel, Canada's largest forest products company, with me as Assistant to the President. Author Karen notes in her Preface that her father was a source of "dry wit . . .laughter. . . and a "moral compass." I cite those same qualities as Irwin Treiger grew and moved through legal, promotional, fund-raising, department store experience and other roles in the Pacific Northwest. At Garfield, he eagerly but quietly moved into writing, editing and committee roles, while I was immersed in athletic and political activity.

Irwin's and my high school years emerged from separate backgrounds, despite the fact we were both "Central Area" kids: I was raised in Denny-Blaine, with its over-whelming views of Lake Washington and Mt. Rainier; attended Sunday School at Epiphany Parish (Episcopalian), and scrambled across the playground at hilltop Madrona Grade School; Irwin attended Washington Middle School, several blocks from Thrifty's, his family's hardware and 10 Cent store near the trolley lines that aimed downtown. While I was swimming and biking among the hills of Denny-Blaine, Irwin was writing poetry and becoming acquainted with Seattle characters, such as a chimney sweep and his stovepipe hat, corn cob pipe and summer shorts, and attending Bikur Cholim Synagogue. Irwin's Ukrainian ancestors found opportunity by boarding old ships, first to New York, then on rattling Canadian railcars across the continent to Vancouver, B.C. The Rochesters also crossed the Atlantic Ocean, first settling on the rich land of Northern Neck Virginia, then boarding the rails to Portland and Seattle.

Clarion calls for both families were celebrations in a raw, new land: Portland, Oregon's 1905 Lewis & Clark's Centennial and the 1909 Alaska-Yukon-Pacific (AYP), a "world's fair" in Seattle. Irwin's family, starting as peddlars and fishmongers, entered schools and colleges such as Reed (Portland, OR), Portland Hebrew School and the University of Washington

(Seattle, WA). Originally named Yisroel Aryeh, Irwin was born on September 10, 1934, the first night of Rosh Hashanah in the Jewish New Year. Irwin's life, a bundle of ancestors, education and travel, exemplifies the brusque new cities of the Pacific Northwest, with their surrounding peaks, great and small rivers and the hundreds of deep ports for products to the world. Irwin Treiger, my high school classmate, took advantage of it all. And this grand setting allowed two boys, born in 1934, to attend school, laugh out loud and raise families within the same neighborhood.

— Junius Rochester, Historian; Author of eight books.

Standing on the Crack

The Legacy Of Five Jewish Families From Seattle's Vibrant Gilded Age

coffeetownpress
SEATTLE, WA

coffeetownpress

Coffeetown Press published by Epicenter Press

Epicenter Press
6524 NE 181st St. Suite 2
Kenmore, WA 98028.
www.Epicenterpress.com
www.Coffeetownpress.com
www.Camelpress.com

For more information go to: www.epicenterpress.com
www.karentreiger.com

Standing on the Crack: Legacy of Five Jewish
Families from Seattle's Gilded Age

ISBN: 9781684924004 (trade paper)
ISBN: 9781684924011 (ebook)
LOC: 2025932315

Table of Contents

To those who came before me. I am humbled and grateful.

Acknowledgments

I am deeply grateful to all those that helped me reach this point.

I am grateful to my father for saving all those photos and scraps of paper and my mother for answering my endless questions about the family.

I am grateful to my ancestors who decided to leave their homes in Europe and travel across an ocean and a continent to settle in the Pacific Northwest.

I am grateful to my nephew Avraham Treiger for interviewing my dad and his cousins, Shim (Mark) Elyn and Sheldon Steinberg so many years ago. I am also grateful to my daughter Shoshana Goldberg for interviewing my parents years ago.

I want to thank all those that sat for interviews with the author for this book, including, my mom, Betty Lou Treiger, my aunt, Jackie Goldfarb, Victor Alhadeff, Norman Rice, Henry Aaronson, and my dear cousin, Shim (Mark) Elyn.

My spouse, Shlomo Goldberg, is a huge part of my life story and is part of my journey in researching and crafting this book. Shlomo, thank you for your love and support.

I want to thank Rudy Ramos for his endless patience as we created the maps and family trees for this book. An additional thank you to Rudy for formatting the print and e-book and making it look fantastic.

Thanks to Nathan Chu for his expert copy editing and proof-reading.

Finally, a huge thank you goes to my friend and consultant, Jennifer McCord. Jennifer has taught me everything I know about publishing a book and has guided me now for some 10 years through my transition from attorney to author. It was Jennifer who embraced the book and agreed to publish it through Epicenter Press. I am forever indebted to you.

"We live as long as memories about us live."

Penny Walters

"What you leave behind is not
what is engraved in stone monuments
but what is woven into the lives of others."

Virginia Woolf, *Modern Fiction*

PREFACE

My father, Irwin Treiger, died on October 20, 2013. He was my touchstone, my rock. I wanted so desperately to hold onto the security that emanated from him, the love I could always count on. I faltered as I walked on the balance beam of daily existence. Without my father's shining presence, I was left in the darkness, haunted by the existential questions of where I came from and where was I going? This inner conflict over meaning and identity led me to the watering hole of history.

About a year after my father died, I pulled out files that had gathered layers of dust. These old photos and papers were waiting for my father to write the family history that he promised us after his retirement. He never retired. I blew the dust away and found a treasure trove. I stared at the photos and documents, believing somehow that they would bring me closer to my father.

Because the search begins with me, I challenged myself to explore why my father's death led me to this historical exploration. As with many, my relationship with my family changed over time. When I was a teenager, I resented always being asked whether I was the daughter of Betty Lou and Irwin or Louis's (my older brother) sister, or Jack Friedlander or Rose Treiger's granddaughter.

Yes, I would sigh in response. I got sick of it all. I went 3,000 miles away, attending Barnard College in New York City. No one in that school knew me and no one knew my family. It provided a four-year opportunity for me to mature and find my own sense of purpose and self.

By the time I graduated, I was proud to be introduced as the daughter of, or the granddaughter of, or the sister of. My first job out of college was working as a Legislative Assistant for Senator Slade Gorton in Washington, D.C. I'd be lying if I said that my family connections – Treiger and Friedlander – had nothing to do with getting that job. Then after law school, I returned to Seattle and entered the legal community. I wore the Treiger name with pride and purpose. When I was asked, "are you related to Irwin Treiger?" or "are you related to Louis Treiger?" I proudly answered, "yes indeed."

With my father's death, everything changed again. I felt a wish to return to childhood and a desire to sit and ask him all of my unanswered questions – about the family, about his experience, about life, about myself. I missed his wise counsel, his dry wit, his laughter, his moral compass, and mostly, his embracing hugs that always filled the empty spots in my soul.

So I opened those dusty files from my father and began.

I spent hours combing through the documents and photos of grandparents, great-grandparents, uncles, aunts, and cousins. Those photos transported me, providing a window into the lives of people, who either I never knew, or I knew, but not in the way the photos portrayed them. As I time-traveled with these black and white and sepia toned photos, some cracked from age, some beautifully framed, my mind opened in wonder. How have these people affected my life? What happened in the 150 years before my birth to form the unique person that is me? It wasn't just the DNA they passed down, it was also their courage, their resilience, their determination.

After combing through these files, my ancestors were firmly a part of my life. I heard them asking me not to forget them, not to allow the final nail to be hammered into their coffins. In my dreams, they urged me to keep one nail out, and if you learn about our lives and tell our stories, then we live on.

Is this why so many people are interested in genealogy? Ancestry.com, the largest database of genealogical information, has three million paying subscribers, and it seems like everyone I know is spitting into a vial and sending it to Ancestry or 23 and Me to find out what their DNA shows and to locate long lost cousins. There are genealogy societies in every major city, with thousands of members. Could looking backwards be another way of looking deeper into ourselves? And what do we hope to find?

This widespread interest in genealogy tells me that I am not the only one interested in digging into my family history, and as I go on this journey, I hope to inspire you and give you a road map to delve into your own family history.

"In personalizing the past," Penny Walters explains, "genealogy accounts for the self in the present, signifies existence and provides meaning... It could perhaps be concluded that, '[f]amily history research offers the reflective space to think about our own behavior, personality and expectations based upon those who went before.'"[1]

As I looked into the past, I began to recognize similarities between myself and my ancestors. Many of my ancestors involved themselves in the Jewish and civic community of Seattle – I see that perhaps it was my fate to grow into a community leader. The desire to make a difference burns inside me and won't let up. It's part of my family legacy.

My ancestors had this same fire. They came to America with nothing in their pockets and most succeeded beyond their wildest dreams. These early immigrants and their children shaped and influenced the civic, business, and Jewish Seattle I live in today. The value of leadership has been passed through the generations down to me and onto my children.

The tale of my family involves five separate links in the chain. Each family, Singerman, Staadecker, Friedlander, Steinberg, and Treiger, has a unique, colorful, and gripping past. They were part of a mass migration from Central and Eastern Europe in the nineteenth and twentieth centuries to the United States. They came to escape persecution, seek family and business opportunities and find a better life for their children. Though they encountered antisemitism and struggled to find their place, they forged ahead with a new life in a new land. What they found differed for each; their stories are distinct and yet universal.

This book tells each family's story and how the five strands came together on a sunny day – the 18th of August, 1957, when my parents were married. That's where East met West, where Temple De Hirsch met Bikur Cholim;[2] where a poor, smart guy married a cool, gorgeous, rich woman. Being the child of Betty Lou (Friedlander) Treiger, the great-granddaughter of Paul

Me and Steven Goldfarb outside Pioneer Association building (Goldfarb Collection).

Singerman, I firmly lay claim to my status as a fifth generation Seattleite. I wear this as a badge of honor, though I did nothing to earn it.

With this personal history, I took the step of joining the Washington State Pioneer Association.[3] To join as a lineal descendant one must have an ancestor who lived in Washington Territory before it became a State on November 11, 1889. I qualified.

Strangely, I agree with Penny Walters – knowing my ancestry grounds me in time and space. I feel more centered and understand better how I fit into my family and the world. This grounded feeling fills me with optimism because as I learned about those that came before me, I gained faith that those after me will be resilient, fascinating, involved members of the civic and Jewish communities.

The stories of these five families echo the stories of many immigrant families, leaving home to find opportunity and a new life. Imagine how scared they must have been to come to a strange land with a different language. They often began their sojourns as peddlers or manual laborers[4], but they dreamed of the promise of a new land for their children and grandchildren.

Because these are my family's stories, this book does not focus on the lives of indigenous people, the Duwamish Tribes, who inhabited the land we now call Seattle before white settlers arrived in the 1850s. Further, it doesn't emphasize other immigrants that came to Seattle to settle or for work opportunities, such as people from Asia, especially China and Japan. Finally, except for the concept of red-lining, this book does not address the discrimination which affected and continues to affect all non-white peoples, especially those in the Black community.

Sadly, in many ways Seattle is an example of how non-white peoples were excluded from the story of upward mobility, and we who live here still feel with the consequences of those racial policies. You can find an discussion of some of these issues in Megan Asaka's 2022 book, *Seattle from the Margins: Exclusion, Erasure, and the Making of a Pacific Coast City.*[5]

Each of us has a family story to tell and I encourage you to use this collection of stories as a guide to explore your own family. Some stories contain more history, while others contain more personal anecdotes. Some were easier to write and others harder – especially the section about my parents.

But how best to begin? I say, start by being curious about yourself. Please use this book to reflect on your own life. It will deepen the experience and make it more meaningful. In Appendix A, you will find a list on how to get started.

I utilized many tools to put together the family histories and stories you will read. Each one led to a new discovery and an understanding of what my ancestors experienced. They came from distant lands and learned a new language and a new culture. A common theme to all these families is their drive to be to work hard and be "present" in all their endeavors. "Standing on the crack" is family code for not being distracted from what is most important and being ready when opportunity presents itself.

Upon arrival, decisions were made – to stay, to go, to marry or not, to have children or not, to do this or that to put bread on the family table, to be selfish or generous, to love wholeheartedly or not. Themes repeat generation after generation – someone isn't good enough; someone isn't rich enough; someone isn't smart enough; someone isn't Jewish enough. Yet, each of these five families matured and flourished, ultimately, strangely, bizarrely leading to me living in the same city that Paul Singerman adopted as his own in 1874.

Join me on this journey into myself. My hope is that you will find something of yourself along the way.

CHAPTER 1

SINGERMAN FAMILY

I entered "Singerman" into the Seattle Public Library online search bar and hit enter. What came up changed everything.

The search bar read:

Manuscript History of Seattle's First Department Store, Embracing San Francisco Store, Toklas & Singerman, MacDougall & Southwick, Costello, Gilbert S.

Format: Book
Year: 1947
Availability: In-library use only

What the hell? I thought to myself. *Is* it possible that there is a book all about Paul Singerman and the store he built? I felt that I had just won a lottery.

The next day, I went downtown to the Seattle Public Library on 5th Avenue, between Spring and Madison. I approached the information desk and showed them the words I had copied onto a piece of paper.

"Can you tell me where I can find this book?" I inquired.

"Let me check," the librarian said. A few seconds later, she told me, "that's on the 10th floor, in the Seattle collection."

"Thanks," I said as I almost ran to the elevators.

Exiting the elevator, I found a long desk with two computer screens and a librarian sitting on the other side.

"I'm looking for this book and was wondering if you can help me find it?"

Singerman Family Tree

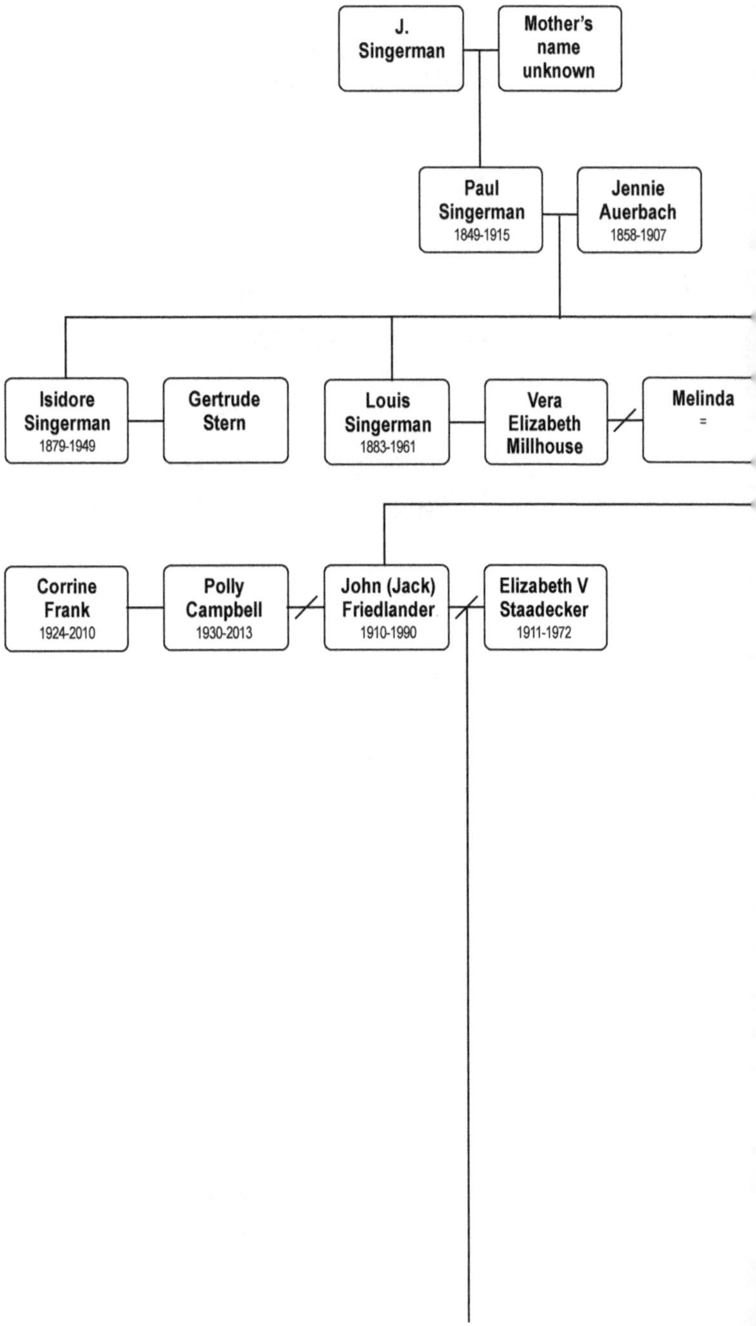

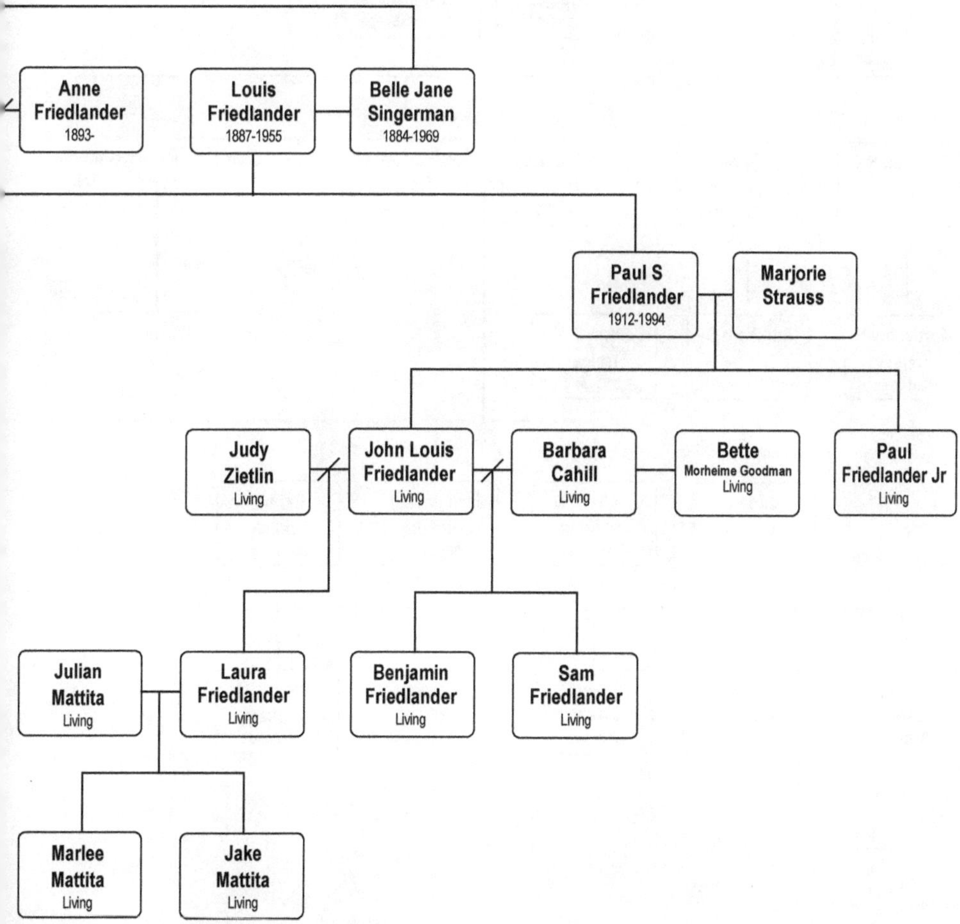
Anne Friedlander 1893-
Louis Friedlander 1887-1955
Belle Jane Singerman 1884-1969
Paul S Friedlander 1912-1994
Marjorie Strauss
Judy Zietlin Living
John Louis Friedlander Living
Barbara Cahill Living
Bette Morheime Goodman Living
Paul Friedlander Jr Living
Julian Mattita Living
Laura Friedlander Living
Benjamin Friedlander Living
Sam Friedlander Living
Marlee Mattita Living
Jake Mattita Living

Singerman Family Tree, continued

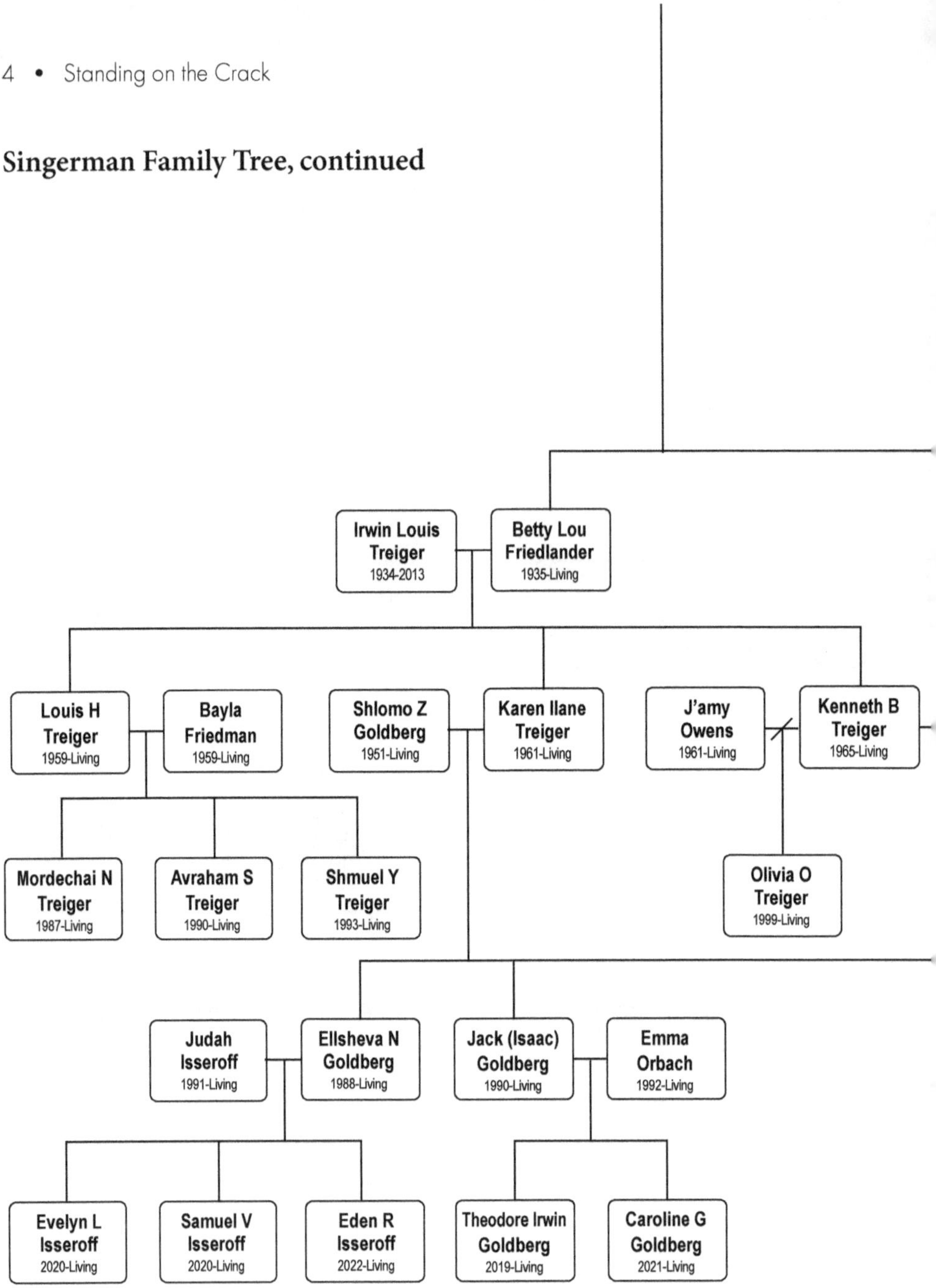

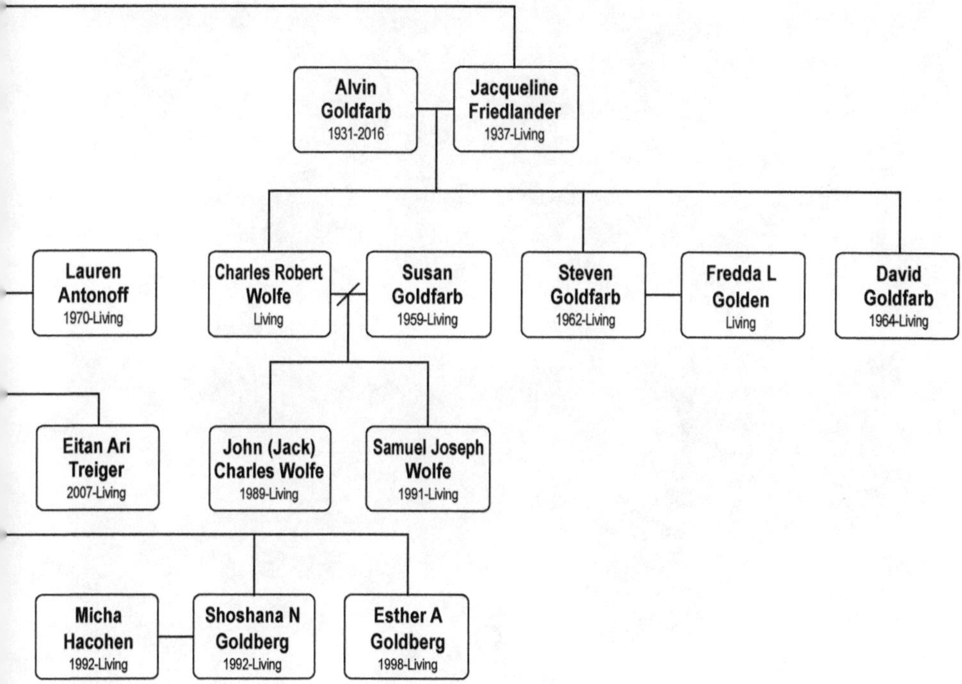
Alvin Goldfarb 1931-2016
Jacqueline Friedlander 1937-Living
Lauren Antonoff 1970-Living
Charles Robert Wolfe Living
Susan Goldfarb 1959-Living
Steven Goldfarb 1962-Living
Fredda L Golden Living
David Goldfarb 1964-Living
Eitan Ari Treiger 2007-Living
John (Jack) Charles Wolfe 1989-Living
Samuel Joseph Wolfe 1991-Living
Micha Hacohen 1992-Living
Shoshana N Goldberg 1992-Living
Esther A Goldberg 1998-Living

Singerman Map – Stores

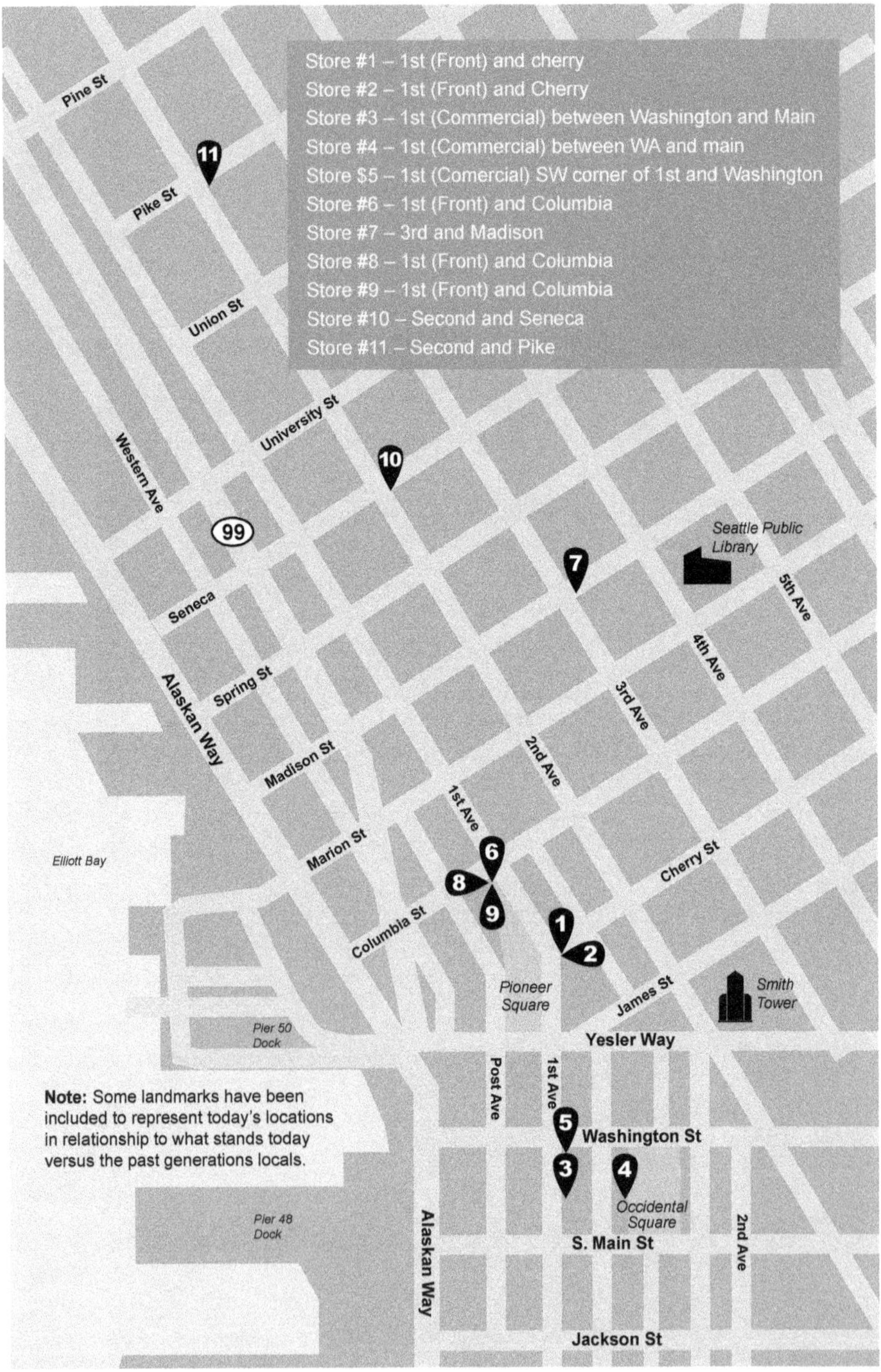

Singerman Map – Homes

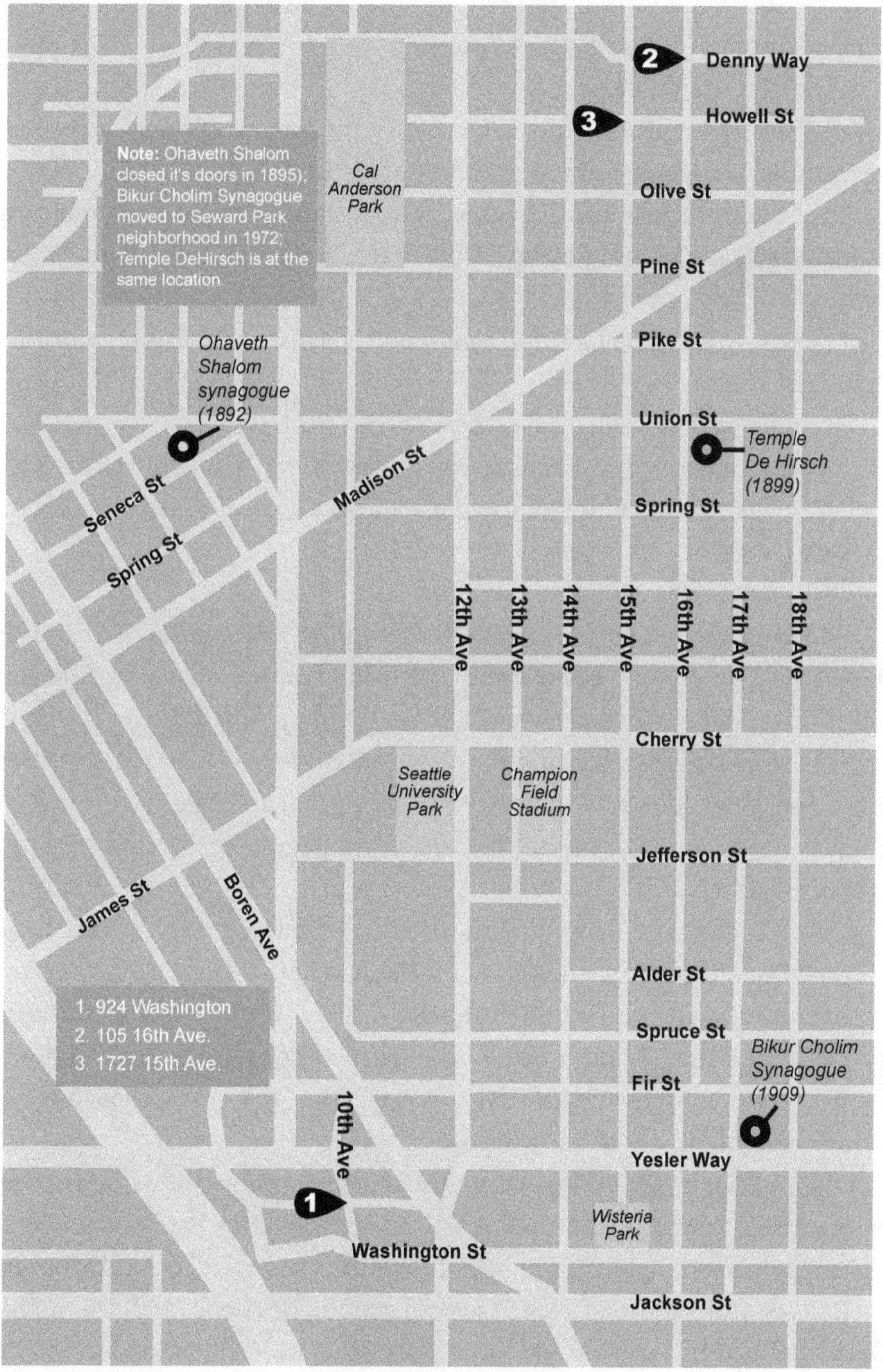

"Yes," she nodded as she looked at my scribbles. "But before I can give you this manuscript," she continued, "you must give me your driver's license. I will hold it until you return it."

"Ok," I stuttered, fishing for my license.

She stored my license in the drawer of the long, imposing desk, took her bundle of keys, nodded at me and quietly said, "follow me."

Obediently, I followed her down a few stairs to a glass case. Slowly unlocking it, she looked for the designated file, and carefully pulling out a brown file folder, she handed it to me.

"Here you go," she said. "You can't leave this floor with this manuscript, it's one of a kind."

"Can I make copies?" I asked hesitantly.

"Yes, we have a copy machine, or you can scan pages to a flash drive."

"OK, thanks." Thinking of the *The Da Vinci Code*, I asked: "Do I have to wear gloves or something to touch the pages?"

"No, that is not necessary," she said.

Holding my breath, I opened the folder, and became instantly absorbed in the pages before me. I couldn't believe what I found. This sixty-seven page manuscript, written in 1945, provided me an in-depth history of Paul Singerman and the eleven stores he ran in Seattle between 1874 and 1915. This rare manuscript was a prize and I hadn't even gone to a far-away land to find it. I made a copy, page by page, and took my treasure home.

The story Gilbert Costello writes in these pages opened my heart and mind to my great-great grandparents, Paul and Jenny Singerman and the pioneer town that was Seattle in the late 1800's. Reading this manuscript propelled me into action. I began to look further into the archives of the *Seattle Times* and the *Seattle Post-Intelligencer* (PI). I searched out old photos and books about early Seattle.

Subscribing to the online *Seattle Times* granted me access to the archives where I found amazing old photos, articles, and ads from Paul's stores. I also discovered new things in the University of Washington Archive and Museum of History and Industry's (MOHAI) collection. The books I chose to read about Seattle's history told the same story from different perspectives: *The*

Story of Seattle[6] written by Roberta Fry Watt, Arthur Denny's granddaughter; *History of Seattle*[7] by Clarence Bagley; *Sons of the Profits*[8] by William Speidel; *Seattle Past to Present*[9] by Roger Sale; and *Seattle at the Margins: Exclusion, Erasure, and the Making of a Pacific Coast City*[10] by Megan Aska. Each book gave me a different view on the place I call home.

The Singerman's story was just beyond my doorstep. Gilbert Costello became my tour guide as I set out on my bike one crisp April morning. I rode down to Pioneer Square, the oldest part of Seattle. I was determined to find the sites for all eleven stores.

However, between Seattle's Great Fire in 1889 and "modernization," all the old buildings that housed Paul's merchandise are gone. Still, I yearned to find some remnant and hoped that my great-great grandfather Paul would speak to me in the eerie emptiness. Empty because the streets and shops were abandoned, some shops even boarded up. Empty because it was April of 2020, and the COVID-19 pandemic was raging. The governor had ordered all shops and office buildings shuttered and told us all to "stay home."

Detour To Raczki, Poland

Though I'm excited to take you on my journey to the heart of early Seattle, the place our story begins isn't accessible by bike. Paul Singerman was born in Raczki, Gubernia Swalki[11] on February 9, 1849.[12] It lies not far from the current Polish-Lithuanian border, 100 kilometers north of Bialystok, Poland.[13]

Costello's manuscript and Bagley's *History of Seattle* state that Paul was from "Poland, Russia." Not very specific. I searched the Ancestry.com database and found a passport application that listed the name of his birth town. Because passport applications are completed by the applicants themselves, it's a perfect place to unearth critical information. That application was filled out by Paul when he was 54 years old. He listed "Ratzk, Gubernia, Suwalki, Russia, Poland" as his place of birth. With this information, the website JewishGen furnished a wonderful surprise – the existence of a *Yizkor* book from the Suwalk region. *Yizkor* books are memorial books written by those who survived the Holocaust

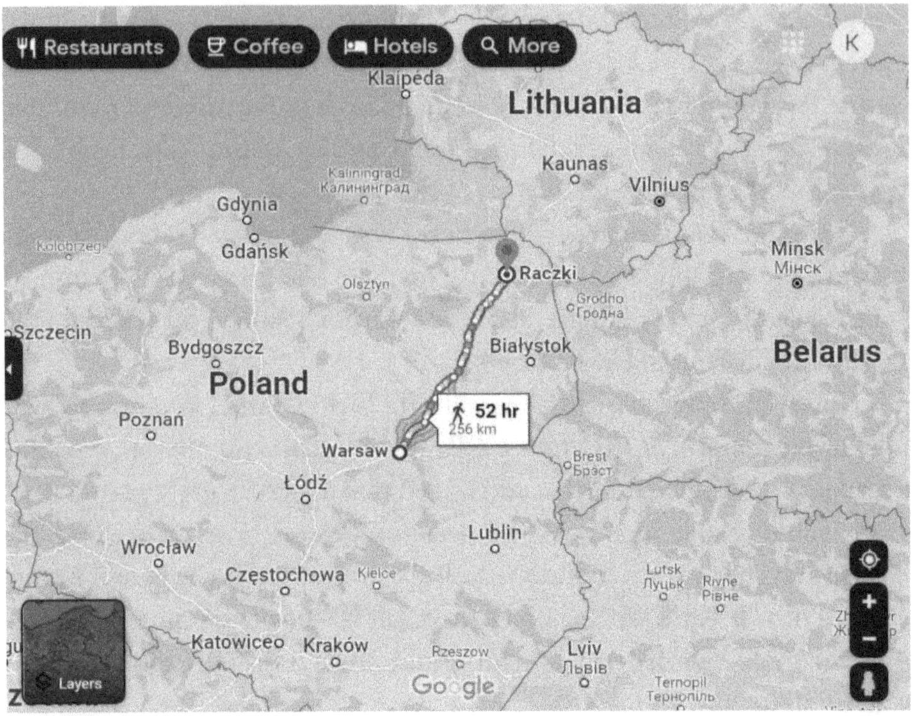

Google map Razcki

from a particular town or region. Amazon informed me that there was an English translation of the Suwalk *Yizkor* Book. I ordered it.

"The town of Ratzk [Raczki in Polish] bears the name of the Ratzkevitshk family which received permission to buy land there in 1507," states the Memorial Book of Suwalk.[14] This region of Poland suffered a two-year famine around 1847, leading many to emigrate to the United States.[15] In 1856, Raczki was a majority Jewish town with 1,739 Jews.[16] The Jews of this town were mostly religiously observant and lived there until World War II. In 1941 the Nazis conquered the territory and threw the Jews out, murdering any that dared to remain.[17]

The 1850's was a decade of economic stagnation in the Suwalk region, and a series of fires destroyed the town of Raczki, with the residents rebuilding each time.[18] Perhaps Paul's early experience with the cycle of destruction and rebuilding that comes with fires, provided crucial training for 1889, when his sixth mercantile store was incinerated.

I know little about the family Paul left behind. His father was listed on one of his passport applications as J. Singerman and Paul's Last Will and Testament left bequests to his "two sisters in Russia." I know Paul's mother was blind at the end of her life and lived until at least 1903, when Paul visited her.[19] But that's all the information I could find.

Jewish emigration from the Suwalk region increased after an 1863 Polish uprising against the Russians. This uprising led to the imposition of a new harsh tax on the Jews of Raczki.[20] Many Jews said "enough is enough" and skipped town for more welcoming locations. At the age of 18, Paul left with them, sailing across the Atlantic on the ship Nebraska, landing in 1867 in New York harbor.[21]

When Paul arrived in New York, he assuredly found *Landsmen*, people who had immigrated from the same area of Europe. Jews from Raczki were among "the founders of the first congregation of Russian Jews in New York in 1852."[22] Three years later, in 1870, he arrived in Santa Cruz, California.[23]

My grandfather, Jack Friedlander, who we call Papa Jack, said that Paul, traveled to California by covered wagon.[24] I was skeptical because the cross-continental railroad was completed in 1869,[25] but I found corroboration in Bagley's *History of Seattle*. Paul made "his way across the plains to California." Bagley writes "he settled at Santa Cruz where he engaged in merchandizing."[26] Bagley's description of Paul's work as "merchandizing" was a fancy name for peddling. Papa Jack said that Paul "was peddling house to house, with a knapsack like the old-timers did."[27] This humble beginning was common among Eastern European Jewish immigrants.[28]

Most often Jewish immigrants were set up by Jewish merchants in town with packs filled with household goods to sell and a route to follow. To be a successful peddler, one had to learn some basic English and have a friendly personality. Those that succeeded were natural salesmen and were willing to knock on any door to present their wares. Most new immigrants who peddled believed that it was a short-term profession, a way to save enough to open their own retail store.[29]

Sometime over the next few years, Paul left Santa Cruz and traveled seventy-five miles north to the largest city on the West Coast, San Francisco, with a census population of 149,473. San Francisco had a Jewish community of 16,000 with seven Synagogues. It was in San Francisco's Jewish community that Paul met his business partners.

Many stories circulate in our family about Paul's primary business partner, Ferdinand Toklas. He was the father of Alice B. Toklas[30] who, together with her partner Gertrude Stein, took Paris by storm in the early twentieth century and was the creator of the Hashish Fudge recipe (marijuana brownies).[31] Since the company was called Toklas & Singerman, I erroneously believed that Ferdinand and Paul were the only original partners.

"In 1875," the Jewish Museum of the American West states, "Ferdinand Toklas created a partnership with Paul Singerman and Hyman Auerbach. They opened a store in Seattle, Washington on Front Street near Cherry."[32]

When I read this my heart skipped a beat. Auerbach – that was the birth name of my great-great grandmother Jenny. I had wondered how Paul met Jenny and where she was from. A careful reading of Papa Jack's 1975 interview with the University of Washington Jewish Archive informed me that Jenny was Hyman's sister.

The story begins, according to Papa Jack, when "[o]ne day the partner [Hyman Auerbach] said 'I have a sister in Germany, and I would like you to marry her.' My great great-grandfather said, 'get a picture of her.'

This all took time and when the picture came, Paul said he would marry her, and then he sent over the money for her to come.

When she came, she took one look at him and didn't want to marry him. My mother told me all this – Jenny wanted to go back home but she was embarrassed to go back and say she didn't get married, and I don't think there were the finances to send her back anyhow... . So they were married and they were very happy.[33]

In 1874, Ferdinand Toklas and Hyman Auerbach loaded Paul and $2,000 worth of merchandise ($55,000 in today's dollars) [34] on a ship and sent him up to Seattle to test the market. And thus, our time in Seattle commenced.

FIRST STOP: FRONT & CHERRY – 1874

I started my bike tour at the center of old Seattle – 1st and Yesler. This is where Paul Singerman arrived in 1874. Young Paul was short, with broad shoulders and a balding head. His round face was accented by sharp, determined eyes. I found two photos of Paul and both were in newspaper articles.

Paul Singerman – Seattle Times Nov. 22, 1903

What Paul found was a small town with fewer than 1,500 US Census-counted residents,[35] with approximately fifty Jews.[36] Seattle was so young and rugged that coal lighting on the streets had just been introduced.[37] Henry Yesler's sawmill was at the center of town, located at the base of Yesler Way, down by the waterfront for easy shipping.

Seattle didn't have much going on - there were a few hotels, a Territorial University,[38] a bank,[39] saloons, brothels, churches, general stores, cobblers, breweries, barber shops, a school, and homes.[40] Back then, the main road of the town (today's 1st Avenue) was a dirt path that had two different names: north of Yesler Way, it was called Front Street and south of it was Commercial. Seattle's future was murky because just one year earlier the Northwest terminus for the cross-continent railroad was announced – Tacoma. It was a harsh blow to Seattle – a city with dreams of grandeur.[41]

The day of my bike tour, the streets were empty due to COVID-19, so I had the opportunity to stand in the middle of a usually busy throughway. I looked north and south and was offered a new perspective on a familiar landscape. I noticed that 1st Avenue has a gentle curve at Yesler Street. This gentle curve was not here when Paul arrived in 1874. I knew this because I had just finished William Speidel's 1997 book *The Sons of the Profits*. In old Seattle, Speidel writes, "[t]here was a jog of about thirty feet along Yesler Way."[42] This "jog" connected the two parts of the city between Front and Commercial with a series of right angle turns. The locals called it "the Throat."[43]

Standing there in the middle of the street, I recalled that after the Great Fire of 1889, the Seattle City Council "took" a piece of Henry Yesler's property and connected the two parts of downtown, smoothing out "the Throat" with this gentle curve. Henry Yesler, who Speidel describes as a mean bastard, was furious. He called the "taking" a theft and sued the city. A settlement was reached, but, according to Speidel, Yesler was disliked even more after this episode.[44]

I biked the short block from Yesler to Cherry. According to Costello, this was the site of P. Singerman & Co.[45] I dismounted my bike and took my camera out. I stood at what was most likely the spot.[46] Today, there is a short, squat, gray structure - the Emerald City Building, built in 1905. It's sandwiched between a 7-11 and an open-air parking lot. Paul's store must have been smack in the center of town with Yesler's sawmill half a block south and the waterfront half a block east.

Costello described what he saw in a photo of this street taken by Charles Thorndike around 1874: Western Union Telegraph Company, Wusthoff Hardware Store, Masonic Hall Building, Henry Yesler's residence (behind some trees), L.S. Rowe grocery store, Nels Childberg grocery store, Boyd & Pencin, dry goods, and Frenk Plummer, cigars and tobacco.[47] Sadly, I couldn't find this photo, just this description of the photo.

I imagined the 1874 Seattle pioneers walking the dirt streets and saw in my mind's eye the horses and buggies going up and down, people stopping in the stores to buy something, standing on raised wooden sidewalks to gossip and discuss the politics of the day.

In these early years, Paul may have lived at the German House Hotel. There's a record of a W. Singerman "seller of general merchandise" living there at this time.[48] Why Paul might have been listed with the first initial "W." remains a mystery.

Business at store #1 was brisk and within a few months, Paul had sold every piece of merchandise he had schlepped up the coast.[49] He headed back to San Francisco with his cash. He reported to his partners, Ferdinand Toklas and Hyman Aurbach that Seattle was indeed an up-and-coming place with good prospects for merchants. Maybe Paul spent

Pioneer Square – 1878 (UW Special Collection, Neg. #UW5894)

1875 in San Francisco planning the opening of their new store because we don't find Paul back in Seattle until 1876. He returned with plenty of merchandise for the shelves of the newly minted San Francisco Store.

Second Stop: Front & Cherry – 1876

I didn't even have to get on my bike to visit the location of store #2. It was right next to store #1. This second store was opened in 1876 on the west side of Front Street, "just opposite Piper's Candy."[50] Paul's first newspaper ad ran on March 18, 1876, claiming the best prices in town for "Dry Goods – Clothing-Boots-Shoes-Hats-Caps-Cigars and Tobacco. And a full and good stock of Family Groceries, Crockery and Glassware."[51]

Just one year before Paul's arrival, steamship service had begun directly between Seattle and San Francisco. In 1876, the Territorial University graduated its first student - Clara McCarty. Two months later, in August of 1876, the YMCA was founded.

Business for the San Francisco Store was also brisk, and Paul outgrew store #2 in no time. The following year, 1877, the San Francisco Store moved to the other side of the Throat.

Third Stop: Commercial, Between Washington & Main – 1877

I pushed my bike south on 1st Avenue and stopped mid-block between Washington and Main, feeling instinctively that this must be the place of Store #3. There was a mural on plywood with large bold lettering: "*Wish You Were Here*." This message was of course meant for all the people who created the vibrant life that is the norm of Pioneer Square but are now missing because of the COVID-19 pandemic. But the words spoke to me of my great-great grandparents' lost world. I wished I had the opportunity to know them and to ask them all my questions.

If I had that chance, I'd want to know how hard was it to leave their families and move here alone. What were their parents like? What was it like in Razke or Germany? Were their families Jewishly observant? What was it like to live here and raise their children in a pioneer town? What language did they speak to each other? With their kids? What were their hopes and dreams? What was it like to be a Jew in Seattle in the late nineteenth century?

San Francisco Store #3, Commercial Street, between Washington and Main. (UW Special Collection, A. Curtis #32366)

Google map – Kempen, Germany

Paul and Jenny died over 110 years ago, and I'm left to find clues to their lives and thoughts in photos, documents, newspapers, and here on the street. I'm reminded that today, I'm part of their world as I search for traces of their lives and strain to hear their voices.

I paused and imagined my father there with me on 1st Avenue. I felt his love and pride. He would have loved this journey into Seattle's early years and the Singermans' lives. It's the history he never got to explore.

During the three years that store #3 was in existence, Paul and Jenny were married. Jenny came from Kempen, Prussia. The January 11, 1879 edition of the San Francisco Bulletin announced the marriage of "Paul Singerman of Seattle, Washington Territory and Jenny Auerbach of Kempen

Prussia."[52] Kempen, today called Kepro, is 124 kilometers from the border between German and the Netherlands and 41 kilometers from Dusseldorf, Germany.[53] I marvel at the risk Jenny took leaving the old country to start a new life with a man she didn't know. She didn't even have a photo.

Paul and Jenny wasted no time – their first son, Isidore, was born on October 9, 1879. They were living in a house at 924 Washington Street, just one block south of Yesler, on 10th. This was well before the iconic Smith Tower was erected in 1914, but when I visited 10th and Washington and stood on the spot where they lived, I had a spectacular view of that tower.

That spot, and that hill, was in the 1870's and 1880's known as Yesler Hill because it was "home to the city's elite classes, including its namesake, Henry Yesler, and his wife Sara Yesler."[54] As the population of Seattle grew, and people began moving up the hill, "the elites fled Yesler Hill for land tracts farther away on the outskirts of the city, selling their Victorian mansions to buyers who subdivided the properties and leased the cramped apartments."[55] The Singermans remained on Yesler Hill until 1899, when they moved to Capitol Hill.

Paul, a new father, was busy meeting the needs of a growing town. His business grew quickly. He realized it was time to move his store again. Just across the road a new building was going up, and Paul seized the opportunity.

Singerman home at 924 Washington Street - taken in 1940 , just before it was torn down. (Washington State Archive)

Fourth Stop: The Squire Opera House – 1880

By the time the San Francisco Store moved to the Squire Opera House on the East side of Commercial in 1880, the US Census recorded 3,553 Seattle residents.[56] The number of Jews had reached 100.[57] Seattle, writes Roger Sale in *Seattle, Past to Present*, had "a remarkably sophisticated economy. There were the coal and the port, there were meat packing, carpentry, and furniture manufacture, there were foundries and bakeries and breweries, retail stores, banks, law offices, doctors, all of which operated within the city and also exported to the logging towns, mining outposts and farming communities that were performing single operations and so were forced to rely on Seattle to get much of what they needed."[58]

The new Squire Opera House was Seattle's first theater and made a statement about how far this small pioneer town had come. The Seattle PI reported that the theater was "unequal to any showhouse north of San Francisco."[59] Patrons entering for a show or a civic event would pass right by Paul's store, brimming with the latest fashions.[60]

"Two of the immense storerooms there," the PI writes of the new San Francisco Store, "have been thrown, by an arched way, into one, giving them a length and breadth and front nowhere else equaled in the city."[61]

"The south store," Costello writes, "was devoted to the lines of clothing, boots and shoes, and wearing apparel, while the room to the north was given over to general lines of dry goods, fancy goods, etc."[62]

The San Francisco Store offered cotton goods, boots, shoes, and everything a miner would need for his journey. These miners weren't heading to Alaska. They were heading to the Ruby and upper Skagit streams, just north of Seattle. Gold was unearthed and extracted there some twenty years before the Alaska Gold Rush.[63]

By this time, business was booming and Paul needed some help. Ferdinand Toklas sent J.B. MacDougal up the coast from San Francisco in 1880. Proving to be a reliable and hard-working member of the team, Paul and Ferdinand made MacDougal a partner in the firm in 1882. The name was changed to Toklas, Singerman & Company. I wonder what happened to Hyman Auerbach. Jenny was his sister, so why didn't she insist that Auerbach's name be included?[64]

But Paul's plan to move across the street by January 1, 1880 was thwarted by delayed light fixtures. Then, the snow began to fall.

January 8, 1880, saw the beginning of an epic snowstorm. Snow fell for thirty days and spread a blanket of white five to ten feet high. Schools were closed and only essential stores and services were open. Paul's frustration grew and he would wait no longer. On January 18, Paul, who

Store #3 – 1880 snow storm – Commercial between Main and Yesler (UW Special Collection. A. Curtis #22876)

Store #4 – 1880 - Commercial between Main and Yesler (UW Special Collection, A. Curtis UW12563, UW5888)

Squire Latimer bldg., 2020 (Treiger Collection).

was so short the snow must have reached his thighs, hired some men to clear a path through the snow from the west side of Commercial to the east side. They carried all the merchandise across the street, right into the new space. The grand opening of Store #4 was twenty days later on February 7, 1880.[65]

Remarkably, I unearthed two photos from the University of Washington Archive that tell the story of this moment. The first photo was taken during the snowstorm, showing snow piled high on a deserted, quiet street. A sign - "The San Francisco Store" - sticks out of the snow on the west side of the street, just in front of store #3. The second photo shows a snow-free, dirt street and the same sign "The San Francisco Store." But now the sign is securely attached to the Squire Opera House on the east side of the street – store #4. These two photos brought this moment to life. I felt Paul's frustration and marveled at his tenacity.

I crossed to the east side of the street to see if I could sense where Store #4 might have been. Perhaps I might discover another magical mural. What I found was a large, imposing, red brick building in the middle of the block. This building isn't from 1880 because the Great Fire of 1889 burned everything. But it did look old.

I noticed a small plaque:

"The Grand Central Hotel – 1889"

"Originally known as the Squire-Latimer Building," the plaque states, "the structure served as office space until 1897. At that time, the influx of miners on their way to the Klondike Gold Rush brought about the conversion to the Grand Central Hotel. After years of decline, the building was restored in 1973. Site of Squire Opera House."

A moment of triumph. I found the actual location of Store #4 with a current building that was erected just nine years after Paul's store graced this location. I snapped some pictures and envisioned people coming here wearing their finest clothes and fancy hats to enjoy a show and do some shopping.

The 1880s were a decade of explosive growth in Seattle. The city's census population rose from 3,500 in 1880 to 43,000 in 1890. With Paul's store right in the middle of the business district, he couldn't stock the merchandise fast enough. According to Costello, the San Francisco Store grew so quickly that they had to move to a larger space. The perfect opportunity presented itself just a half a block north.[66] This move happened in 1882, the same year that a second son was born to Paul and Jenny. They named him Louis.

Fifth Stop: Commercial & Washington – 1882

Store #5 opened in 1882 in a two-story brick building on the southwest corner of Commercial and Washington. Just a few pedals worth of effort zipped me to the corner of 1st and Washington. Getting off my bike, I realized that my friend Joanna worked on this street. Whenever I used to visit her, I gave nary a glance at these old buildings. I mostly worried about finding a parking space. Now I'm fascinated, especially by the southwest corner and its proximity to the bay.

In 1882, the base of Washington Street was a transportation hub – it was here that the Oregon Improvement Company had its dock, so travelers arriving to Seattle by water would pass the corner of Washington and Commercial as they entered the city. The Walla Walla Railroad that transported coal from Newcastle to Elliot Bay had its depot on Washington Street.[67] Many a young coal miner, needing new shoes or trousers would surely be enticed by the fine window displays at the San Francisco Store.

Toklas, Singerman & Company advanced $10,000 ($308,000 in today's dollars) in cash toward the erection of the new building in exchange for the opportunity to occupy the ground floor at a fixed rental.[68] "The salesroom," wrote the PI, "is the largest on Puget Sound, being 60 feet wide by 100 feet long, and occupies the whole of the first floor of the Marshall Block."[69] This new modern store had lots of space to browse with gleaming brass racks for the displays. It opened its doors on Saturday, September 23, 1882, with $250,000 worth of merchandise ($7.7 million in today's dollars).

It was in store #5 that Paul initiated an annual "Fall Showing." Each fall as the new styles arrived, the San Francisco store opened its doors for one hour in the evening. Lining the street outside, men and women waited for the chance to enter and, with the soft glow of gas lights, view the newest fashions. As no purchasing was allowed, this Fall Showing enticed the customers to return with open wallets.[70]

With the Northern Pacific railroad spur finally connecting Seattle to the cross-continent terminus in Tacoma in 1884, Seattle grew from a town to a city and the world was changing fast. A few years earlier, in 1876, Alexander Graham Bell invented the telephone. This new, miraculous machine was first tested in Seattle in 1878, as reported by the Weekly Pacific Tribune.

The job of a telephone, the Tribune wrote, is "to transmit sound, which is done by the sender holding the instrument about four inches from his mouth, and by the receiver holding the other instrument to his ear. The sounds are carried perfectly so that the voices of acquaintances can be recognized, music rendered heard distinctly, and so forth."[71]

It took five more years to convince enough Seattleites to bring phone service to the city. Toklas, Singerman & Company was the first mercantile store to subscribe.[72]

It was while Paul Singerman was hard at work selling merchandise in store #5 to the men and women of Seattle that the most momentous event, at least for me, occurred. It was August 9, 1884. The third Singerman child was born – a girl, who they named Belle Jane. She grew up to be my great-grandmother, who I knew as Gigi.

When Belle was two years old, electric lights arrived in Seattle.[73] Again, the San Francisco Store was the first store to introduce this new technology. This was an even bigger event than the arrival of the telephone. It all happened on April 24, 1886, when Paul created a spectacle for all of Seattle to see.

"The magic hour was set for 9 o'clock in the evening," writes Costello, "and it was an event that brought practically every resident flocking down to lower Mill [Yesler] and Commercial streets ... And so, as the hour hands of the clock reached the figure of '9' on that April evening in the San Francisco Store, then located at Commercial and Washington, the place was jammed to the doors with spectators; hundreds of others milling around in the street outside; waiting intensely and expectantly. They had been told that this was the moment the store would turn off its old gas lights and turn on the mysteriously new and widely discussed electric lights... . At the same moment the gas lights had been turned off. There was a barely noticeable interval of darkness and as if by magic wand the interior of the store, with a 60x100 foot space, and proudly described as the largest uninterrupted store showroom in the Territory, was flooded with the 'new' light, produced from five 2000-candled power lamps. Every inch of the store was brought into full view with startling clarity. The change from the previous gas light was so marked that those who witnessed the event could hardly believe their eyes. The new lights burned steady and bright. And for hours afterward people thronged in and out of the store to look and marvel, to be followed in turn by others who likewise watched with amazement and almost unbelief."[74]

What a brilliant marketing plan. I would have loved to see all the people dressed up, excited, waiting their turn to enter the store. Upon entering, they would look around and enjoy the many products throughout the store. With no TV or movie theaters, this must have been a big night out on the town.

By the time Belle was six years old, she had already seen many changes in Seattle: the introduction of a horse pulled trolley and then later, its electric trolley replacement; riots in which the white settler population attacked the Chinese residents and forced most of them to board a boat to San Francisco;[75] the establishment of a ferry system; the opening of the Bon Marche, Fredrick and Nelsons, and Bartell's Drug Store; a fire that burned down the entire downtown; the rapid rebuilding and reshaping of the city after the fire; and the opening of the transcontinental railroad in Seattle.[76]

When Belle turned ten, she celebrated with a party, which is not unusual. But what is unusual is that the party was covered in the Seattle PI:

"Belle Singerman was given a birthday party by her mother Mrs. Paul Singerman, in honor of her tenth year, Thursday August 14th. The many young friends of Belle responded to the invitation and a most enjoyable evening was past by all present. The residence 924 Washington Street, had been handsomely decorated for the occasion and together with distribution of prizes and dainty refreshments meant the little folks went away wishing the many returns of such a happy birthday."[77]

Aside from amazing birthday parties, I wonder what went on in their home. Did they celebrate the Sabbath and Jewish holidays? There definitely were music lessons in the Singerman home. Isidore played the piano and Louis played the violin. They both became musicians of note, playing for Seattle audiences.[78]

Belle attended Old South School[79] and the University of Washington. I wonder if she graduated from the University? If she did what did she major in?

Store #5 met Paul's needs for six years, the longest he had stayed in any one location. Those years must have been hectic – running a growing retail business, raising three children, and getting involved in civic life, specifically the Chamber of Commerce and the Masons. Paul was a thirty-third degree Mason and served as the "Almoner."[80]

Paul was also involved in Seattle's Jewish community, which was still informal as the first congregation wasn't founded until 1889. The first recorded celebration of the Jewish High Holidays was in 1884[81]. Services were organized by Bnai Brith Lodge, which had formed one year earlier. In 1887, Yom Kippur services were held at Phythian Hall, Opera House building, led by Rabbi Samuel S. Hymes of Victoria, BC.[82]

Meanwhile, Paul was constantly innovating and working to grow his business. The next opportunity came in 1888. Toklas, Singerman & Company took its most ambitious step yet. I rode my bike three blocks north, to 1st and Columbia.

Sixth Stop: Front And Columbia – 1888

"The house (San Francisco Store) now well under way," writes the Post Intelligencer on July 7, 1887, "will be a veritable mercantile palace, with few equals and no superiors west of the Mississippi River. While thoroughly adapted to the purpose for which was intended, a mammoth store, surpassing anything of the kind West of St. Paul, Minnesota and North of San Francisco, California – it will be a magnificent structure, a monument to the enterprising firm building grit and a credit to the live city in which it is located. ... . The two store fronts will be wholly composed of iron, steel, stone, pressed brick, terra cotta, galvanized iron and glass... . The lower floor will have six immense show windows and great double doors between, all supplied with plate glass of the best description. ... In the northwest corner will be an Otis hydraulic elevator, carrying both freight and passengers, stairs to the upper floors winding around it. ... The whole house will be lighted with gas and electricity and heated from steam from boiler in basement. The cost of this palace of business complete will be $72,000 [$2,267,374 in today's dollars]. The firm paid for the ground $48,000 [$1,500,000 in today's dollars]. The whole expenditure will therefore be $120,000 [$3,7787,000 in today's dollars]."[83]

Store #6 – C. 1880 (MOHAI Illustration of Toklas & Singerman, Wiliam Newton Photographs Lib. 5.41)

Store #6 – 4th of July parade. Store is at end of block with streamers hanging. (UW Special Collection A. Curtis #25173)

The grand opening of store #6 was April 9, 1888. Construction of the four-story building which spanned the southwest corner of Front (1st Ave.) and Columbia, had begun a year earlier. Its exterior was made of brick – a special kind of fireproof brick. Further, it had a telephone, electric lights, and was the first store to have an elevator.[84]

The Northwest Building Review glowed with detail:

"This imposing Toklas, Singerman and Company Building ... had rich Romanesque stylistic details and three stories with an exposed basement as the grade dropped on Columbia. Particularly notable was the arched stone trim above windows on the first and third floors. The facade was divided into three bays, the central one crowned by a decorative pediment rising above the parapet."[85]

Store #6, with hours from 8 a.m. to 8 p.m.,[86] promised to "put forward better goods at lower prices than have yet been quoted ... [s]omething special will be shown on every counter."[87]

As I reached 1st and Columbia I focused my eyes on the southwest corner. My heart sunk in my chest. I saw a large, dull, gray, concrete garage. It was impossible to visualize the beautiful edifice that was constructed here in 1888.

My father, Irwin Treiger, had a reprint of a famous historical map of Seattle in 1889. It hung proudly in his law office. The exciting part of the map is that it showed Toklas & Singerman & Co. at 1st and Columbia – store #6. In the top left corner, it has a picture of the store showing both the outside and inside. Under this picture it says: "Toklas & Singerman & Co. Wholesale & Retail Dry Goods Merchants." The map now, equally proudly, hangs in my home's entryway.

With all the excitement of the grand opening, there was no way for Paul, his partners, and his staff to know that in fourteen months, everything in the store, down to the last belt and hat, would be incinerated by Seattle's Great Fire. Everything would change in a moment. One day Paul was running a large store filled with merchandise and customers in a growing, thriving city. Then a fire that had began in a glue pot in the basement of a carpentry shop near Front and Madison streets ignited an inferno that burned through twenty-five blocks - the entire business district of Seattle. The loss from the fire to Toklas, Singerman & Company was reported at $550,000 ($18.7 million in today's dollars).[88]

Costello, with his lyrical prose, takes us back to that day of shock and horror. "Within minutes," Costello writes, "the flames spread from the carpenter shop to adjoining rooms, then to the entire Denny Block in which the fire originated. Long tongues of flames leaped high into the sky. The air soon darkened with the billowing smoke, through which a former kindly sun now shone red and angry. Only a block to the south stood the magnificent building which housed Toklas Singerman & Company's 'San Francisco Store.' It was deservedly noted as the city's finest retail structure. And within its four walls was a stock of merchandise valued at close to half a million dollars, a fact in which Seattleite's took further pride.

... to begin with, it was the thought of everyone that the San Francisco Store building, as it was commonly known, was completely fireproof. At least, to an extent that would enable it to withstand any ordinary conflagration.

With the blocks of wooden buildings to the north rapidly engulfed in flames as the fire began to rage unchecked; faced with an entirely inadequate water supply which was rapidly being exhausted, other merchants in the immediate vicinity began to carry stock from their own stores and pile the goods in the aisles and on the display room floors of the San Francisco Store.... .

[T]he very walls of the San Francisco Store seemed, in a manner of speaking to be smoking from the scorching heat. Many of the windows had been blown in from the impact following the attempted dynamiting of the Colman Block and though wet blankets were hung to curtain the window spaces they offered little resistance to the hungry flames.... .

[T]he SF Store building was in flames. Brick and stone though it was, and supposedly fireproof, the very bricks and stone seemed to disintegrate as the whirling and angry flames whipped from every window and cornice.... .

It was a tragic scene. The sky was filled with glowing embers and showering sparks with the sky darkened from clouds of smoke which billowed thousands of feet in the air over the business section.... .

It was exactly at 3.10 o'clock p.m., in the afternoon, as later announced by Mr. Louis Singerman, that the San Francisco Store burst into flames. In little more than an hour the entire structure and its stocks were a raging inferno, and soon a mass of ruins, flaming and smoking, so completely razed that only a portion of the south walls remained standing."[89]

The day after the fire, Ferdinand Toklas got on a ship from San Francisco to Seattle with new merchandise and J.B. MacDougal boarded a train for the East Coast to buy additional replacement stock. Other suppliers that Paul had been using responded within 48 hours. Toklas, Singerman & Company received wires from "two of the largest jobbing firms in the East, John B. Farwell & Co. of Chicago and H.B. Chaffin & Co., of New York, offering immediate replacement of stock and cash loans for any amount desired."[90]

Toklas, Singerman & Company announced in the PI (June 12, 1889) that they would "rebuild and planned an even larger building than the one which had burned."[91]

While many merchants erected tents and sold goods, Toklas, Singerman & Co. "reached the decision that it would be out of the question to accommodate the lines and quantity of merchandise which they considered as a minimum in any tent that could be conveniently

June 6, 1889 - looking south on 1st ave. from Spring Street - 30 min after Fire began. (UW Special Collection UW2730z)

June 6, 1889. After Fire, 1st Avenue. (UW Special Collection BAB26)

June 6, 1889 - after fire looking west on 1st between Columbia and Cherry streets (UW Special Collection UW41285)

erected. Instead, the firm entered into a short-term lease of the northeast corner of 3rd and Madison streets and had awarded a contract to F.W. Woodman to erect a one-story frame structure, 75 by 120 feet in dimension."[92]

The PI reported that the building would be completed two weeks and "in forty days the firm will open with a large stock of goods."[93]

As I stood staring at the ugly garage on the corner of 1st and Columbia on this spring day in 2020, I wondered if Paul thought about giving up.

Paul whispered in my ear: "Karen, when you are faced with adversity, you can shrink, shrivel, and give up, or you can attack the challenge head on. That's what I did."

He sent me a message. "Do as I do – when you hit the inevitable bump in the road or even if you find yourself in a burned down city or in the middle of a pandemic, shake yourself off, get a plan and make it happen." I felt loved as I heard Paul speak to me, giving me strength and confidence to keep going. My voyage of discovering my family history was giving me unexpected experiences.

Seventh Stop: 3rd & Madison – 1889

The hill up to 3rd was too steep to ride, so I pushed my bike to the site of store #7. At the corner of 3rd and Madison I found a very tall, non-descript office building, with steel and glass shooting up to heaven. No plaque, no hint of what was here before.

I pulled myself out of my inertness and marveled at how quickly Paul, Ferdinand and J.B. were able to create something from nothing.

"A full and complete stock of silks, dress and fancy goods, notions, hosiery, ladies and men's boots and shoes, cloaks, suits and wraps, children's wear, together with a full line in the art, millinery and domestic departments," the PI wrote. "The choicest patterns in carpets, oilcloths and linoleums will be offered in this stock, while in the gents' furnishing line a fine grade of goods, as varied and complete as anything ever offered in this city will be opened for inspection and purchase."[94]

Remarkably, eighty-seven days after the fire, on September 2, 1889, this ad ran in the newspaper:

"Our public policy, unscathed by smoke and flame, remains the same – HONEST GOODS – HONEST WORDS – HONEST DEALINGS"[95]

Ferdinand Toklas moved his family to Seattle from San Francisco. The Toklas family lived at 9th Avenue and Madison Street.[96] They remained in Seattle for five years and Alice, age 13, attended Mount Rainier Seminary and studied music at the University of Washington.[97] It seems that Mrs. Toklas and Jenny moved in the same social circles, attending luncheons together.[98] But when asked in 1967 about her relationship with Alice, Belle said that she "remembers Alice B. Toklas only vaguely."[99] Papa Jack said that the family didn't talk much about Alice because she was a lesbian and "[a]t that time you didn't talk about those things."[100]

Store #7 – 1890 -3rd and Madison (MOHAI – Willaim S. Newton Photography Lib. 1991 5.47)

1890 Toklas & Singerman Sales Clerks outside Store #7 – 3rd and Madison (MOHAI Lib. 1991 5.46)

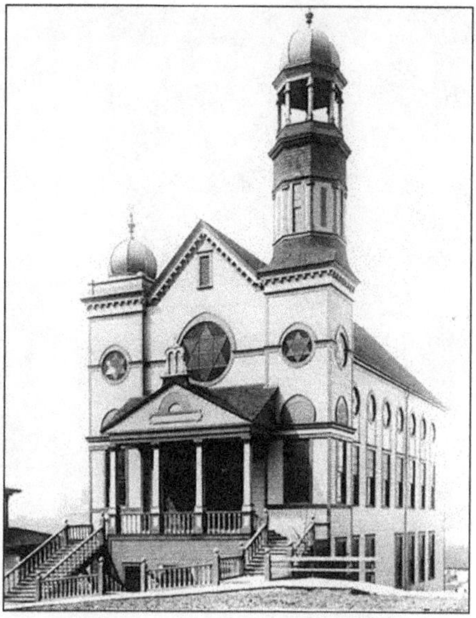

Ohaveth Sholum, 8th & Seneca (UW Special Collection Neg. UW18708)

While store # 7 was getting under way, Washington State was admitted to the Union as the 42nd State[101] and Paul was busy building Seattle's Jewish community. Paul was one of the founding trustees, when on November 4, 1889, the Articles of Incorporation for Ohaveth Sholum were signed.[102] This first Synagogue was established as a "quasi-Reform" Temple – quasi because though men and women sat together and there was an organ, orthodox liturgy was used, and men wore *Kippot* and *Tallit* (prayer shawls). In 1892, Ohaveth Sholum dedicated its first building on 8th and Seneca. This Gothic style building could seat 800, though the membership was only 125.[103] There was a Sunday school and programs to bring the community together.

However, the Congregation didn't last. Ohaveth Sholum closed its doors in 1895.[104] A few years earlier in 1891, an Orthodox Synagogue, Chevra Bikur Cholim, was started. Paul was a "charter member" and active at this new Orthodox Congregation as well.[105] By the end of the decade (1899), a new Reform Congregation, Temple De Hirsch, was founded. Perhaps Paul continued to periodically attend Bikur Cholim, but the family was fully engaged at Temple, with their social lives revolving around Temple happenings. Belle attended the religious school and was in Temple's first confirmation class.

Belle loved Temple.[106] As an adult, she took my mother, Betty Lou Treiger, and my aunt, Jackie Goldfarb, to services every Saturday morning and then out to lunch.

"I loved going with Belle on Saturdays," my mom told me. "Daddy would take us to the store [Friedlander and Sons] in the morning and she would pick us up and take us to Temple services and then out to lunch at the Olympic Hotel. Belle was a wonderful grandmother."[107]

First Confirmation class of Temple DeHirsch. Top Row (l. to r.) Jake Elster, Leah Grunbaum, Sam Friedmand. 2nd Row: Sara Colsky, Etta Dinkelspiel, Belle Singerman, Cora Dinkelspiel. David Himelhoch, Celia Hardman, Rabbi Joseph, Estelle Leopold, Alfred Marks, 1900 (Reprinted with permission of Temple DeHirsch).

The same year Temple De Hirsch was founded, the Singerman family purchased property on southwest corner of 16th and Denny. The purchase of the property for $8,000 ($302,000 in today's dollars) was reported in the PI on March 26, 1899.[108] They built a home on the property and moved in towards the end of 1900.[109] I visited this corner on Capitol Hill. The house is gone. The lot is now part of Kaiser Health's office complex.

Eighth Stop: Front & Columbia – 1890

Exactly one year after the Great Fire, June 6, 1890, store #8 opened to great acclaim.

"The opening of the new store of Toklas, Singerman & Co., at exactly ten minutes past three o'clock,"[110] the PI describes, "was the event of the afternoon. Long before the time set for the opening, a crowd of several hundred ladies had gathered on the sidewalk in front of the building. It was understood that the celebrated Belgian actress, Mlle Rhea, was to participate in the opening and when at exactly ten minutes past three two carriages dashed up to the sidewalk a pathway was opened in the crowd and Mlle Rhea ... alighted and walked to the main entrance. There they were met by Mr. J. B. MacDougal and at this moment the doors were thrown open. It is estimated that at least 5,000 people visited the store between the hour of opening and 6 o'clock last evening."[111]

Five thousand people in one day. That was twelve percent of Seattle's 43,000 residents. As these excited shoppers entered the store, they were met by a mix of electric and gas lights, an elevator to take them to all five levels and a welcoming staff of over 100. The shelves and counters were bursting with merchandise. The staff were "actively engaged in supplying the wants of the ever-increasing throng of customers surrounding their counters."[112]

"The first floor," writes the Northwest Real Estate and Building Review, "contained dress goods, domestics, notions, ladies' furnishings, clothing and hats. On the second, one found cloaks, millinery, children's clothes and ladies' shoes. The third story contained sales floors for carpeting, the fourth for the storage of carpets and the sewing of carpets and shades."[113]

Heading back to 1st and Columbia on my bike was very quick, as it was all downhill. The street upon which I stood was high above where store #6 had been. After the Great Fire the streets were built on higher ground, in some places, as high as eighteen feet above the old one.[114] I grew up knowing that the street level was lower before the Fire because there are underground tours of Seattle that take you through the tunnels. These tours were started in 1965 by Bill Speidel, who is credited with saving the old buildings of Pioneer Square. He petitioned the city to turn the whole neighborhood into a landmark.

As a Girl Scout, my troop took an underground tour once. I was terrified in the dark, dirty tunnels. The lighting was minimal, and the soot was still on the walls from the fire, some 80 years before. I was sure rats were nipping at my heels. After the tour, I told my mom that I never wanted to go back down into those tunnels again. Too scary. But, in the name of research, I descended the stairs to the tunnels in October 2021.

It was a completely different experience. The tunnels, all 33 square blocks of them, are no longer scary, they are cleaned up for the tourists with nice lighting and not a rat in sight.

On this tour, I learned that after the fire, merchants like Paul were in a hurry to rebuild and couldn't wait the seven years the city engineers said it would take to fill in the streets with dirt to raise the level. So, they built the streets 10-18 feet above the old ones and used a combination of trestles and arches to support the elevated streets. A series of skylights were built into the new streets so that a bit of natural light would seep into the tunnels below. I've noticed these square, glass-like pieces on 1st Avenue before, but I didn't know that they were 1890 skylights.

After the fire, the tunnels were used for commerce – imagine an underground mall. But the "mall" was closed in 1907 when the bubonic plague arrived. The rats that lived in the tunnels were passing the disease. The city's solution was to close the tunnels and encase the dirt streets below in cement to trap and kill the rats. It remained closed until Bill Speidel re-made the neighborhood in 1965.

I always thought that the pioneers didn't want to clean up after the fire and just made a new street above it, leaving the ash and the mess below. Thanks to Speidel, I learned the real reason for the elevated streets – sewage.

"The blunt truth," Speidel writes, "is that before the fire you had to climb a ladder to use the plumbing facilities in the heart of Seattle's main business district."[115] In fact, even as early as 1882, Dr. Edward Loomis Smith, the city health officer, reported that the sewers were "worthless." Smith showed how the sewers "flushed in reverse twice a day when the tide came in."[116]

Store # 8 was successful – so successful that the Northwest Real Estate Review called it "the busiest and most profitable acre and one-third in the northwest."[117] But for some reason that I don't understand, one year after the opening, Paul sold his interest in the company to his business partner J.B. MacDougal and another gentleman, Mr. Henry Southwick. The change of name from Toklas & Singerman to MacDougal & Southwick was announced in the newspaper on July 16, 1891.[118]

Ninth Stop: Front & Columbia – 1892

Even though Paul sold his interest in the department store, he wasn't ready to retire. One year after the sale, in 1892, he opened a men's clothing store (store #9), on the same block, retaining the name Toklas & Singerman.

Five years later on July 17, 1897,[119] the steamer Portland sailed into Seattle's harbor – filled with gold. This was the beginning of the Klondike Gold Rush and residents of Seattle rejoiced. It was a gift for merchants like Paul. An economic slowdown had depressed Seattle's economy, but the gold in Alaska was a game changer. One hundred thousand men descended on Seattle – the "gateway to Alaska." It's estimated that each miner dropped $500 ($19,000 in today's dollars) on supplies before heading north.[120] The hotel business boomed and the port expanded to accommodate people arriving and then heading up the coast to Alaska.[121]

"The real dough," Speidel states, "was made by the guys who outfitted the miners on the way out and gave the lucky ones some place to spend their money on the way back."[122]

In 1900, Paul's oldest son Isidore joined the business. It seems that Isidore, known as Uncle Billy in the family, was musically talented. He not only played piano, but also wrote a famous two-step song in honor of the University of Washington class of 1899. The song was "The Purple and Gold" (the colors of the University) and Isidore often played it at college dances.[123] Isidore (on piano) and Louis (on violin) seemed to have played together quite a bit. For example, on February 16, 1906, the Seattle Times noted that the Seattle Operatic Quartet Club was to have a concert and one of the pieces "is to be performed by Mr. Louis Singerman accompanied by Mr. Isidore R. Singerman."[124]

The Singerman family's life was filled with musical performances, luncheons and parties. The PI Society Page described Paul and Jenny's wedding anniversary celebration. Friends were invited to their home and "[t]he rooms were decorated for the occasion. The afternoon was spent at cards. Prizes were distributed for the winners of progressive whist."[125]

At this same time, the center of Seattle's downtown was shifting north and the six-story Lumber Exchange Building was under construction at the southwest corner of 2nd and Seneca. Paul and Isidore saw the future and decided to move.[126]

Tenth Stop: Lumber Exchange Building – 1902

My bike ride to 2nd Avenue and Seneca Street was brief, but I still pedaled for a few blocks. What I saw there was entirely unsatisfying. I wanted to cry when I saw the building that replaced the magnificent Lumber Exchange Building in 1990. In place of the handsome red brick structure sits what is comically known as "The Ban Roll-On Building," or the "R2D2 Building." It deserves these names because the edge of this modern building is a short, squat cylindrical monster that looks like a ban roll-on bottle or R2D2. It's not attractive and its nicknames tell the story of how the citizens of Seattle make fun of this uninspiring piece of real estate.

In 1903, the Lumber Exchange Building graced the corner. The Seattle Daily Times described it as a "vestibule and hallways finished in white onyx and marble quarried in northeastern Washington.... [The stonework] is not exceled in beauty by the marbles from the most famous quarries in the Old World."[127] Paul etched the store's name in the stone above the street level windows and filled the shelves with "top-notch men's spring and summer suits for fifteen to twenty-five dollars... [$535 to $900 in today's dollars] [whose] fabrics are of the purest wool, in grays, browns, stylish

Lumber Exchange bldg. 2nd and Seneca. Hard to see, but the black banner in the corner, says: Toklas & Singerman & Co. (MOHAI PEMCO Webster & Stevens Collection 1983.10.6676)

plaids and fancy mixtures. The tailoring is of the highest class, insuring faultless fit."[128]

By 1903, Paul was comfortable enough with his sons running the store to travel to Europe with Jenny and their daughter, Belle. I have a hunch that the trip had something to do with a broken engagement between Belle and Benjamin Gordon. The paper announced the engagement of Belle and Ben in September of 1902. Paul and Jenny held a "reception" to celebrate.[129]

"The house was most handsomely decorated for the occasion. On the large piazza was arranged a variety of palms and tropical plants, to which in the hall was added many vases of roses, carnations, and other flowers all in pink, while behind the gorgeous bank of pretty Japanese lilies came sweet strains of music from a stringed orchestra. In the front parlor the flowers were yellow roses, while in the next room, where the young couple were congratulated, was all in green and white. A large bay window had been converted into a regular paradise of flowers by placing dark portieres at the windows, shutting out the daylight, and literally covering them with such flowers as hydrangea, grandflora, roses and carnations. On each side of the bay window was a curtain made from pretty green; interwoven with flowers in such a manner as to resemble lace curtains, while at the top, at the intersection of the curtains was suspended a large, beautiful letter 'B' made of maidenhair ferns, roses, etc. which represented the initial letters of each of the couple."[130]

Quite the engagement party. However, there was never an article in the Seattle Times or the PI about a wedding between Belle and Ben, nor any news of a divorce. Thus, my inference that the engagement was broken. I will never know the details of this failed relationship, but it couldn't have been easy for Belle and the Singerman family. One year after the newspaper announced the engagement, the Singermans sold their home on 16th to the General Investment Company[131] and left for Europe to visit Paul's elderly mother and vacation in Carlsbad and Wiesbaden.

My grandfather, Papa Jack, didn't know about his mother's broken engagement. When asked about young people's activities when his parents were single, Papa Jack responded, "Well, my mother told me about some fellow that took her out, but there was nothing serious. And I think my mother was the first Jewish woman my father met, and he married her."[132]

It seems that Belle's brother Louis was the *Shadchan* (matchmaker). "Seattle was very small," Papa Jack explained, "and his father ran into Lou Singerman, who said 'I want you to meet my sister.' I think they were married within a matter of months."[133]

The 1903 European voyage was likely Paul's first trip back to Europe in 35 years. He had not seen his family since he was eighteen. Paul's mother was blind by this time,[134] and during his visit he wrote to his sons directing them to prepare a Thanksgiving feast for the blind residents of Seattle.

"Every blind man, woman and child in Seattle," writes the Seattle Times, "will be given an opportunity to partake of a delicious Thanksgiving dinner at the expense of one of Seattle's oldest and best-known businessmen, Mr. Paul Singerman who is now visiting his aged mother in Europe… . Mr. Isidore Singerman explained that it is a thanks offering of his father because he has been able to see his mother alive and well in so advanced years."[135]

After six months in Europe, Paul, Jenny, and Belle returned to Seattle. They arrived in Seattle in April of 1904.[136] Having sold their home before the trip, they moved into the Lincoln,[137] a new luxury apartment-style hotel on 4th and Madison.

"It was a towering presence on the skyline," writes the Pacific Coast Architectural Database, "having seven stories on its east façade and nine on its west. At this vantage point and with its height, most rooms had commanding views of Elliott Bay and the Olympics on the west, Mt. Rainier (south), and Cascades (east)… . The roof garden had grass, flowers, shrubs and pergola, providing a pseudo-bucolic setting in the middle of downtown."[138]

This modern apartment was a temporary dwelling for Paul and Jenny. They were looking for a place to build their dream home.

Side Trip - The Singerman House – 1904-1907

One month after their return to Seattle, Paul and Jenny purchased land on Capitol Hill.[139] The plot was just a block and a half from their home on 16th. It was purchased for $2,100 ($74,000 in today's dollars) from

Winnifred C. Filson and C. C. Filson on May 31, 1904.[140] Paul and Jenny filed plans with the building inspector to build a two story and basement stone and frame residence at 1727 15th Avenue. The cost was estimated at $7,000 ($247,000 in current dollars).[141] The home was completed in 1905 and the family moved in.

This stunning home still graces 15th Avenue. Thanks to its Landmark status, the home retains its original glory, and I drove by it in my car on a separate trip, wanting to check it out. I noticed a sign that indicates it's an inn – the Gaslight Inn. I peeked through the sparkling cut glass on the beautiful dark wood door. It looked gorgeous. I couldn't help myself; I knocked.

"Hi," I said, "I am Karen Treiger, the great-great granddaughter of the Singermans, who built this house. I was wondering if I could come inside?"

"Wow," said Joelle, one of the current owners, "that's amazing. I am so happy to meet you. I know all about the Singermans. But right now isn't a good time. Here is my card, call me and we'll set up a time. My husband, Ryan, will be so excited to meet you."

It was October 22, 2022 when my mom and I visited Ryan and Joelle. This time Joelle opened the door and welcomed us with hugs. She and her husband Ryan live in the basement with their two kids. They run the eight-room inn on the top three floors. They were thrilled to give us the grand tour.

Rich, glowing dark wood panels in the entryway, the ballroom, the living room, the dining room, and the grand staircase transported me to another era. The lighting was dim, but it didn't feel dark. It felt expansive and welcoming; the serenity of the space enveloped me.

The house is full of stained-glass windows. The most spectacular one sits at the center-point of the main staircase, going from the entryway to the second floor, where the Singerman family had their bedrooms. At the base of the staircase, attached to the stair-post sits a statute of a woman that is described as "[t]he most unique feature of the house." The post "rises to hold a cast bronze light fixture ... [depicting] a maiden with a basket of roses and shower of light overhead, while monks' faces are depicted in other cast bronze fixtures." [142]

We made our way up the staircase to visit four bedrooms. One, clearly the master bedroom, has a stain-glass window and a fireplace with a sitting room that opens to the sleeping area. Across the hall, there was a room that must have been my great grandmother, Belle's room. It was the only one with a sink in the room. The other two other rooms must have been for Isidore and Louis. They showed us the space in the hallway that was the common bathroom.

The maid's room on the first floor was well thought out – it connects with a narrow stairway up to the bedroom wing, so that the maid need not enter the family's living space to get upstairs. To get to the third floor, we went up a narrow stairway. There we found three smaller rooms, clearly designed for the help, that now serve as guest rooms.

Visiting the Singerman home with my mom, I quickly realized that I was no longer researching history, but living it. I felt the history of my family running through my veins. My body had a light tingly sensation as I envisioned Belle here in this home, sleeping in her bedroom, telling her brothers to hurry up in the bathroom, inviting friends to visit, and entertaining larger groups. In fact, Belle didn't wait long to throw her first party. Shortly after they moved in, the Seattle Times Society Page reports:

"Last Wednesday evening, the home of Mr. and Mrs. Paul Singerman 1727 Fifteenth Avenue was the scene of a brilliant dancing party, given by Miss Belle Singerman in honor of Miss Esther Lesser of Portland Ore. The ball room was beautifully decorated for the occasion. A large number of guests were present."[143]

"See, we made it," Paul and Jenny whispered to me. "We didn't even speak English when we got off the boat and look how far we came."

After putting so much thought, effort, and money into this home, why did Paul and Jenny sell the house only two years after they moved in? It was sold in May of 1907 to the Miller family for $17,000 (approximately $568,000 in today's dollars)? [144]

The Landmark Designation Report suggests that the Singermans sold the home in 1907 because Jenny was upset that new condominiums were being constructed across the street.[145] Is that plausible? The house was so lovingly designed. I wonder, instead, if it had something to do

Singerman House (permission from owners of home)

(Left) Betty Lou Treiger and Karen Treiger outside Singerman Home, 2023 (Treiger Collection)

with Jenny's health; she died just two months after the sale on July 9, 1907, at the age of 52.[146]

Though Jenny didn't live to see any of her children married, it wasn't long after her death that all three children tied the knot. Isidore married Gertrude Stern, from New York, in 1908.[147] Gertrude and Isidore lived in Seattle but didn't have children.

A year later, on June 28, 1909, Louis and Belle were married in a double ceremony. Yes, a double ceremony – but it gets better – the two Singerman siblings married two siblings – the children of Sam and Augusta Friedlander, owners of a 1st Avenue jewelry store. In a ceremony

Gertrude and Isidore Singerman, Seattle Times, November 27, 1908.

conducted by Rabbi Koch of Temple De Hirsch, Louis married Anne Friedlander[148] and Belle married Louis Friedlander. Belle and Lou lived in Seattle, raising their family here. Anne and Louis moved to Salt Lake in 1910. Their marriage ended in 1917 with a divorce.

Besides the double wedding ceremony, 1909 was a banner year in Seattle. The summer and fall months saw over three million visitors to the Alaska Yukon Pacific Exposition – Seattle's first world's fair.[149] The Expo gave Seattle worldwide publicity and fueled the growth of the city.

Eleven months after the double wedding, Belle and Lou gave birth to their first child (my grandfather), John Morton Friedlander (Hebrew name - Mordechai), who they called Jack. I imagine he was named for Augusta's father, whose first name was Morton, likely Mordechai in Hebrew.

"Mr. and Mrs. Louis Friedlander," writes the Seattle Times, "became the parents of a fine baby boy on Monday, May 9, at 5:30 p.m. an incident commonplace in itself, although of vastly more than passing importance to the many friends and acquaintances of the proud and happy parents. To Paul Singerman, father of the young mother, this event brings especial cause for happiness, which is the dignified and honored title of 'grandfather.' So overjoyed was Mr. Singerman when apprised of the event that he immediately wrote his check for $5,000 [$165,000 in today's dollars] in favor of the child's mother."[150]

A second son was born on July 9, 1912. Belle and Lou named him Paul, after his grandfather Singerman. I knew him as Uncle Paul.

Grandfather Paul didn't sit home after Jenny's death. In 1912, he took a trip to Europe. Ancestry.com shows that he traveled westward on July 6, 1912, on the Cleveland with Hamburg Amerika Line. On his return trip, he departed Hamburg, Germany and arrived in Cherbourg, New York.[151] When he returned to Seattle, he and his son Isidore, opened their final store.

Eleventh Stop: The Annex – 1913

The final stop on my bike tour was 2nd and Pike. I rode north on 1st Avenue and turned right, traveling east on a short city block. It was here in 1913 that

Singerman Annex – 2nd and Pike (UW Libraries Item #SEA0198; Public Domain)

Paul and Isidore opened the Singerman & Sons Annex. The Pike Place Market opened in August of 1907 and Paul and Isidore saw the future of Seattle in the Pike Street corridor. The Annex occupied an entire city block.

A headline in the Times read: "Oldest Clothing House Opens on Pike Street: Singerman & Sons Branch Outgrowth of Forty Years in City – Senior Member Active Here Since 1874."

"One of the most reassuring signs of the stability of business conditions in Seattle for the past four or five years," writes the Times, "has been the steady growth and frequent expansion of many of the old-established retail stores along the downtown avenues. These institutions are under the direction of men who have had their hand on the pulse of prosperity throughout all the changes that have transformed Seattle from a village into a great business and industrial community that it is today. Since 1874 the name of Singerman has stood over the entrance of a Seattle clothing house, and Paul Singerman is probably entitled to the distinction of having been in the retail clothing business in Seattle longer than any other merchant in the city.

For the past ten years the present firm of Singerman & Sons which succeeded the Toklas-Singerman Company, has carried on business at the southwest corner of 2nd Avenue and Seneca Street. This issue of the Times contains elsewhere the announcement of the opening of Singerman & Sons Annex at 223 Pike Street, and Isidore Singerman, upon whose young and capable shoulders rests the general management of the firm's interest, is thoroughly optimistic concerning the new venture. He expects to see Pike Street within a very few years as busy a thoroughfare as is 2nd Avenue today. He does not contemplate anything else but a full measure of success for the new store.

For some reason or other, the combination of father and sons in business partnership as a rule withstands all the 'jinx' and the 'hoo-doos' that infest the highway toward success in business, and this particular one which has written the name of Singerman & Sons into the business history of Seattle is no exception to that rule.

The new store is owned entirely by and will be under the direct management of the old well-known firm specializing in popular-priced reliable brands of clothing."[152]

This assessment of Singerman & Sons as an exception to the rule of "jinx" and the "hoo-doos" was perhaps premature and provided a jinx of its own.

As I stood on the corner of 2nd and Pike, my view was of a Target and two non-descript office buildings. Then I saw a ray of hope – an old building – the State Hotel. I looked it up on my phone and indeed, a stately seven story, terra cotta tiled structure was built in 1904. It was here when the Singermans opened the Annex. I took a few photos and gave my camera a rest.

Paul's Story Ends

It was only one year after opening the Annex that Paul fell ill and moved in with his daughter Belle and her family at the home he had built for them at 709 15th Avenue.[153] The Seattle Times reported that Louis Singerman returned to Seattle (from Salt Lake) on August 15th to visit his father.[154] Paul died thirteen days later on August 28, 1915.[155]

The headline in the Seattle Times on August 30, 1915, read: "Friends Pay Respect to the Late Paul Singerman."

"In the presence of an usually large number of pioneer friends," the Times reported, "business acquaintances and blind persons, in whom he has always taken great interest, funeral services for the late Paul Singerman, pioneer merchant and philanthropist of Seattle, were held today at the home of the daughter, Mrs. Louis Friedlander, at 709 15th Avenue North.

A huge mass of floral remembrances filled the residence. Rabbi Samuel Koch officiated. Many automobiles accompanied the remains to the Hills of Eternity Cemetery where Masonic services under the auspices of St. John's Lodge No. 9 F. & A.M. were held. Mr. Singerman was a member of this lodge for many years."[156]

After Paul's death, the newspaper was quick to report the value of his estate: $110,445 ($3.4 million in today's dollars).[157] Paul's will, which he executed on March 28, 1912, gave his two sisters in "Russia" annuities of $100 and $200 ($3,000 and $6,000 in today's dollars) with the remainder of the estate divided among his three children.

"Isidore Singerman," the Times writes, "is bequeathed 300 shares of the capital stock of the company Singerman & Sons and the remaining

200 shares providing he pays his sister Mrs. Friedlander $15,000 [$466,000 in today's dollars] in ten yearly installments of $1,500 [$46,650 in today's dollars]. The Will states that Louis Singerman and Mrs. Friedlander each received property and cash valued at $20,000 [$622,000 in today's dollars].

If an attempt is made to disturb the provisions of this instrument the testator directs that the contestant shall receive $1 [thirty-one dollars today] and no more. The real estate is equally divided among the children and Isidore Singerman is named executor without bond. The Will was signed March 28, 1912 and witnessed by Rudolph C. Miller and James B. Metcalf."[158]

Once Paul died, the store was not the same. By November, Isidore had to hang the family's dirty laundry out for all of Seattle to see. A large ad in the Seattle Times read:

"A Frank Statement from I.R. Singerman: A Crisis in Affairs Induces Executor of the Paul Singerman Estate to Put His Situation Plainly Before the Public.

As executor of the estate of the late Paul Singerman, I find it necessary to raise a considerable sum of money in order to meet certain conditions in the will and to permit of the rearrangement of the business. To do this I must sell out a large part of the stock of Singerman & Sons.

I well realize that under present business conditions drastic cuts must be made in prices if I am to attract trade enough to raise the needed money. BUT IT MUST BE. Tomorrow the sale starts – everything in the store will be sacrificed (except contract goods), but in every detail of the sale credit will be reflected on the reputation of Singerman's – gained in forty-one years of right dealing with Seattle people.

I.R. Singerman, Executor."[159]

It went downhill from there. It seems that Isidore struggled to keep the boat afloat and by 1923, the great history of the Singermans as merchants in Seattle ended in defeat and embarrassment. Another ad in The Seattle Times ran on December 6, 1923. It announced a huge sale:

"The business community of Seattle was stunned when the high-grade Singerman stock was assigned to the 'benefit of the creditors.' It is positively shocked now by the forced sacrifice of this great clothing stock.... We are ready for the big rush. Come, select your suit or overcoat while there is still time."[160]

They made it through the Christmas season, but on December 27 people learned that Singerman's had, "failed to meet its obligations. By LEGAL PROCESS the Singerman stock was assigned for the BENEFIT OF THE CREDITORS – now the balance of this great clothing stock has been turned over to us and must be closed out at once. The end of the year is here and with it comes the end of this great sale. Singerman's stock will soon be but a memory."[161]

Now I more fully understand why "Singerman" was a name spoken in only hush tones in my grandfather's home.

"I had two uncles, Lou Singerman and Isidore Singerman, my mother's brothers," Papa Jack said in his 1975 interview, "but they were not very good businessmen and they failed. It would still be good and worth a lot of money today but it all went down the tube... . They went through bankruptcy. They were not good businessmen. They argued and couldn't get along. Their wives fought too, which happens in a lot of families."[162]

"My mother's father", Papa Jack explained, "died a very rich man. And then my two uncles took over the business. In about seven or eight years, they lost it."[163]

This explains why Belle always insisted that her sons – Jack and Paul – get along. Papa Jack used to recite the poem his mother made him memorize – "I love you well my little brother and you are fond of me ..." When I asked my Aunt Jackie Goldfarb how the rest of the rhyme goes she said "... da da da da da da da, the family." Well, I found the rest of the words:

I love you well, my little brother,
And you are fond of me;
Let us be kind to one another,
As brothers ought to be.
You shall learn to play with me,
And learn to use my toys;
And then I think that we shall be
Two happy little boys.

I suppose after watching her brothers destroy Singerman & Sons, Belle was laser focused on that eventuality not repeating. When asked whether his mother was active in the community, Papa Jack said:

"My mother was not a great one for meetings. She put most of her time into my brother and myself. And I put the responsibility at her feet for this business being so successful. She used to preach that Paul and I had to get along and not fight or there wouldn't be a business."[164]

Belle Singerman was the only one of the three Singerman kids to have children. She lived until 1969 and saw the birth of six great grandchildren, including me. Isidore died at the age of 70, in Seattle on June 3,1949, and Louis, who moved to San Francisco and remarried a couple of times, died there at the age of 79, on January 1, 1961.

Belle (Singerman) Friedlander with six of her grandchildren, back row: Karen Treiger, Ken Treiger, Belle (Singerman) Friedlander, David Goldfarb, Steven Goldfarb. Front row: Louis Treiger, Susan Goldfarb. (Treiger Collection)

Final Thoughts

The Singerman wealth was not passed on to future generations. Nonetheless, Paul and Jenny's work ethic and belief in the promise of tomorrow was passed through their daughter Belle onto her son Jack, to his daughters Betty Lou and Jackie, and finally to me, my brothers and my cousins. Belle made sure that her boys worked hard and built a successful jewelry business. The legacy was not one of cash or stock, but of honor, belief in hard work, and a promise of something better.

As I visited the sites of the eleven stores and three residences, I heard their voices in the empty streets of Pioneer Square, 2nd Avenue, Pike Street, and Capitol Hill. The Gaslight Inn is the only structural testament to Paul and Jenny's immigrant success. But there is a deeper and more meaningful legacy: two grandchildren,[165] four great-grandchildren,[166] nine great, great grandchildren,[167] thirteen great, great, great, grandchildren,[168] and, as of this writing, five great, great, great, great grandchildren,[169] two of whom were born in Seattle, making them seventh generation Seattleites.[170]

Looking back at my ancestors' lives is an opportunity to look deeper into myself and attempt to understand my place in time and space. What have I learned; what have I discovered? I learned that Paul Singerman, who came from Raczki, Gubernia, crossed the Atlantic Ocean and the North American continent, and overcame obstacles by seeing them as challenges to conquer. When the Great Fire decimated his magnificent store, Paul immediately said we will rebuild, bigger and better than before. Paul emerged from the ashes, shook himself off, and kept going. I hope that there is a special piece of DNA for resilience and that it was passed down to me. Paul was a civic-minded businessman, who watched Seattle grow from 1,500 in 1874 to 285,000 in 1915 when he died. His active involvement in the nascent Jewish community inspires my passion for volunteering.

Jenny Auerbach took a huge gamble leaving her home in Europe and traveling across the world for a promise of marriage. After she met Paul, she wasn't convinced that this short, stocky, Jewish man was the best match. Nonetheless, she made it work, building a life together with Paul and raising a family to be proud of.

After I am dead and gone, what trace will there be of my life? Will anyone care about me in 150 years? Maybe this is what pushes me to write these stories – hoping, dreaming, that someone will remember me and my name will be mentioned among the living. I leave these words and stories here for people to follow me backwards in time.

CHAPTER 2

STAADECKER FAMILY

"Something's happened to Nanny," my mother, Betty Lou Treiger told me. "You stay here with Susan until we get back." My mom said this as she dropped me at her sister, Jackie Goldfarb's, home, just up the street from our house in our quiet suburban Mercer Island neighborhood.

My Aunt Jackie Goldfarb and my mom were gone before I could even take off my coat, leaving my cousin Susan and me alone. I don't remember where our brothers were, but I was 11 and Susan was 13 years old, and we were scared. We agreed that something bad must have happened.

It turns out that something worse than bad had happened – something terrible – unimaginable. A chain smoker, my grandmother, Elizabeth (Staadecker) Friedlander, who we called Nanny, had finished her cigarette in bed before going to sleep in her apartment in Bellevue, Washington. But the cigarette was not fully extinguished, and the sheets caught fire. Nanny woke with smoke all around her. She could hardly see. Feeling her way out of the room, she found a fire extinguisher and came back to put the fire out. Black smoke filled the room making it hard to breathe and impossible to see. She opened the door and entered – but the room she entered was not the bedroom; it was a small, smoke-filled closet and the door was closed. She tried to get out, scratching the door with her nails, but she couldn't, and she died in the closet, holding the fire extinguisher.

Most of my memories are of Nanny sitting on the couch in our living room, smoking a cigarette or visiting her in a small apartment in Bellevue with my mom. As I began to research the lives of Nanny and the Staadecker family, I was worried. Worried because my relationship with Nanny was

Staadecker Family Tree

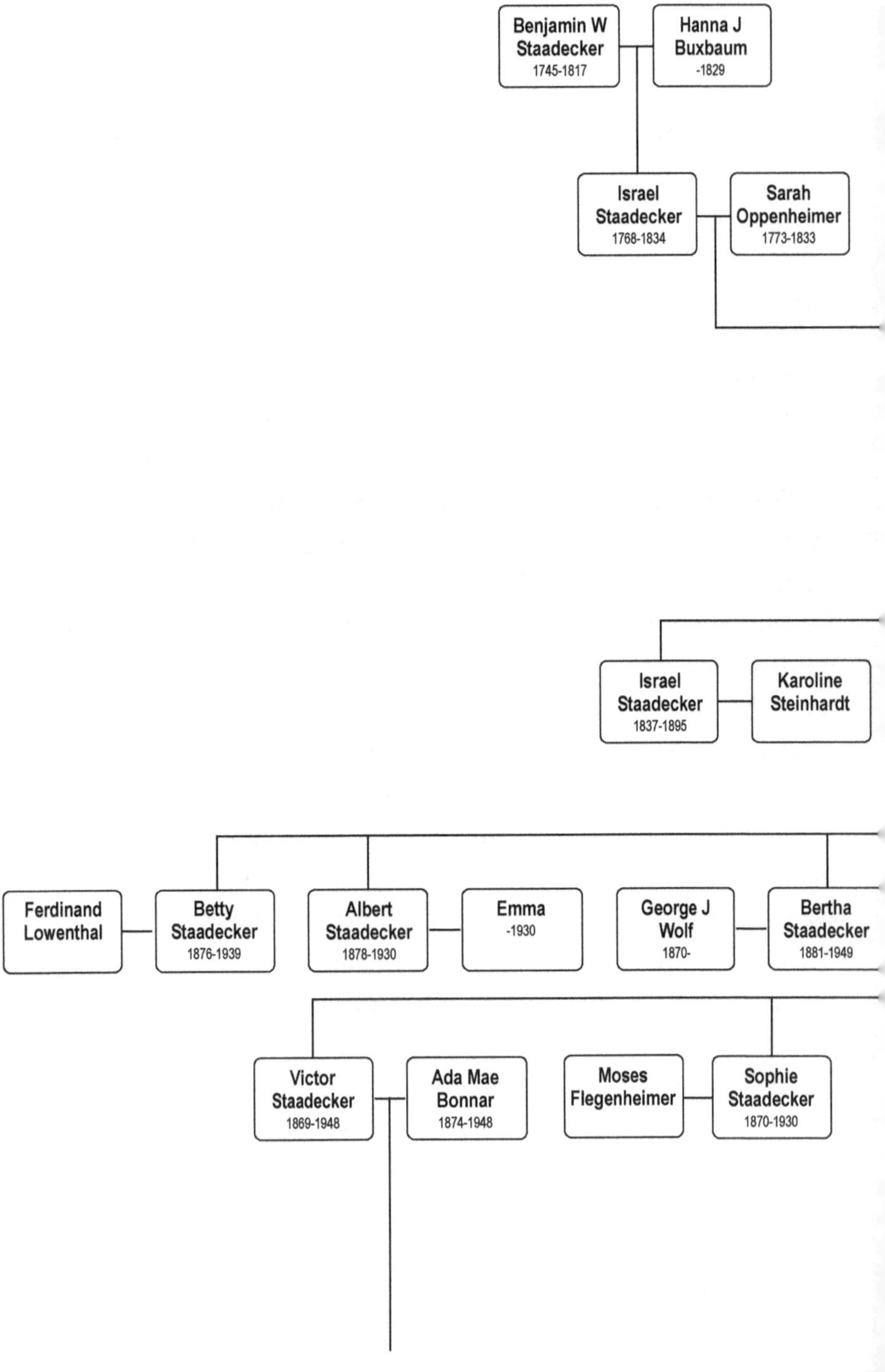

Benjamin W Staadecker 1745-1817
Hanna J Buxbaum -1829
Israel Staadecker 1768-1834
Sarah Oppenheimer 1773-1833
Israel Staadecker 1837-1895
Karoline Steinhardt
Ferdinand Lowenthal
Betty Staadecker 1876-1939
Albert Staadecker 1878-1930
Emma -1930
George J Wolf 1870-
Bertha Staadecker 1881-1949
Victor Staadecker 1869-1948
Ada Mae Bonnar 1874-1948
Moses Flegenheimer
Sophie Staadecker 1870-1930

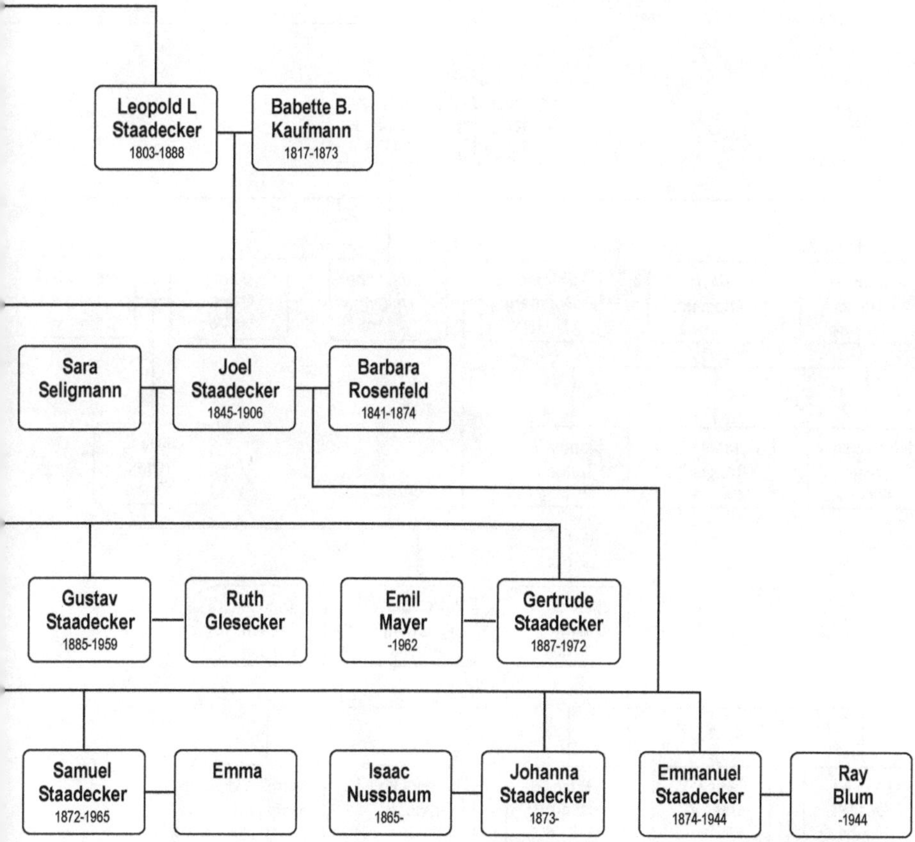
Leopold L Staadecker 1803-1888
Babette B. Kaufmann 1817-1873
Sara Seligmann
Joel Staadecker 1845-1906
Barbara Rosenfeld 1841-1874
Gustav Staadecker 1885-1959
Ruth Glesecker
Emil Mayer -1962
Gertrude Staadecker 1887-1972
Samuel Staadecker 1872-1965
Emma
Isaac Nussbaum 1865-
Johanna Staadecker 1873-
Emmanuel Staadecker 1874-1944
Ray Blum -1944

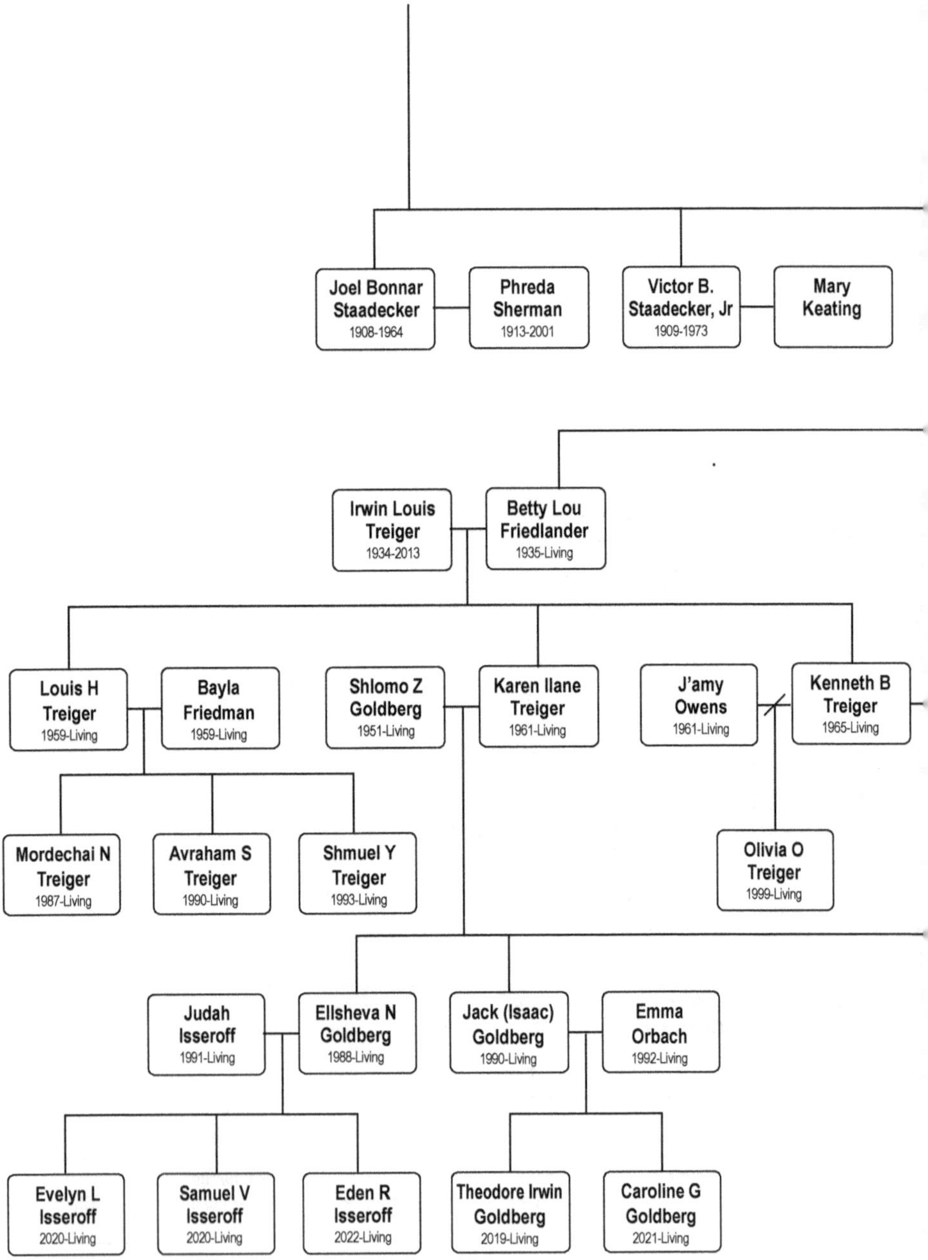
Joel Bonnar Staadecker 1908-1964
Phreda Sherman 1913-2001
Victor B. Staadecker, Jr 1909-1973
Mary Keating
Irwin Louis Treiger 1934-2013
Betty Lou Friedlander 1935-Living
Louis H Treiger 1959-Living
Bayla Friedman 1959-Living
Shlomo Z Goldberg 1951-Living
Karen Ilane Treiger 1961-Living
J'amy Owens 1961-Living
Kenneth B Treiger 1965-Living
Mordechai N Treiger 1987-Living
Avraham S Treiger 1990-Living
Shmuel Y Treiger 1993-Living
Olivia O Treiger 1999-Living
Judah Isseroff 1991-Living
Ellsheva N Goldberg 1988-Living
Jack (Isaac) Goldberg 1990-Living
Emma Orbach 1992-Living
Evelyn L Isseroff 2020-Living
Samuel V Isseroff 2020-Living
Eden R Isseroff 2022-Living
Theodore Irwin Goldberg 2019-Living
Caroline G Goldberg 2021-Living

Staadecker Family Tree, continued

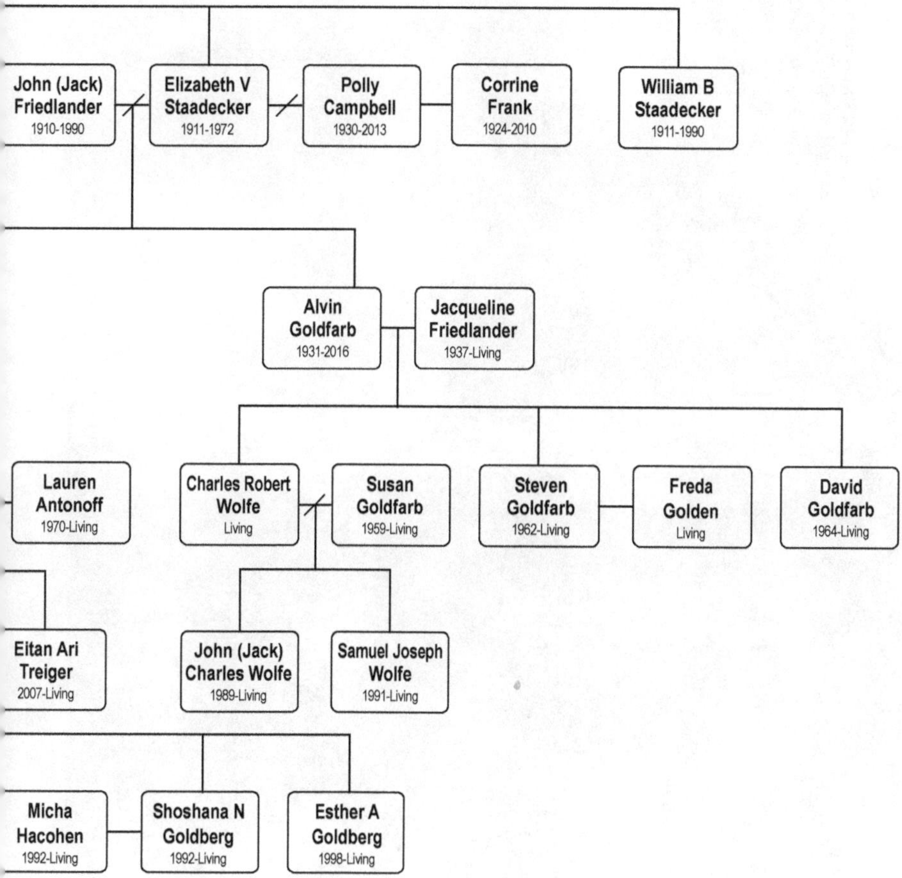

Staadecker Map – Stores And Homes

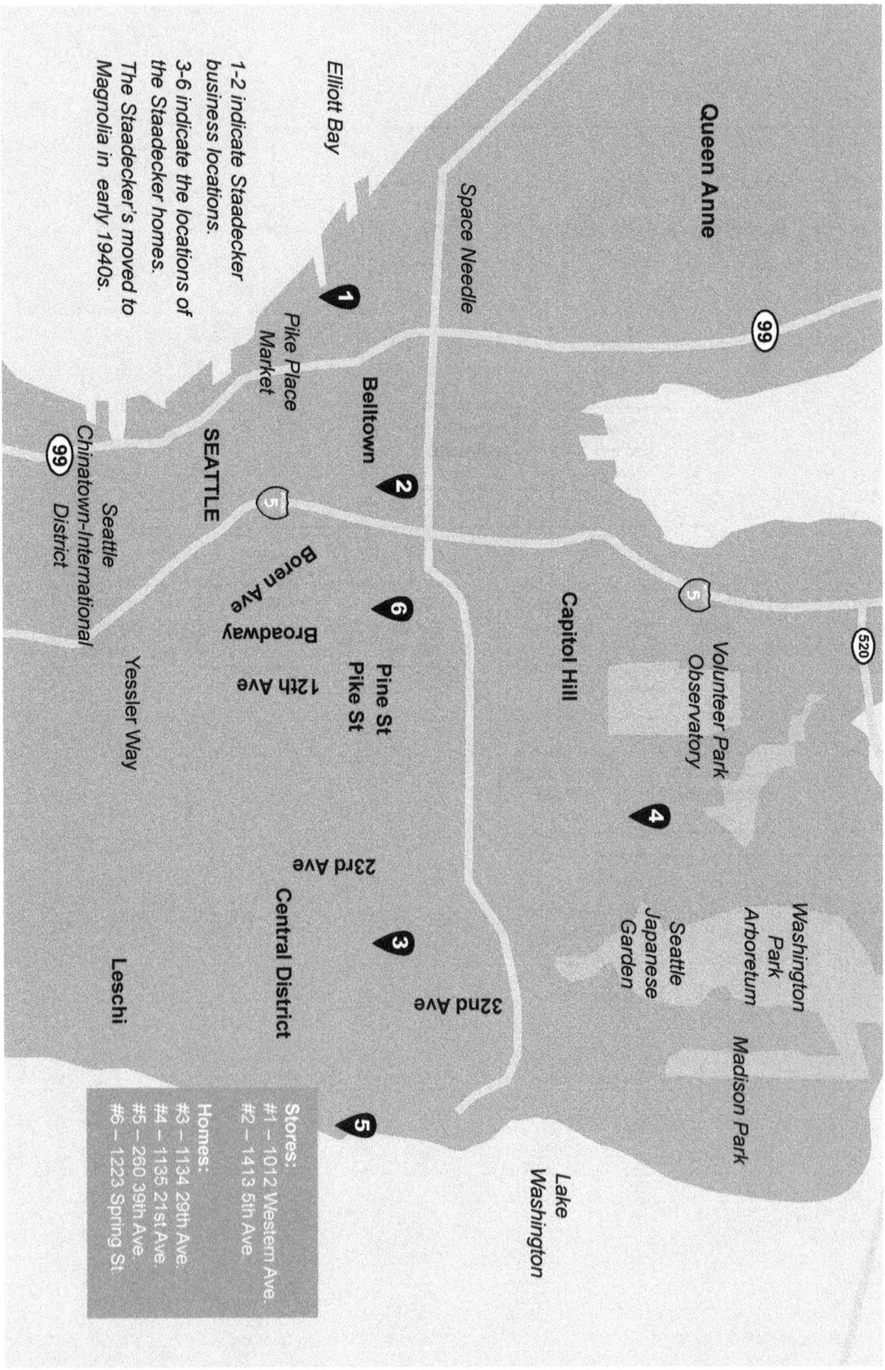

not warm nor loving. I have no memories of ever spending time alone with her. Researching and learning about the lives of Victor and Ada Staadecker made me reckon with my grandmother's early life and later struggles. I was given the gift of meeting Nanny as a child and seeing her life through a new lens. I hoped I might get to know her in a new way.

The Staadecker Story Begins

Sixty-one, that's the number of years Nanny lived.[171] Before her marriage at the age of 22, she lived a storybook life: beautiful homes and servants, magnificent gardens, loving parents, three doting brothers, including her twin brother (who we called Uncle William), gorgeous dresses and hats, luncheons, private school, dance lessons,[172] Temple De Hirsch junior choir, summer camp, sororities, classes at the University of Washington, parties, parties, and more parties. Nanny's parents were self-made immigrants who came to Seattle dreaming of success.

Nanny's father, Victor Staadecker, was the eldest child of Joel Staadecker (1845) and Barbara (Rosenfeld) Staadecker (1841). They lived in Merchingen, Baden, Germany, a small, picturesque town close to Germany's current western border with France. Among the townsfolks living in white wooden homes with red tiled roofs, lived three hundred Jews. Small Jewish-owned shops lined the town square and Jewish-owned farms circled its outskirts. There was trading – lots of it – in timber, cattle, and agricultural produce. The Baron of the city allowed the Jewish community to have a Synagogue, a Jewish guest house, and a Jewish school.[173]

Joel, a grain handler, and Barbara married in 1867. Though Uncle William, Nanny's twin brother, said that the Staadecker family in Germany was poor,[174] they lived in a large home in the center of the town.[175] Until 1857, Joel's uncle, Zacharias Staadecker, served as the Rabbi of the town.[176]

Joel and Barbara brought five children into the world: Victor (1869), Sophie (1870), Samuel (1872), Johanna (1873), and Emmanuel (1874). Barbara died in 1874, the same year Emmanuel, was born, but I couldn't confirm if she died in childbirth.

Bereaved and responsible for five young children, Joel quickly found a new wife. He married Sara Seligmann, "The Brave." I dub her "The Brave"

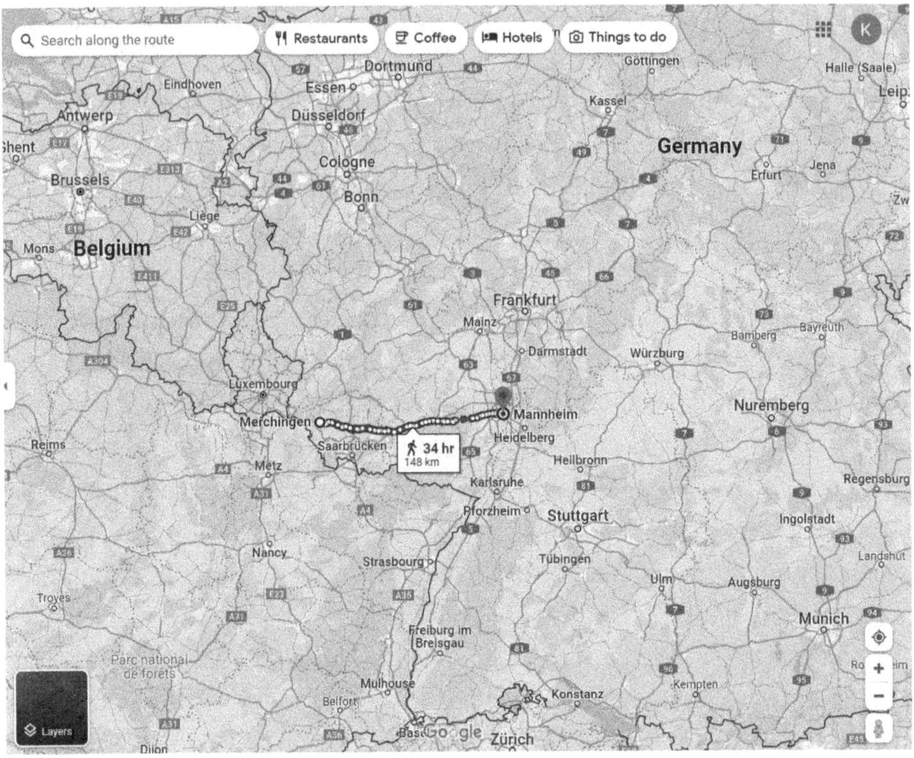

google map – Merchingen to Manheim

because Sara stepped into the intrepid role of stepmother of five children, all under the age of six. However, Sara was not deterred. Over the next fifteen years, she gave birth to five children of her own: Betty (1876), Albert (1878), Bertha (1881), Gustav (1885), and Gertrude (1887), making what Jews would call a *Minyan* (quorum of ten for Jewish prayer) of Staadecker children.

I imagine my great-grandfather Victor, as a smart, hard-working *Yekke (German Jew),* who liked to wear crisp-ironed shirts and made his bed every day. He learned to read Hebrew and according to Uncle William he was religious and his family in Germany "celebrated the Sabbath every Friday night."[177]

To study in Gymnasium, Victor traveled sixty miles east to Mannheim and lived with his father's brother, Abraham Staadecker and his wife Mina.[178] Perhaps the educational opportunities were better in Mannheim, but my imagination runs wild with stepmother stories – you know –

too many children from the previous mother – need to thin the ranks. Mannheim, with a population of 53,000, was home to one of the largest Jewish communities in southern Germany.

An attorney by trade, Victor's Uncle Abraham was also a Talmud[179] scholar. I envision him sitting at the dining room table studying *Gemarah* (Talmud) with his nephew Victor. The thought of this brings a smile to my face as I doubt that Victor packed his *Gemarah* when he left Germany at age 17. When he got on that ship to America, he left his large family behind and many of their traditional Jewish practices.

Crossing The Atlantic

Victor crossed the Atlantic at the age of seventeen. He disembarked in New York Harbor in 1885 with, as Uncle William described, "some cheese and a dollar in his pocket."[180] Victor joined approximately 1.3 million New Yorkers.[181]

Perhaps Victor started his American journey in *Kleindeutchland* – Little Germany. This was the name for the Lower East Side in the mid to late 1800's. Cramming into tenements, German immigrants created the third largest "city" of Germans in the world – 500,000 by 1855. These hard-working Germans became bakers, butchers, cigar makers, brewers, carpenters, and furniture makers.[182] The unpaved, dirt streets, jammed with peddlers and vegetable sellers, buzzed with energy and activity.

By 1880, there were 60,000 Jews living in lower Manhattan."[183]When Victor arrived in 1885, many of the *Kleindeutchland* Germans were heading uptown, seeking better living conditions. Many of the German Jews, however, stayed in the Lower East Side where they had set up synagogues, temples, and fraternal societies. Victor found a job as a Western Union boy and sent most of his earnings back to Germany for his sisters' dowries.[184]

After four years on the crowded streets of New York, Victor traveled West. He was 21 when he boarded a train to Weisser, Idaho, where he "had some relatives."[185] Victor worked and slept in his relatives' dry goods store. It didn't take long for him to continue his westward journey, probably by train. His destination was Portland, Oregon where "a crony of his from Germany," Ignatz Lowengart, lived.[186] Uncle Ignatz, as the Staadecker children later called him, was in the wholesale millinery business, selling hats to Portland's fashionable stores. In those days, hats were big business as it was scandalous to leave the house without one. Women chose from an array in their closets.[187]

Upon Victor's arrival in Portland in 1900, he rented a room at the Portland Hotel. His stay was recorded in the Oregonian "New Arrival" section.[188] Victor joined 90,426 U.S. Census-counted people in this growing town.[189] The Portland Hotel was smack in the middle of the rebuilt Portland on 6th, between Yamhill and Morrison. There had been a fire in 1873 that destroyed the center of downtown. [190]

Ignatz Lowengart was the proprietor of Lowengart & Co. [191] where over the next five years, Victor learned the millinery business. Ignatz lived just north of downtown, in what is today known as Old Town. The US Census Report indicates that Ignatz, his wife, daughter, mother-in-law, brother, two servants, and a chef, all lived in a home in the area around Davis or Everett Street.[192] I visited the area in March of 2023 with my children Esther and Shoshana and we found little evidence of the mansions that, in Ignatz time, graced those tree-lined streets. Today, it's filled with upscale apartments, restaurants, coffee shops, and bookstores.

Portland's early German-Jewish settlers, first arrived in 1849.[193] They were successful businessmen and politicians. In fact, by the time Victor arrived in 1900, three Jews had served as Portland's mayor.[194] The Jews who settled in Portland "brought with them knowledge of English,[195] familiarity with frontier society and connections to San Francisco-based trade networks that positioned them well to join with fellow pioneers and help create new communities."[196] By 1860, while Jews made up a mere half a percent of Oregon's U.S. Census-counted people population, approximately one-third of Portland's 146 merchants were Jewish.[197]

This success stemmed in part because the early pioneers' "racial anxieties [were] focused on Native Americans and, later, on Asians. Jews – with their European origins, American experience, and English language skills – were generally viewed as white pioneers, not as foreign interlopers."[198]

Three years after Victor's arrival in Portland, a letter arrived. Victor's half-sister, Bertha, pleaded for escape from an unwanted marriage arranged by their father. Victor rescued her with a ticket on a steamer and brought her to Portland in 1903. Bertha, it seems, was not opposed to marriage in general, just to the man her father chose. In May of 1904, Bertha met a young Jewish German merchant, George Wolff, who had just opened a general store in Aberdeen, Washington and was visiting Portland on a buying trip.

"They were a case of love at first sight," stated their daughter Sylvia (Wolff) Epstein, "and in 1904 they were married and came to Aberdeen and I was born in 1905."[199] Sylvia wasn't kidding; Bertha and George were engaged three days after they met.[200]

Go North Young Man, Go North

Sensing opportunity 173 miles north of Portland, Uncle Ignatz proposed that Victor head to Seattle and, in partnership, open a wholesale millinery shop, copying the success at Lowengart & Co. In 1900 there were 80,000 U.S. Census-counted people in Seattle and by 1910 it jumped to 237,000.[201] Victor's arrival in 1905 was smack in the middle of this growth spurt.

The Alaska Klondike Gold Rush, which began in 1897 catapulted Seattle from a town to a city. The Gold Rush was a goldmine for Seattle's business community as these dreamers came to Seattle to stock up for the journey north. Between 1900 and 1910, Wallin and Nordstrom shoe store opened, interurban rail service began, the Seattle Symphony performed for the first time, King Street Station opened, the Seattle Children's Hospital began operating, and the Yukon Pacific Expo (Seattle's first world's fair) was held in 1909 with over three million visitors.[202]

New buildings were popping up everywhere. It was one such new building, the National Building, located at 1012 Western Avenue,[203] that Victor rented for his millinery shop. One block from the pier, this handsome, six-story, red brick building, which still stands today,[204] was emblazed with STAADECKER & COMPANY on the side.

"My father," Uncle William said, "had a very large business in ribbons and in hats and in feathers and flowers and in felt bodies."[205]

Victor continued building his millinery empire. Needing more talented employees, he placed an ad in a New York paper in 1907 seeking an experienced millinery designer. The ad was answered by one Ada May

Staadecker & Company – Western Avenue (sometime between 1905-1909) (Joel Staadecker Collection).

Bonnar, born on February 16, 1874 in Lucknow, Ontario, Canada. The Bonnar family was originally from either Ireland or Scotland, depending on which of our family members you ask. Ada moved from Lucknow to New York in 1895, honing her millinery design skills for some twelve years before accepting the position at Staadecker & Co.

As far as I know, Ada had never been married and was likely, at the age of 33, considered a "spinster." Bags packed, she boarded a train and traveled across the continent to begin her new job and her new life. Ada had fair skin, a soft face, intelligent eyes, and hair stacked high on her head. She had broad shoulders and looked like a woman who wouldn't hesitate to tell you what was on her mind. She began to work for Staadecker & Co. in 1907 and on February 27, 1908, she shed her spinster status and "married the boss."[206]

My great grandmother, Ada, is a legend in our family because at a time when marriage between Jews and Christians was rare, Victor, a German Jewish man married Ada, a Canadian Protestant. My mom, Betty Lou

Treiger, has a cherished letter, carried by Ada from her home in Lucknow, Canada to the United States. The envelope reads:

Ms. Bonner – Certificate of Membership.

The letter is dated April 17, 1890, from Tillsonberg and is written in old fashion cursive script:

This is to certify that the bearer Ms. Bonner leaves the Presbytenau Congregation in Lullodeu, Oxford Co. a member in full communion and good standing. She is affectionately commended to the fellowship of God's people wherever her lot in life may be cast.

M. M. Gregors

Ada and Victor were 34 and 39 respectively when their first child, Joel Bonnar Staadecker, named for Victor's father Joel, was born November 5, 1908. Joel's birthdate gave me pause. Between February

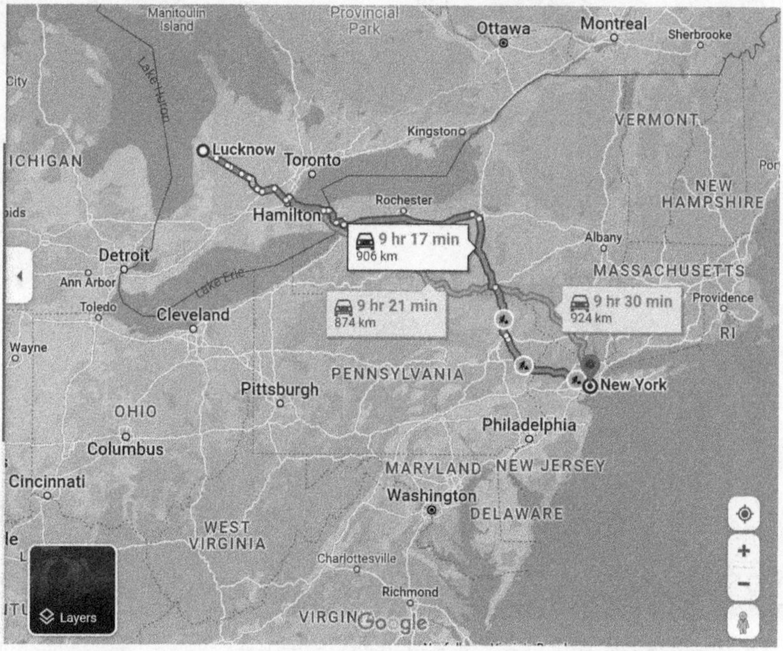

Google map – Lucknow , Canada to New York

27, 1908 and November 5, 1908, there are 252 days (36 weeks). A typical pregnancy is 280 days (40 weeks). Perhaps Ada gave birth four weeks early or perhaps there was some *shtupping* going on and she became pregnant leading to a quick marriage. Of course, there is no way to know, but this adds color to the rare intermarriage between a Jew and Christian. [207]

If this was a "shotgun marriage," Victor and Ada certainly made it work. They had three more children: Victor Bonnar Staadecker Jr. born on October 18, 1909[208] and the twins, Elizabeth Jane and William Bonnar, born April 29, 1911.

It was a busy household, but Ada and Victor took time to volunteer with Temple De Hirsch. Ada served on the Board of the Temple's Women's Auxiliary,[209] and Victor served on the Board of Directors, rising first to the office of Vice President[210] and then to the Presidency. Though Ada didn't convert to Judaism, she involved herself in the charitable work of

Ada (center) Joel (back row), Elizabeth and Victor, Jr. (to right of Ada), and William (to left of Ada). (UW Libraries, Special Collection, UW1425, Jewish Archives Collection).

the Jewish women of the day. According to Uncle William, she was well accepted by the Jewish community.

"It was very rare incident where a Gentile lady would be so well accepted," Uncle William said. "Nobody ever thought of her as a Gentile lady. They always thought of her as a Jewish lady. The only difference between her and being a Jewish lady was she never affirmated to the faith. She [could] even ... read Hebrew from the Temple and was very close to the rabbi."[211]

Though Uncle William felt that his mother was accepted into the Jewish community, this mixed marriage didn't go unnoticed by other family members.

"My Uncle [Victor]," Sylvia (Wolff) Epstein, stated, "married someone who was not Jewish ... . She went to Temple all the time. They think of themselves as Jewish but there was no observation [sic]."[212]

Despite murmurs against her, Ada was active in the Seattle Chapter of the National Council of Jewish Women (NCJW). This was a national organization with over 50,000 members in the 1920s. These Jewish women saw themselves as role models. The Seattle Chapter put out a yearbook in 1927-28 and it includes reports on all the activities of the chapter. The foreward to the Seattle yearbook is penned by Mrs. Estelle Sternberger, the national Executive Secretary, and in which she articulates:

"[T]he Council's vision is the vison of a Jewish womanhood keeping eternal watch over the body and soul of every Jewish mother and daughter, the vision of every Jewish woman playing a role of dignity and achievement in her community, her country, her faith, all in the comity of humanity."[213]

The Seattle chapter of NCJW had thirty-four clubs, including Dramatic Club, Mother's Club, Sports Club, Embroidery Club, and more. There was a Blue Bird Group under the leadership of Mrs. Alphred Shemanski, "who instruct[ed] them in hygiene and behavior."[214] There was a sewing school, a Sabbath school (175 enrolled); English classes, and vocational scholarships given to needy Jewish students.[215]

The 1927-28 Yearbook lists Ada as a member of the "Social Committee."[216] Also serving on the Social Committee were Mrs. Emil

Mayer (Victor's sister Gertrude) and Mrs. Louis Friedlander (my great-grandmother Belle).[217] In 1928, Ada was nominated to serve on the Board of NCJW.[218]

Ada worked at the Educational Center to help acculturate (read assimilate) Jewish emigrants from Eastern Europe. The already established Jewish communities of the United States, primarily of German Jews, looked down on these newcomers from Eastern Europe. These new arrivals were poor, religiously observant and spoke Yiddish, not German or English. Though the established Jewish community provided assistance and classes, they wouldn't dream of inviting them over for dinner. This was still very true when my parents, Betty Lou Friedlander and Irwin Treiger, who were from these different parts of the Jewish community, decided to marry in 1957. It was a rough bridge to cross.

In her work with the NCJW, Ada often went down to the docks or over to King Street Station where the trains came in to welcome the newcomers.[219] In my imagination, Ada was one of the women who welcomed my grandmother, Rose Steinberg (from Belarus) when she arrived at the train station in 1911.

"[My mother] was a great gal," Uncle William summed up his thoughts, "Everybody liked her... she was very jovial, very attractive lady, and very artistic.... lots of fun at a party."[220]

Ada was not only a mother of four and active in charitable and social organizations she was also the Vice President of Staadecker & Co. I learned this from a 1930 article in the Seattle Times, entitled "A Seattle Magician Who Takes Payroll Dollars from Hats."[221] After an interview with Victor and a description of the process of hat making, the journalist concluded:

"And just a word of warning – don't refer to the officers of this company as the Staadecker brothers just because their names are listed as Victor, A.B. and Sam Staadecker.[222] The second name – in addition to being that of the Vice President – is the President's wife."[223]

SUNDAY MORNING, MARCH 16, 1930. THE SEATTLE SUNDAY TIMES 9

A Seattle "Magician" Who Takes Payroll Dollars *from* Hats

The "double-date" frock, a Jenness success that has become as much of a "hit" in the Middle West as in Seattle, worn by Miss Marjory Rhind

"The average well-dressed woman buys twelve hats a year," says Victor Staadecker (at right), president of Staadecker & Co.

A view of the makers' table (at right) in the hat factory, each employe working from an original model which stands before her

THE Story of Staadecker & Co., Queen City Specialists in Style as Expressed in Headgear to Frame Woman's Face and Frocks to Catch Her Fancy

By BETTY STEWART.

A WOMAN'S hat!

Is anything more important to her—except, perhaps, her face? Can anything bring her more joy or sorrow?

Like dashing Iris March, Michael Arlen's

Seattle Sunday Times, March 16, 1930, p.9 , Victor's picture is bottom right. (Permission for Use - Seattle Times).

Staadecker & Co.

With Ada by his side, in 1909 Victor was ready to expand his business. He made a deal to lease a new six story brick building under construction on 5th Avenue between Pike and Union. According to Uncle William, 5th Avenue was a wooden street at this time.[224] The new building was called the Staadecker building and would house the largest millinery factory in the city. The new home for Staadecker & Co. was built over five months and cost $50,000 to $60,000 ($1.7 - $2 million in today's dollars).[225] From this impressive factory, Staadecker & Co. produced hats sold in Oregon, Washington, Idaho, China, Honolulu, and Alaska.[226]

Though it's hard to know exactly what went on inside the Staadecker Building, thanks to Mimi Lee, Uncle William's childhood friend,[227] we have a glimpse of its inner workings. It's due to a remarkable 1929 essay Mimi wrote in high school. Uncle William passed it on to my mom, Betty Lou Treiger,

Staadecker & Co – 5th Avenue (MOHAI #1983.10.6480).

informing her that it "is really quite accurate."[228] I found this essay among the dusty files saved by my father, who somehow knew just what to save and what to throw away. This scrap of paper is particularly spectacular.

"Staadecker & Co.," Mimi writes, has "many different departments. Each department has a different style, make and type of hat."[229] Staadecker & Co. employed 125 full time employees. The lowest paid apprentice paid nine dollars per week ($165 in today's dollars) and the highest paid hat maker was paid sixty dollars per week ($1,100 in today's dollars).[230]

The highest quality hats made by Staadecker & Co. were called "the Beth hats," Mimi writes, and they "have [a] small picture of the owner's daughter, after whom they are named."[231] These hats, Mimi explains, are "made by hand, and are sold and displayed on the fourth floor. There are three French Rooms where the hats are shown to the customers, either by the saleswoman or fitted on Parisian models. The entire show room is decorated in black and red. The rugs are black and gray, and furniture is wicker. Some of the hats shown in this department cost as much as seventy-five dollars wholesale [$1,370 in today's dollars]."[232]

During the busy season, Staadecker & Co. employed additional workers to help make these hand-made hats. Up to 200 at one time are known to have been employed to make Beth hats.

Then there are the less expensive Kenmore hats, made in two rooms, on one-half of the third floor, which is filled with "artistic pictures, most of which were painted by the manager of the department."[233] These Kenmore hats were "medium priced" and were partly made by machine. "The flowers, ornaments and materials from which the hats are made for all the departments," Mimi writes, "are stocked on the other half of [the 3rd] floor."[234]

The second floor of the Staadecker building is where the "Job hats" are produced. "These hats," Mimi explains, "have very little trimming or decoration of any kind. These ready to wear hats occupy the entire second floor of the building, except the space in the front of the floor where the office is situated."[235]

"The making of a hat," Mimi continued, "is extremely interesting and equally complicated. It is always started on a frame. The frame is either wire, buckram or crinoline. It is covered with velvet, satin or straw, depending upon the present styles, and the time of the year."[236] After the hats are completed, they go to the shipping department, where the "articles are itemized, and the order is then brought to the credit manager, who is the secretary treasurer of the firm. He considers the financial possibilities of the customer, and passes on the bill of goods, making the best terms possible. The order then goes into the hands of the floor manager. When the order is assembled, it is taken to the fifth floor, where the shipping department is located."[237]

Because the millinery business is "mainly a style business," Mimi writes, the products must be shipped by express, because "freight is too slow" for the changing trends. The express shipping company picks up twice a day and the, "packages are sent through the back entrance on the first floor. There is a long, narrow room on the first floor where the boxes of merchandise layed down without being pilled [sic] upon one another. Every package, that is sent out or brought in, is checked in the downstairs freight room."[238]

"I think I have taken in everything that was explained to me," Mimi concluded her paper, "and I hope you can visualize this establishment. FINIS."[239]

It was one year after Mimi's visit to Staadecker & Co. that the Seattle Times ran the Magician article which furnished even more description of the hat industry and Victor's millinery factory.

"Is there anything more important to her," the Seattle Times writes, "except perhaps her face? Can anything bring her more joy and sorrow? ... Deprived of their hats who knows but that all womenkind would hibernate and never see the sunlight again."[240]

In this illustrated article, the journalist described how Staadecker & Co. created 150 new hat styles each month and "[t]hose of the previous month are entirely discontinued."[241] In conversation about the importance of hats to a woman's wardrobe, Victor stated that "the average well-dressed woman buys twelve hats a year."[242]

This 1930 article included a photo of Victor, showing a handsome man with a receding hairline and a prominent forehead. In the photo, round spectacles sit on his nose and he is impeccably dressed in a suit and tie. Uncle William reported that Victor was often mistaken for Woodrow Wilson. Victor made four or five trips a year[243] to the East Coast and on one occasion when the train stopped in Chicago, photographers began taking Victor's picture because, as Uncle William explains, "they all thought he was the President. The resemblance was remarkable. He was very severe and stern man. He brought up his family very strictly. Most of those Germans did. He ruled the roost. He was a good father."[244]

Victor Staadecker, 1935 (UW Libraries, Special Collection, UW1424).

The four Staadecker children were a privileged and well-mannered group. Remarkably, they were featured in a national publication – *The Illustrated Milliner*. The author of the piece, Grosvenor K. Glenn, wrote an article titled *From Coast to Coast*. The year was 1915 and Grosvenor's assignment was to travel across the country to see what the milliners were up to and report on the lucrative world of hats. Arriving at King Street Station, Mr. Glenn called Victor Staadecker who greeted him warmly and gave him a top to bottom tour of Staadecker & Co. Then, Victor invited Mr. Glenn home for a home-cooked meal, by the cook of course.

Glenn commented on Staadecker & Co., on 5th Avenue, as a new building of concrete that "was arranged to excellent advantage. The showrooms are in Frenchy gray. The stocks are in fine shape reduce to small quantities, though the assortment of novelties is very comprehensive embracing the latest eastern success in each department."[245]

After two pages about Staadecker & Co's millinery factory and the world of hats in Seattle, Glenn veered from his usual prose.

"I must be pardoned for introducing an unusual personal note," writes Glenn, "but I cannot content myself without saying that four of the most charming children I have ever known are those of Mr. and Mrs. Staadecker, three boys and a girl. All are under six years of age, the youngest boy and girl and twins are nearly three years old. The grace of the children are a reflection of their unusually talented and gentle mother and the kindly character of Victor Staadecker, gentleman."[246]

Ellizabeth Staadecker (Treiger Collection).

A few years after Mr. Glenn's visit, Nanny (Elizabeth) was photographed in ballet clothes. Adorned in a full blown, spaghetti-strap, tutu, she could have been on the cover of Junior Ballet America. Her toe shoes, laced with ribbon that wrap around her ankle and socks that reach mid-calf give off a serious air. Nanny's attempt at a graceful ballet position, however, was not successful, as her arms stick out from her body like stiff branches of a tree. Her shoulder-length hair is adorned with a bow the size of the top of the space needle, giving the whole picture a lopsided feeling. The hint of a smile makes me wonder whether she was enjoying herself.

I connect viscerally to this photo and the ambivalence it conveys. As a girl, I too took ballet lessons. I didn't enjoy my ballet lessons and the photos of me in a pink tutu look just as ridiculous as Nanny. Although Nanny and I share this common awkward experience, two generations apart, this doesn't make me feel closer to her. Instead, it somehow makes me feel more sorry for her.

Staadeckers Establish Themselves In Society

Staadecker & Co. produced millinery masterpieces garnished with colorful ribbons, felt, and bird feathers. When the journalist Mr. Glenn visited in 1915, he saw many trimmings, but he didn't see feathers of aigrettes, snow herons, grebes, or any wild fowl, other than game birds. This is due to vigorous lobbying by the Audubon Society.

In 1909, the Washington State Legislature passed a law prohibiting the use of such feathers for millinery design. After the law's enactment the Audubon Society warned milliners to cease and desist. Many milliners didn't take heed and were "caught with thousands of dollars' worth of feathers and plumes, which from the sales standpoint was practically valueless. . . Several had been caught, the goods have been confiscated and the milliners prosecuted."[247]

Something had to be done. The milliners organized, and with Victor Staadecker as their chairman, a deal was cut on July 27, 1909. The agreement made between the milliners, the State, and the Audubon Society, granted the milliners five months to sell the stock of rare bird feathers they had on hand.

"It is estimated," the Seattle Times reports, "that fully $25,000 [$863,000 in today's dollars] worth of the forbidden merchandise is held by the establishments of Seattle alone."[248] With this negotiated deal, the women of the State of Washington, have five additional months to "freely purchase and adorn their hats with the brilliant plumage of any or all wild birds."[249]

Ada and Elizabeth Staadecker (Treiger Collection).

The outlawing of such rare bird feathers didn't mean that women's hats would be feather bare. Other feathers, some of which were quite valuable, were used for adornments. The feathers were so valuable that some resorted to stealing. In an article dated July 30, 1912, the Seattle Times reported that Staadecker & Co. was victim to a "carefully planned" robbery. "Thieves," the Times reports, "took upwards of $2,000 [$64,700 in today's dollars] worth of ostrich plumes and feathers of bird of paradise from the Staadecker & Co. Store, 1413 Fifth Avenue, last night."[250] The article describes that the thieves entered the building from a fire escape and a "manhole in the roof." The "loot" was taken away in an "automobile hidden in the alley in the rear of the building."[251]

Victor's leadership was not restricted to the Milliners' Association. He was a Mason of the twenty-seventh degree,[252] a high honor. He also served on the board of the YMCA.[253] Besides his involvement in Temple De Hirsch,[254] Victor took on leadership roles in *Bnai Brith*,[255] Glendale Golf & Country Club,[256] the Community Fund,[257] and the Caroline Kline Galland Center (home for Jewish Aged).

Temple De Hirsch was the center of the family's social life. They held a celebration when their eldest son, Joel, turned thirteen and became Bar Mitzva. On November 16, 1921, the Seattle Times reported that the "family would welcome guests in their home at 1134 29th Avenue to celebrate." [258]

Their son, Victor Jr., was confirmed in 1924[259] and William followed with confirmation in 1926.[260]

It appears that in November of 1921 (when Joel celebrated his Bar Mitzva), the Staadecker family lived at 1134 29th Avenue. That same month, they purchased a lot on 21st Avenue North.[261]

"Mr. Staadecker," the Seattle Times writes, "will start the erection of a handsome residence ... to cost in the neighborhood of $25,000" ($438,000 in today's dollars).[262]

However, inexplicably, only one year after the announcement, the Staadecker family moved to a mansion in Denny Blaine. It sits, still today, just across the road from the shore of Lake Washington. It was built in 1922 by someone who never lived there.[263] Victor bought it the same year – 1922. There must be more of a back story here of why Victor and Ada began to build a new home but moved into the Denny Blaine one instead, but I couldn't uncover it.

The Denny Blaine mansion, nestled among trees on a quiet street had a garden, with "maybe two, three thousand tulips every year."[264] One-third of the home was reserved for the servants' quarters which housed six-in-help, including two maids, a cook, and gardeners for the large grounds. The kitchen was housed in the servants' quarters which leads me to believe that Ada didn't do much cooking. The home was the scene of many a grand party.

"Those days," explains Uncle William, "in the early twenties and thirties were rather affluent times for the community of Jewish people. They all seemed to be doing well. They enjoyed parties."[265]

Just a brief glance at the Seattle Jewish Transcript Social Page makes it clear that Seattle's Temple Jews of the 1920s and 1930s loved parties. It was constant entertaining – dinners, concerts, lunches, teas, birthdays, anniversaries, visitors from out of town – any excuse for a party.

"My mother was a good party giver," Uncle William explained. "She knew how to do everything beautifully. Her tables were always much talked about. The way she entertained was outstanding. We had a beautiful home [in Denny Blaine] of about 20 rooms, on Lake Washington Blvd. It was an easy house to entertain in because it was so large."[266]

One of the grandest moments of entertaining in the Denny Blaine home was the marriage of my grandparents, Elizabeth Staadecker and Jack Friedlander. Elizabeth (Nanny) was the very same "Beth" from the Beth Hats described by Mimi in her Garfield Essay #4, now no longer a girl, but a young woman.

My Grandparents Marry

Elizabeth Staadecker (Nanny) and Jack Friedlander (Papa Jack) were married in the Staadecker's Denny Blaine home on December 27, 1933. Excitement abounded when my grandparents announced their intention to marry.

"Both Miss Staadecker and Mr. Friedlander," wrote the Seattle Jewish Transcript, "are favorites of the young socialites in the city."[267]

This was to be a union of two of the most prominent Jewish families in the city.[268] The Friedlanders were jewelers and owned a large, marble-fronted store just down the street from Staadecker's millinery factory, on the corner of 5th and Pike. A full-page article in the Jewish Transcript covered the wedding. From the white calla lilies and red roses to the "tall wrought-iron candelabras shedding a mellow glow over the bridal party."[269]

The article spun a vision of the bride:

"Blond and very slender, the bride looked charmingly ethereal in a bridal gown of cream magnolia satin. Godets flared from the tightly fashioned skirt and spread into the soft lustrous folds of a fan shaped train. The bodice was cut with a high cowl neckline and long sleeves. A long veil of rose point fell over the frock, and was arranged about the head simply, with a short wreath of orange blossoms at the nape of the neck."[270]

Nanny's mother, Ada Staadecker's dress was described as "a smart frock of black chiffon velvet with train, and wore a shoulder corsage of orchids."[271] Jack's mother, Belle Friedlander, was "gowned in a stunning formal gown of apricot brocade made en train and also wore orchids."[272]

The "Lohengrin wedding march[273] ... added solemnity," after which Rabbi Koch, of Temple DeHirsch officiated at the ceremony. The ceremony was limited to a small number but was followed by a reception where many guests were welcomed.[274]

This magnificent description of Nanny as a bride seemed incongruent. My memories of her are of an old woman with long, thin fingers, holding a cigarette, wearing a large, floppy hat. When I knew her, Nanny was very skinny, I thought she might be blown over by the wind. She had no body fat, hips so small that there was no way she could ever hula hoop. But as I now think about her early years, I see someone who was raised as the only girl in a very successful immigrant family. I imagine that Victor and Ada placed their hopes and dreams on all of their children, but especially their daughter, to carry on the family traditions and status.

However, nothing in her first 22 years prepared Nanny for what was to come – an unhappy and difficult marriage, two bouts with Tuberculosis, a bitter divorce,[275] aversion therapy at Schick Shadel Hospital for alcoholism, and death by fire in her apartment.

My grandparent's marriage was a miserable failure, a "mismatch from the beginning," Aunt Jackie told me. "Mother and Daddy were never happy," she continued, "they always argued."[276]

Alvin and Jackie Goldfarb; Betty Lou and Irwin Treiger (Treiger collection)

I see now that Nanny went from the bosom of her parent's home where she was the princess and was adored by her parents and brothers, to an unfortunate married life. She must have felt alone, though she gave birth to two daughters, my mom Betty Lou in 1935 and Jacqueline (Jackie) in 1937 and she volunteered with Temple and the National Council of Jewish Women. She was, however, never able to find her footing.

Perhaps because their parents' marriage was unhappy, the sisters, Betty Lou and Jackie are very close. They both married Seattle men[277] and bought homes near each other. Aunt Jackie's house was a second home to my brothers and me, so long as we took our shoes off at the door.

A Visit To The Staadecker Home

In the fall of 2021, I invited Aunt Jackie and my mom to go with me to Victor and Ada's Denny Blaine mansion and knock on the door. I hoped to look inside.

"We can't just knock on the door," Aunt Jackie said.

"Yes, we can," I assured her, "if the people who live there don't want to let us in, they can say no."

"Ok," she sighed, "I'll come."

The three of us set out one sunny October afternoon. We parked and walked up to the Halloween bedecked front door and knocked. Flanked by two eighty-something year old women I thought, how can they say no?

Magically, the door opened. Two people stared at us quizzically.

"Hi, I'm Karen Treiger, and this is my mother, Betty Lou Treiger and my aunt, Jackie Goldfarb. Their grandparents used to live in this home and we were wondering if we could come in and look around."

Well, they opened the door wide and welcomed us in. I was surprised to learn that my mom and aunt had never been in this home. We walked into a grand entry with the original wide staircase leading up to the second floor. Just off the entry to the left was the guest bathroom, and the stunning marble floor with cream colored ivory flower inlays was part of the original 1922 home.

To the right was an expansive living room with the original delicately ornate fireplace before which Jack and Elizabeth were married. Thanks to the newspaper's description of the wedding, I closed my eyes and was able to see the beautifully dressed women, the men in their fine suits, people excited to congratulate the young couple. Entering the dining room, I noticed the fireplace that warmed the guests at the many dinner parties, luncheons, and teas described on the Seattle Times and Jewish Transcript Society Pages.

The current residents of the home explained that they had bought the house a few years before and renovated the servant's quarters, transforming it into a spacious kitchen, family room, and game room. The sunlight shone through the windows and glass doors which led directly out to the yard. The yard and the garden were sources of pride for Ada and Victor, with thousands of tulips popping up each spring. It's said that sightseeing buses would pull up in front of the Staadecker home and people would ooh and aah over the house and garden. If Victor was home when one of these buses stopped by, he would invite all the passengers off the bus and give them a tour of the garden.[278]

"This is the most beautiful house I have ever seen," my mom exclaimed once we left and the door was shut behind us. My mom and Aunt were

Betty Lou Treiger (left) and Jackie Goldfarb (right) outside Staadecker's Denny Blaine home (Treiger Collection).

Staadecker House – Denny Blaine -front (Treiger Collection).

Staadecker House – Denny Blaine - back (Treiger Collection).

both thrilled that we had been invited in and were visibly moved to see the place where their mother had lived and where their parents were married.

I was overjoyed that my plan had worked. Victor and Ada lived in this beautiful home and built a happy and secure world for their children. Victor and Ada sold the house to Emil Sick[279] in 1932,[280] before my mom and Aunt were born. Victor and Ada moved, with their son William, to a three-year old upscale apartment building at 1223 Spring Street. The apartment building had twelve stories and was built in a style that reflected "a transition from Neoclassical to the popular Art Deco."[281] The top floor was a "palatial" penthouse, while the other floors had two large apartments with "a foyer, reception room living room, dining room, tile kitchen, pantry, tile bathroom with enclosed glass showers, and a maid's room, complete with its own bathroom."[282]

This building still stands today at the corner of Spring and Minor. Coincidentally, my mother's apartment building, First Hill Plaza, which was built in 1982, is across the street. I pass by this apartment building all the time and until now, didn't know that I had any connection to it. I doubt my father knew that Victor and Ada lived across the street when he lived here. He would have loved to know that fact.

Victor and Ada helped build Seattle into the business center of the Pacific Northwest. Their active involvement in the civic and Jewish community helped create the vibrant city of today. Growing up I knew little about the life of Victor and Ada, but now I know that I stand on their immigrant shoulders.

Succession

Victor's journey from Merchingen to New York, and then on to Ohio, Portland, and Seattle, has much to teach me. His hard work, business savvy, and good luck led to his affluent, successful life in a stunning home with 3,000 tulips. I can hear Victor urging me not to be afraid to follow my dreams. However, Victor didn't achieve all his dreams – he failed to pass a successful business onto his children.

Victor had high hopes that his sons would join the business and carry on after he retired. In the late 1920s, Joel and Victor Jr. attended

Yale, graduating in 1930 and 1931 respectively. This achievement was particularly noteworthy given the antisemitism at Yale during their enrollment. A 1922 memo from the admissions chairman labeled "Jewish Problem," urges quotas on the "alien and unwashed element."[283] After this memo, Jewish enrollment was held to 10% for four decades.[284]

After finishing Yale in 1930, Joel wanted to attend law school, but his timing was terrible. The Great Depression[285] hit and people had less money to spend on hats. "There was no money for further education," Joel's son, Joel Jr. said. "My grandfather told my father to 'get a job.' My dad came back to Seattle and got a job as an insurance agent."[286]

Victor Jr. came home after he graduated from Yale and worked with his father at Staadecker & Co. before joining the Navy Reserve. He served in the Navy during World War II and "came out a full commander."[287] By the time the war was over, hats were out of fashion and Staadecker & Co. was no more.

Uncle William, who looked strikingly like his father, attended the University of Washington after graduating Garfield High School. "I didn't even finish the University of Washington," Uncle William said. "I was not a good student. It didn't interest me. I liked business. I couldn't wait to get in it. I did get in it. I've been in it ever since... some many, many years."[288]

After dropping out of University, Uncle William joined his father at Staadecker & Co. As the Great Depression hit Seattle, they downsized. They no longer needed the entire building, so they rented out the Mezzanine to Best's Apparel, a women's clothing store, which opened in Seattle in 1925.[289] The connection between Staadecker and Best's was likely made by Uncle Ignatz, in Portland, who was one of the initial co-investors in Best's.[290]

"After several years," my father, Irwin Treiger writes, "Best's Apparel overshadowed the millinery operation and the two switched spaces, with Best's occupying the main floor."[291] Perhaps because Victor was the largest stockholder in Best's, Best offered to sell his business to Staadecker in 1940. [292] However one of Victor's sons, "who had been the 'designated heir' to the business, declined, thinking that there was no future in the apparel business. The rest is history, with Best's ultimately selling to Nordstrom, giving Nordstrom its entree to the world above the foot."[293]

After the United States declared war in 1942, Uncle William was on his way home from a buying trip in the East. He was in the club car and "was the only human in the car that wasn't in uniform.

The next day, I went down and enlisted. Then I told my father what I had done. He felt very badly. ... I entered the army in October of '42 and was in it for three years and nine months. At that time, the time I went in the army, my father was in his seventies. I didn't know if they'd be making hats during the war. As a matter of fact, today, they don't even wear them. I just put an ad in the paper, 'Well established business for sale. Partners gone to war.' We sold it the following Monday. My father retired. I stayed in the Army, my brother in the Navy. I didn't get out 'til 1946. I signed a deal [with the buyer of the millinery business that] I wouldn't go back into the millinery business for five years. I wouldn't have gone back in the millinery business anyway because it wasn't a very good business then."[294]

During the War, Uncle William served as a major in the Army, stationed at Fort Lawton.[295] Though he performed with the original Seattle Repertory Theater and had always wanted to be an actor,[296] when the war was over, he opened a jewelry store in Northgate Mall, called Staadecker Jewelers. He ran that business until he retired. Though it wasn't discussed when I was growing up, Uncle William was gay. He had no children, so the great nieces and nephews served as surrogate grandchildren. We would visit him often, first in his Capitol Hill home and later in his assisted living facility in Bellevue.

Each Christmas Eve, he took the Treiger and the Goldfarb families out to dinner at Trader Vics. Each child received a thoughtful gift that was wrapped like it contained crown jewels. Most of the gifts were picked up on one of his many trips abroad, and many of them still adorn my Seattle home to this day.

Uncle William always had people laughing. In fact, my mom and Aunt Jackie told me that when he would come over for dinner to their home in Magnolia, he would sit at the dinner table and make the girls laugh so much they didn't eat their dinner.

"Mother would get furious with Uncle William," my mom told me. "He would disrupt our dinner, but Jackie and I loved it."[297]

For some reason, Uncle William spoke with the royal we and in the third person.

"How are we today?" he would ask. And then without missing a beat, not waiting for a response, he would say, "William is fine."

Uncle William was a true gentleman, treating everyone with respect and kindness. He lived with his parents Ada and Victor until their deaths. Uncle William himself lived to the age of 79, dying in 1990. My house is full of Uncle William's art and furniture, which I inherited when he died. Two of those pieces belonged to his parents before him. Uncle William also collected art of Pacific Northwest artists like Mark Toby, Helmy Juvonen, Richard Gilke, and Morris Graves. As I walk around my home and look at the art on my walls, I think of Uncle William.

Though Ada was sick for years, it was Victor who died first – January of 1948. Ada followed six months later, on July 18, 1948. She was seventy-four. The Seattle Times reported that Ada left an estate worth $50,000 ($651,000 in today's dollars), which was to be split evenly among her four children. Victor and Ada moved to Magnolia in the early 1940s to be close to Elizabeth and the rest of the family.[298]

"Mother was very close with Ada," my mom told me. "We would go over there often to visit. What I remember is that Ada was in bed a lot."[299]

Before Victor and Ada died, they saw three of their children married. Nanny was the first to marry in 1933. Joel married Phreda Sherman. Though Phreda was born in Seattle, Joel met her in Portland, Oregon. They married in the fall of 1938. Finally, Victor married Mary Keating in 1939.

Joel followed his parent's footsteps by being active in the

William Staadecker (Treiger Collection).

Jewish Community. He served on the boards of Temple De Hirsch, Kline Galland Home, the Jewish Federation, and Glendale, where he was a golf champion.[300] Aunt Phreda was a smart, beautiful, gregarious woman who volunteered with the Jewish Community Center and the Council House.[301]

Joel and Phreda had two biological children, Joel Jr. and Bonnie Jo, and adopted another son, Charlie, who ran an unsuccessful campaign for mayor of Seattle in 2013. Joel died in 1964 and Phreda, lived another thirty-seven years. She died in 2001. While I have no memory of Joel, I remember Aunt Phreda with great warmth. She was the center of any room she was in. Humor and love exuded from her very being, always making us laugh.

Victor Jr. and Mary gave birth to one son, Victor Keating Staadecker III.[302] In 1944, Victor Jr. and family moved to Berkeley, California. Victor Jr. died on January 12, 1973.[303]

Final Thougths

Reflecting on the death of Victor and Ada seventy-seven years ago, I wonder about the "what ifs." What if Victor remained in Germany and made a life there. Would he have married and had children, been rich or poor, been murdered in the Holocaust or somehow survived? What if he never left New York or Idaho or Portland? What if Ada had never left Canada, never answered that ad, never traveled 3,000 miles across the continent to join Staadecker & Co.? What if she married someone else, maybe someone of her own faith?

Victor's decision to leave Germany affected so many in his family. Over the course of thirty-four years, Victor sponsored and paid for six of his siblings to make the long journey to America. Bertha, who arrived in Portland in 1903, lived in Aberdeen with her husband George Wolff. Then came Sam and Gertrude in 1906,[304] both of whom worked for Staadecker & Co. In 1907, Gustav arrived, settling in Aberdeen and working with his brother-in-law, George Wolff. Emmanuel arrived in 1910, married, and moved to Texas.[305] Johannah came in 1937[306] as Hitler's rise to power made life for Jews a nightmare.

Of the remaining Staadecker children, his sister Sophie and Albert died in Germany before WWII. Tragically, three of Sophie's six children were murdered during the Holocaust: Leon, murdered at Auschwitz; Samuel, murdered at Dachau; and Ella, whose place of death is unknown.[307] Victor's half-sister, Betty, refused to leave Germany. She was the only one of ten Staadecker siblings murdered by the Nazis.[308] Certainly, if Victor had not left and brought his siblings over many more Staadeckers would have perished in the Holocaust.

Uncovering the past and peeking into the lives of Ada and Victor allowed me to fit some puzzle pieces together. The courage of Victor and Ada leaving their homes in Germany and Canada to start lives in the remote Pacific Northwest fills me with strength and pride. I now know that I come from cultured people, yet they were tough as nails. In many ways, they lived the immigrant dream in America. There is, however, a sober recognition that dreams you have for the future and for your children may not turn out as you hope. The story may not end as you dreamt or wished it.

Contemplating Elizabeth's life, my gratitude increased. I learn from Nanny's experience that a childhood of privilege and wealth isn't a guarantee for a happy adult life. Though there were plenty of bumps in the road for Nanny, I now see her more fully. Life was far from perfect for her, but she made a difference. Raising two amazing daughters, helping new immigrants settle, caring for her parents, and centering her life around community brings her life's values into focus. Her death in a fire started by her own cigarette, turned a sad life story into a tragedy. She died alone, gasping for air.

This grim story pushes me to examine my own life and how I live each day. I try to face my insecurities and fears, knowing that we must strive to shape the world around us. Being alive is to struggle and we must learn from those struggles, to help us find meaning and continued purpose in life.

Nanny's name was passed on to our eldest daughter. We gave her the English name Elizabeth, which is derived from the Biblical name Elisheva. I think Elisheva wonders why we chose to name her for Nanny. The simple answer is that Shlomo Goldberg (my spouse) and I feel strongly about the Ashkenazik Jewish tradition of naming babies for deceased grandparents.

At the time, Elizabeth was the only deceased grandmother whose name had not already been taken. Shlomo's grandmothers both died in the Holocaust and Fay (Faiga Bracha), his older sister, bears their names. My paternal grandmother, Rose (Steinberg) Treiger was still alive in 1988 when Elisheva was born. Even if Nanny was not the perfect role model, there is much to learn from Nanny's life about fortitude and resilience.

In fact, I now believe Elisheva was destined to be named for Elizabeth, because in the fall of 2020, Elisheva and her husband Judah brought fraternal twins (boy/girl twins) into the world, tugging us back in history some 109 years to the birth of Elizabeth and William, the Staadecker twins. But Elisheva's connection to the Staadecker family continues, as she and Judah chose to name their third child, born in 2022, after Ada Bonner Staadecker, naming her Eden. Our task is to find meaning in the past and allow the connections to resonate through the generations.[309]

As I reflect on the shallowness of my relationship with Nanny, I feel that Nanny lost her opportunity to get to know me and my cousins before she was taken from this world. I am doing things differently now. This time of life feels fleeting and my grandchildren are a gift that opens my heart and nourishes my soul.

My mom has very few memories of Victor or Ada, but by breathing life into their stories, I hope they will live on. Victor and Ada left a legacy of family, hard work, and community leadership. It's part of our family DNA. The family business didn't survive, but their values did. They show us that we can each make a difference.

At least, I am inspired to try.

CHAPTER 3

NANNY'S TUBERCULOSIS

"Patients must not read. Patients must not write. Patients must not talk. Patients must not laugh. Patients must not sing. Patients must lie still. Patients must not reach. Patients must relax. Patients must ... Patients must never take medicine without the Doctor's permission.... [Patients must] keep nothing on your stand but your water glasses and sputum cup. Never keep pictures or flowers on your stand... Keep your stand neat and clean. An orderly patient is a helpful patient."[310]

This is Betty MacDonald's description of the rules at the Tuberculosis (TB) sanatorium depicted in her novel, *The Plague and I*. Betty, the mother of two young children, was a patient at Firland Sanatorium, just north of Seattle, for eight months. "As we drove off," MacDonald wrote, "I turned and waved and waved to the children. They stood on the sidewalk, squinting against the sun. Young, long-legged, and defenseless. I loved them so that I felt my heart draining and wondered if I was leaving a trail behind me like the shiny mark of a snail."[311]

I was searching for just such a memoir. I longed to know what my maternal grandmother, Elizabeth (Staadecker) Friedlander, who we called Nanny, felt as she left her two young daughters and entered Firland, a Tuberculosis sanatorium. Children, according to MacDonald, were only allowed to visit once a month, for ten minutes. My mom, Betty Lou Treiger and my Aunt Jackie Goldfarb told me that they visited Firland once a month. Aunt Jackie was not allowed to go inside because she was only ten. My mom, who was twelve, got to go inside, with her father, Jack Friedlander, who we called Papa Jack, for a ten-minute visit.

Left: Elizabeth (Staadecker) Friedlander holding Betty Lou (UW Libraries Special Collection, UW41897).

Bottom: Betty Lou Friedlander and Jackie Friedlander (UW Libraries Special Collections, UW41898).

"I waved to mother through a window," Aunt Jackie recalled. "These visits were very sad, because I would see my mother through the glass, and she was in some kind of machine with only her head sticking out."[312]

Neither my mom nor my Aunt remembers exactly when their mother was a patient at Firland. So, Aunt Jackie's description of the buildings is crucial to pinpoint Nanny's admission. Had Nanny been a patient before November of 1947, she would have been hospitalized in a Downton Abbey type mansion, surrounded by thirty-four acres of farmland. However, after November of 1947, Firland moved north to a much larger, refurbished Naval Hospital.[313] This was a different story.

The original sanatorium opened in 1913 and was the project of the Seattle Anti-Tuberculosis League, formed seven years earlier. Through a mix of private donations, state, and county funds, including, remarkably, half of the profits from Seattle's first World's Fair, the 1909 Yukon-Pacific Expo, Firland was built. It opened with two patients. By 1937, it had hit its maximum of 250. This was, however, inadequate to meet the need; Seattle had one of the highest incidences of TB per capita in the country.[314] By the time Betty MacDonald was admitted in 1938, there was a waiting list of 3,000. She, like other mothers of young children, jumped to the head of the line. City officials were pressured to find a way to treat more patients.

To achieve this goal, Firland moved in 1947, to an old Naval Hospital. Capacity jumped to 1,350; the wait list evaporated. But this uninspired facility had none of the charm of the old mansion and the nurses had no time to give patients individual attention. Patients "were lined up like soldiers in the long, impersonal bunkhouses and given sponge baths assembly-line fashion."[315] Windows were still open and outdoor "rest cure" was still the Firland norm, but, after November of 1947, sanatorium life sounds harsh, cold, and, yes, sanitized. This was the location of Nanny's convalescence.

I live seventeen miles south of Firland, so I decided to drive there. Since 1959, the campus has been home to Fircrest, a residential facility for people with intellectual and developmental disabilities.[316] To get there, I followed directions on my phone. As I took the final turn into the wide-open gate, my phone sang: "You've reached your destination." I immediately noticed that the sprawling ninety acre campus was eerily empty.

"Wow, this is ugly," I thought. Most of the buildings would feel right at home in Minsk under Soviet control – rectangular, off-white, characterless buildings.

"I don't think there's been much remodeling since Nanny was here," I mumbled to myself.

As I continued to drive, I found a few sad-looking, slant-roof cottages. My heart sank as I thought of Nanny stuck on bed rest in one of these. The whole campus felt like a sci-fi movie, devoid of human life. I only saw four people – one resident sat alone outside one of the cottages, another walked across the grass, assisted by two aides. The road wound up a hillside and there, nestled among some tall pine trees was the only charming building in the place. It was made of old red brick with moss growing on the side and a steeple on top. I didn't need the sign – "Chapel" – to alert me to its religious purpose.

I tried to visualize Nanny, at the age of thirty-six, among these depressing buildings, without family or friends, only getting to see her daughters and husband for brief monthly visits. She must have hated it.

Nanny, as I knew her, was an enigmatic, quiet, chain smoking, rail-thin, reformed alcoholic. Her life of sixty-one years was a bumpy ride, with a tragic end. But of all the bumps, it was her encounter with Tuberculosis

Chapel at Firland (Treiger Collection).

that fascinated me. I wanted to know more. I wanted to understand what it might have been like.

I read Thomas Mann's *Magic Mountain*, the fictionalized experience of a young man at a European Sanatorium, and MacDonald's *The Plague and I*. With this background, I drew a mental picture of Nanny's experience at Firland. She was a patient there for six months. However, not long after her discharge, she relapsed and was re-admitted for another six months.

Perhaps my interest in Nanny's TB[317] was triggered by my experience as a child. At the age of six, I had Nephritis, an inflammation of the kidneys. My "rest cure" lasted three months. The first month I had to stay in bed – I could only get up to go to the bathroom. The second month I could get up, but I could only be in the house. The third month, I could do anything I wanted, except go to school. I didn't mind the whole thing at all. In those days (1967), we had a black and white TV on wheels. When one of us kids got sick, it was rolled into our room to watch from our bed. I got to watch a lot of TV and drink 7 Up – the other sick treat.

The only exception to my "rest cure" was the weekly visit to the doctor where I peed in a cup and had my heart listened to with cold, metal stethoscope. After the appointment, my mom and I proceeded to an old-fashioned coffee shop. I had a doughnut and hot chocolate from one of those machines that spurts and spits milk, chocolate, and air into the paper cup below. Those moments sitting across from my mom with no brothers to bother me are some of my happiest childhood memories and made the whole Nephritis business very positive.

This early experience with Nephritis and hot chocolate led me to try a similar tactic. In 1992, at the age of four, my daughter Elisheva, was diagnosed with Acute Lymphocytic Leukemia. Her treatments over two and half years were administered at Seattle's Children's Hospital. She was poked and prodded with needles and fed toxic chemicals through a white plastic tube that stuck out of her chest. Periodically, the doctors put her to sleep and poked her with a very long and scary needle to extract a bone marrow sample. After each appointment, we stopped at Baskin and Robbins ice cream shop, just down the street from the Hospital. Elisheva could order whatever she wanted, usually a chocolate milk shake.

My hope was that when she was older, she would remember her illness not for the needle pokes and the bone marrow test, but for the sweetness of the ice cream and the fun we had in stopping there. Each time we entered the ice cream store, my memory of the doughnut shop flashed through my mind, and I was somehow comforted from the worry and exhaustion that came with a four-year-old in cancer treatment and a toddler and infant at home.

After these sweet thoughts of hot chocolate and ice cream faded, I was still left wondering why I spent weeks researching Tuberculosis. Ultimately, I had to face the possibility that perhaps my interest in Nanny's TB arose from the COVID-19 pandemic. While working on this TB research in July of 2022, COVID had sickened over 565 million people worldwide, with over six million dead.

My spouse Shlomo, son Jack, and I had contracted the disease for our first time in November of 2020, before a vaccine was available. We were worried because the virus can settle in your lungs and as the immune system responds to this viral invader, you could get sicker. Sometimes the immune response is so virulent that the patient can't breathe on his or her own. Further, if a person has underlying conditions, such as diabetes, asthma, or obesity, the chance of complications and the possibility of death increases. I'm pleased to report that we had none of those additional risk factors, but we were still anxious.

Some of the symptoms of COVID-19 include fever, night sweats, loss of smell and taste, malaise, difficulty breathing, and coughing. We didn't have difficulty breathing or any other symptom that would land us in the hospital. I lost my sense of smell and taste and suffered fevers, chills, and what became known as "brain fog," where it felt like there two helpings of oatmeal inside my head. Our son Jack had symptoms similar to mine, while my spouse Shlomo got off the easiest – a cough, fatigue, and bit of brain fog.

Of course, TB is bacterial, not viral, but like COVID-19, it spreads through droplets in the air and can attack the lungs of its host. "Tuberculosis is spread by the expelled secretions from the lungs of larynx (voice-box) of the patient," explains Helen Bynum in *Spitting Blood: The History of Tuberculosis.*

"Coughs, sneezes, and even speech create aerosols of tiny airborne particles. These evaporate to 'droplet nuclei' of less than 1 micrometer in size, which contain the tubercle bacilli and are inhaled. The minimum time one must spend with a single active tuberculosis patient – the index case – before acquiring the disease is unknown, but evidence suggests that it can be brief... Smokers, alcoholics, and injecting drug users, are in greater danger, as are those who suffer from diabetes, end-stage kidney disease, and another lung disease such as silicosis or who have a depressed immune system most commonly today as a result of medication or HIV infection." [318]

Wanting to know how my grandmother contracted TB, I asked Aunt Jackie.

"It was because she volunteered with the National Council of Jewish Women," my Aunt told me. "She helped sort the clothes of the newly arrived Jewish immigrants."[319]

My physician spouse informed me that it's not likely that Nanny contracted TB from clothing. Perhaps she caught it from a recent immigrant, but I have no way to know. I also don't know what symptoms Nanny experienced, but the list of horrible possibilities is long: "[F]ever, night sweats, malaise, weight loss, loss of appetite, difficulty breathing and a cough. The coughing can be so extreme that it causes soreness in the ribs. The coughing can also produce blood."[320]

Before an antibiotic treatment was found for TB, it was thought that the best "cure" was rest and fresh air. Patients would rest for hours outdoors, regardless of the weather. During the cold months, they wrapped themselves in blankets, sat outside and shivered. Nanny had no extra body fat to keep her warm; she must have been freezing sitting outside those distressed cottages.

In the pre-antibiotic era, TB was also treated with more invasive treatments. One common treatment was artificial pneumothorax, a procedure in which the lung was collapsed, allowing it to "rest" and therefore, hopefully, heal. To accomplish this, Betty MacDonald writes that the Doctor, "injected Novocain and then forced a hollow needle, about as large as a big darning needle but much longer, in between the lung and the pleura. After it was in, he attached it to a contraption that forced air in."[321] As the Medical

Cottages at Fircrest School, Formerly Firland Sanitorium (Treiger Collection).

Buildings at Fircrest School, Formerly Firland Sanitorium (Treiger Collection).

Director explained to Betty MacDonald, collapsing a lung was like putting a splint on a broken leg, allowing it to rest and heal more quickly.

In Thomas Mann's *Magic Mountain*, the patients would spend the first four weeks in bed, after which they were allowed to get up and eat relaxed meals and take a daily mandatory walk. After the walk, the afternoon was spent resting outdoors on their patios.[322]

Original Firland Sanitorium, 1927 (Courtesy of Seattle Municipal Archive).

Upon admission to Firland, patients were sent to the bedrest hospital. During those first weeks on bedrest, "[p]atients were not permitted to read, write, speak, or cough. Coughing was prohibited because it was feared that it would start a coughing frenzy among other patients. Coughing was only permitted to produce a sputum sample for testing. Because fresh air was considered to be key in the treatment of tuberculosis, windows were kept open all year long. In addition to fresh air, nourishment was also extremely important, and hearty meals were provided for all patients."[323]

Time at a sanatorium had a different feel to it; each day was the same without much to do and, certainly, with no rush to do it. "What people call boredom," Thomas Mann puts in the mouth of his protagonist Hans Castorp, "is actually an abnormal compression of time caused by monotony – uninterrupted uniformity can shrink large spaces of time until the heart falters, terrified to death. When one day is like every other, then all days are like one, and perfect homogeneity would make the longest life seem very short, as if it had flown by in a twinkling."[324]

What did Nanny do every day at Firland? I imagine that those first few weeks in bed were terribly hard. But Mann assures us in *Magic Mountain*, that, "it is enough for us to remind everyone how quickly a number of days, indeed a great number, can pass when one spends them as a patient in bed. It is always the same day – it just keeps repeating itself."[325]

Mann explains that when our usual cues of time passage are removed, we are incapable of estimating how much time has elapsed. "A group of miners buried by a cave-in," Mann writes, "and cut off from observing the sequence of day and night, were rescued at last and guessed the period of time they had spent in the dark, between hope and despair, at three days. And it had been ten. One would think that in such an agonizing situation time would have had to have seemed longer to them. And yet it had shrunk to less than a third of its objective proportions."[326]

Mann's descriptions of the warping of time resonates with those of us who lived through the months of COVID-19 lockdown. Each day the same; not going to work, not seeing friends and family, afraid to say hi to people on the street; all so isolating and lonely. Time changed its meaning and made many of us re-evaluate our relationship to it. The months of COVID lockdown were as Mann described one long day – melded together.

Perhaps Nanny used her "time" at Firland to perfect her sewing skills. She was an excellent seamstress. After all, once the period of bedrest was complete, the patients were required to do occupational therapy (OT). They were up for eight hours a day; the remaining sixteen were "resting."[327] One of the categories of OT offered was the "domestic arts center."[328] Sewing was likely one of the "domestic arts." I have two pillows that Nanny made for me when I was a girl. Their sewing is masterful. The pillows have delicate butterflies and flowers sewn onto them and the borders are thick and beautiful.

Antibiotics were introduced to Firland in 1947. I imagine that Nanny received antibiotics there and perhaps that explains why her initial stay was only six months. Before antibiotics, a typical stay was two years. However, Nanny relapsed and was re-admitted for an additional six-months. I can't imagine the dread of having to be re-admitted to the sterile, monotonous life at Firland. I imagine Nanny saying goodbye yet again to her family and enduring a second bed rest and the slow march to healthy lungs.

I envision the deep and lasting mental scars from having TB and being separated from her family. Did Nanny feel the heartache and pain of separation from her children that Betty MacDonald described? Did she leave a trail behind her like the shiny mark of a snail? Was time warped during her stay? Did she experience six months as one long day? She didn't leave a diary or letters that help me understand how she felt or what she was thinking. She didn't even talk about her experience with her daughters.

The feelings I'm left with are sadness and grief. Sadness that her adult life was not filled with happiness, joy, and love. Grief in the lost relationship I never had. I now understand that my deep dive into TB was a last-ditch effort to try to connect with my grandmother, to have a relationship, even one built on her illness and loneliness. While I have a deeper understanding of TB and of life in a sanatorium, I have no better sense of who she was than when I began.

This exploration, however, surprised me in what it did open up. It pried open a door in my heart to see my own mother with more clarity and compassion. My mother built a wall around her heart – not to stop loving – she loves openly and wholeheartedly – but regarding expression of emotion, especially when talking about her childhood. She doesn't talk about how she feels or her emotions and they have never been part of her vocabulary. When I ask about her own mother, she usually doesn't want to speak about it.

I see now that, as an adult, my mother made a choice not to be like her mother. She chose to be a warm, loving, hands-on, funny, fun mom. Her every activity, from making dinner to shopping to her charitable work, was infused with energy, intelligence, and excitement. She made our family the center of her life and she was at the core, holding it all together. She has exquisite taste in clothes, art, furniture, and homes.

She accepted the family legacy of active participation in the Jewish and civic community. She volunteered with diligence and was a role model for me and my brothers. She didn't just volunteer herself – oh no – she *schlepped* us along. We learned by example, action, and discussion.

As a parent raising four children of my own, I recalled all the wonderful parts of my childhood and learned from my mother to be the rock-solid center of the storm that swirled around a busy household. I worked hard to infuse our home with joy, warmth, fun, and love. My mother passed on the values that came down to her from the branches of her family tree: Staadecker, Singerman, and Friedlander. She showed me how to raise a family of interesting, smart, community-minded, good-hearted people. And how to have fun along the way.

CHAPTER 4

FRIEDLANDER FAMILY

My First Career

"What do you have there, Nini?" My grandfather Jack Friedlander's baritone voice boomed, using my childhood nickname.

"I found salt and pepper shakers over there, with all the plates," my seven year old responded. "They match my parents' fancy dishes, and I think they would be the perfect anniversary present for them. Can I buy them? How much do they cost?"

"Well, let me see them," Papa Jack said. Slowly turning them over, he inspected the price tags.

"How much money do you have?" he asked.

"I have one dollar," I stated, puffing up my chest and showing him the dollar bill clutched in my hand.

"Well, that's perfect," he told me. Removing the price tags, he handed them back. "They cost fifty cents a-piece," he said. "Take them downstairs and have the girls wrap them."

I gave my grandfather the dollar and took the Lenox, gold-rimmed salt and pepper shakers down the steep stairs to the basement of Friedlander & Sons Jewelers. I was sure I got the deal of the century. I sure did.

Jack Friedlander was a complicated grandfather. By the time I was born, he and Nanny were divorced and he was married to his second wife, Polly. He was a handsome man, who stood about 5'9" and had a full head of hair and shoulders as broad as a high school football star.

My childhood memories of Papa Jack are of a fun, sweet, loving,

Friedlander Family Tree

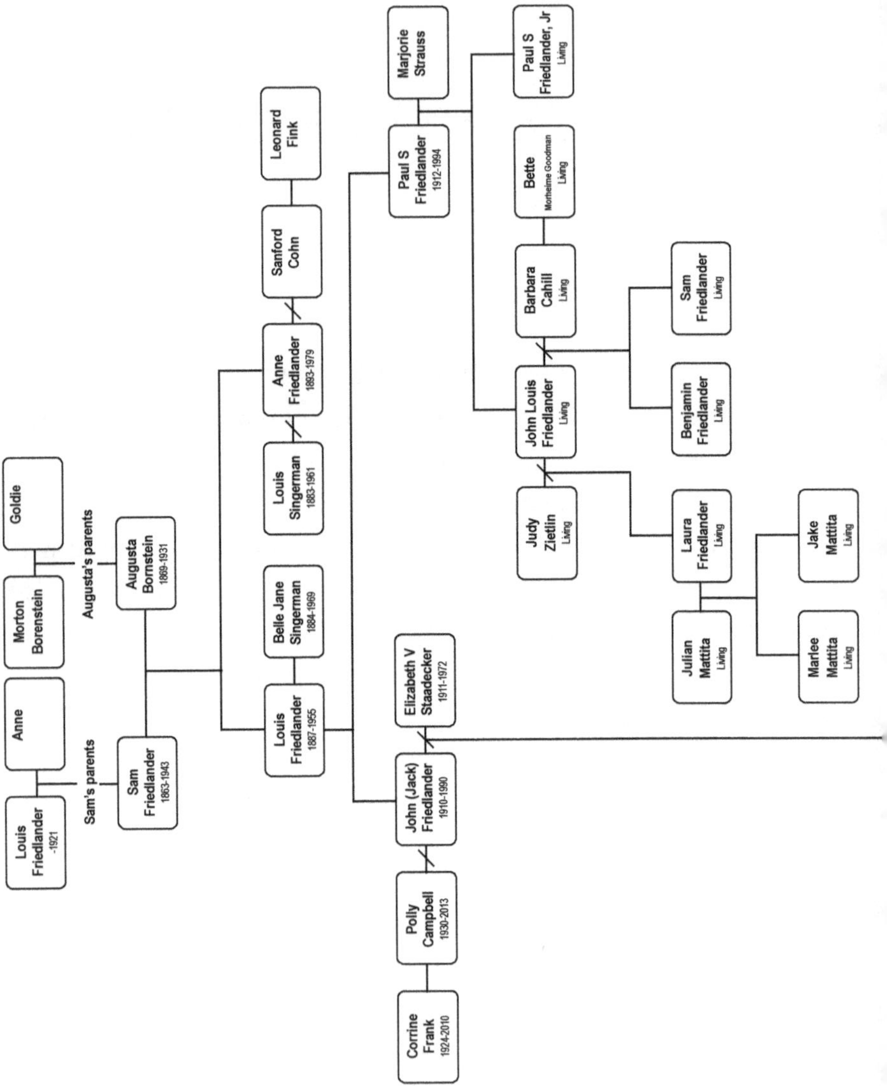

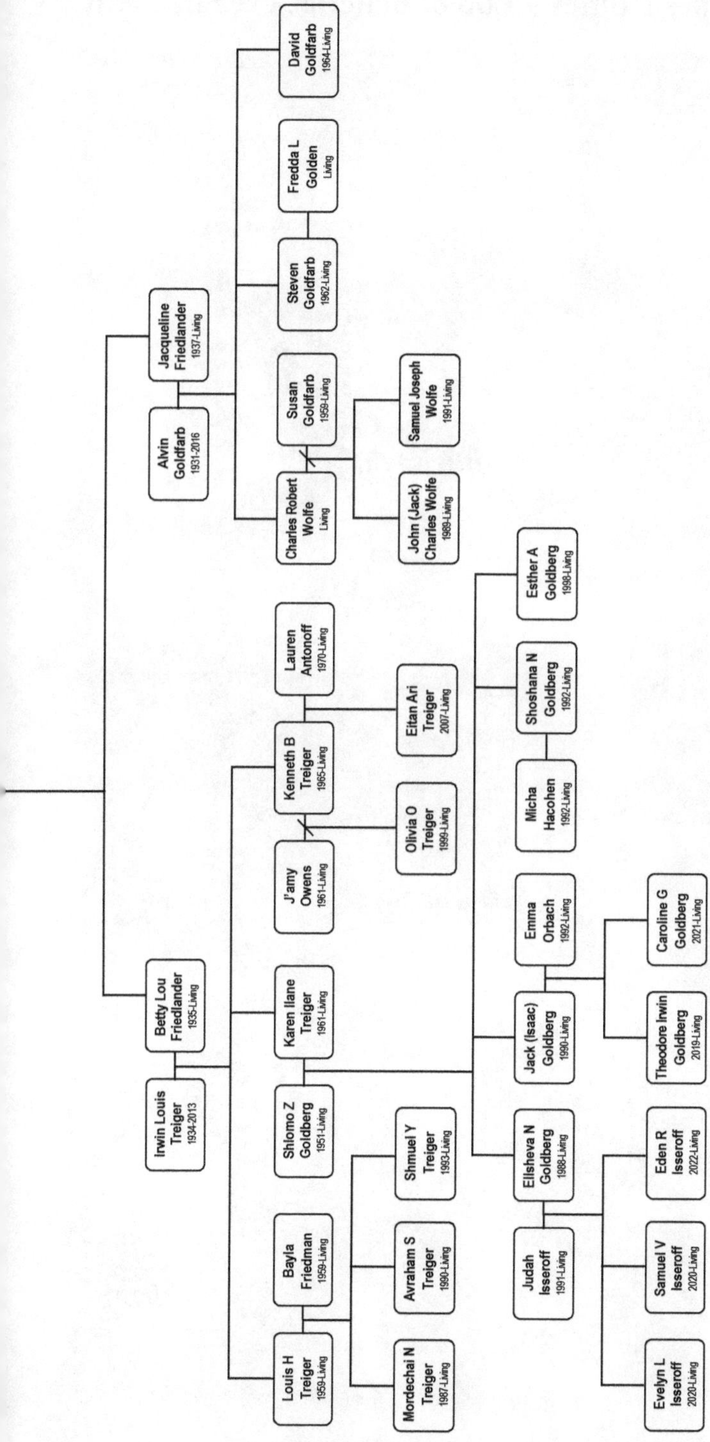
Irwin Louis Treiger 1934-2013
Betty Lou Friedlander 1935-Living
Alvin Goldfarb 1931-2016
Jacqueline Friedlander 1937-Living
Louis H Treiger 1959-Living
Bayla Friedman 1959-Living
Shlomo Z Goldberg 1951-Living
Karen Ilane Treiger 1961-Living
J'amy Owens 1961-Living
Kenneth B Treiger 1965-Living
Lauren Antonoff 1970-Living
Charles Robert Wolfe Living
Susan Goldfarb 1958-Living
Steven Goldfarb 1962-Living
Fredda L Golden Living
David Goldfarb 1964-Living
Mordechai N Treiger 1987-Living
Avraham S Treiger 1990-Living
Shmuel Y Treiger 1993-Living
Olivia O Treiger 1999-Living
Eitan Ari Treiger 2007-Living
John (Jack) Charles Wolfe 1989-Living
Samuel Joseph Wolfe 1991-Living
Judah Isseroff 1991-Living
Elisheva N Goldberg 1988-Living
Jack (Isaac) Goldberg 1990-Living
Emma Orbach 1992-Living
Micha Hacohen 1992-Living
Shoshana N Goldberg 1992-Living
Esther A Goldberg 1998-Living
Evelyn L Isseroff 2020-Living
Samuel V Isseroff 2020-Living
Eden R Isseroff 2022-Living
Theodore Irwin Goldberg 2019-Living
Caroline G Goldberg 2021-Living

Friedlander Map – Homes – Lou & Belle/Jack & Elizabeth

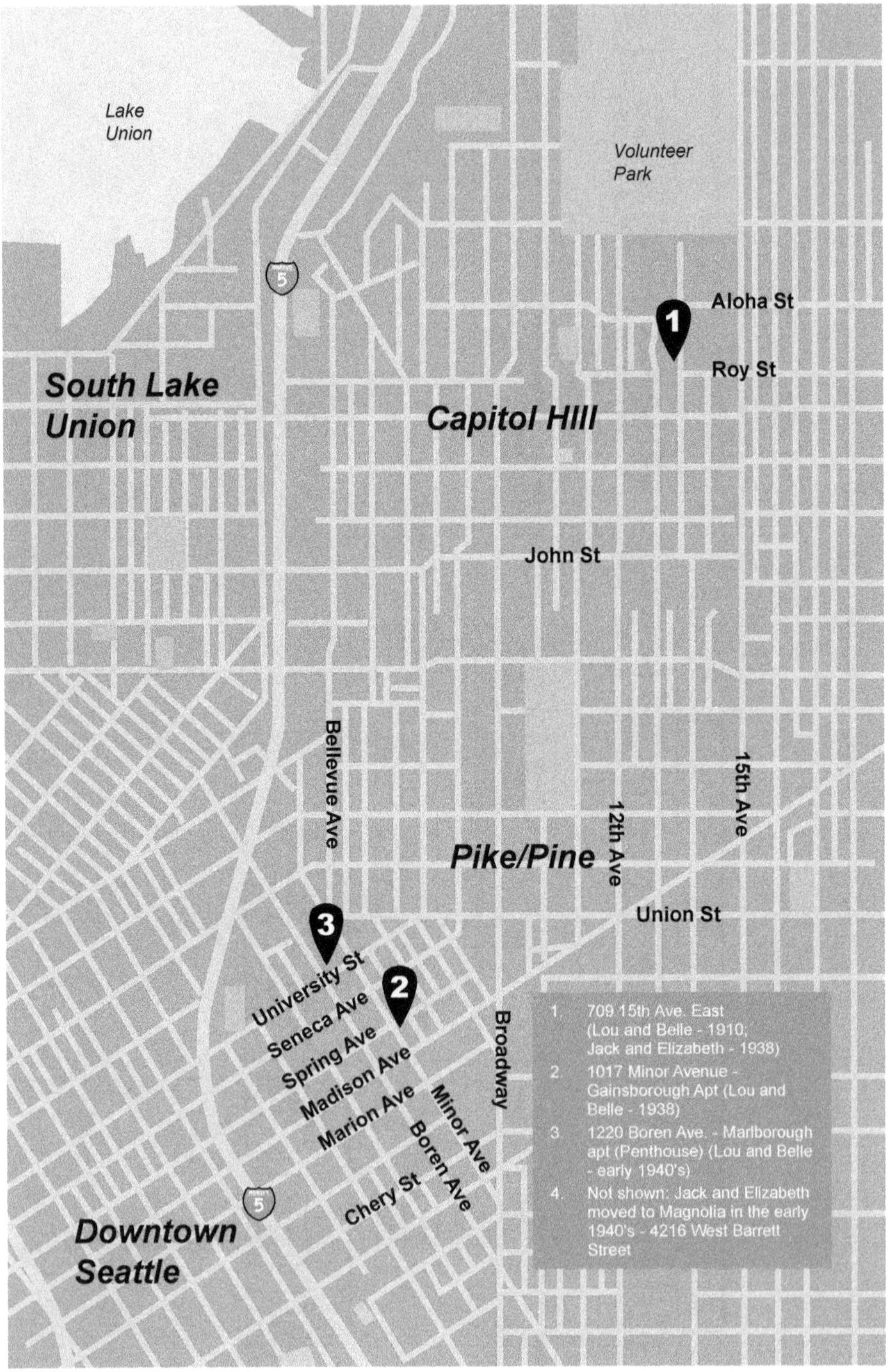
Lake
Union
Volunteer
Park
Aloha St
1
Roy St
South Lake
Union
Capitol HIll
John St
Bellevue Ave
15th Ave
12th Ave
Pike/Pine
Union St
3
2
University St
Seneca Ave
Spring Ave
Madison Ave
Marion Ave
Minor Ave
Boren Ave
Broadway
Chery St
Downtown
Seattle
5
1. 709 15th Ave. East (Lou and Belle - 1910; Jack and Elizabeth - 1938)
2. 1017 Minor Avenue - Gainsborough Apt (Lou and Belle - 1938)
3. 1220 Boren Ave. - Marlborough apt (Penthouse) (Lou and Belle - early 1940's)
4. Not shown: Jack and Elizabeth moved to Magnolia in the early 1940's - 4216 West Barrett Street

Freidlander Map – Homes – Sam & Augusta

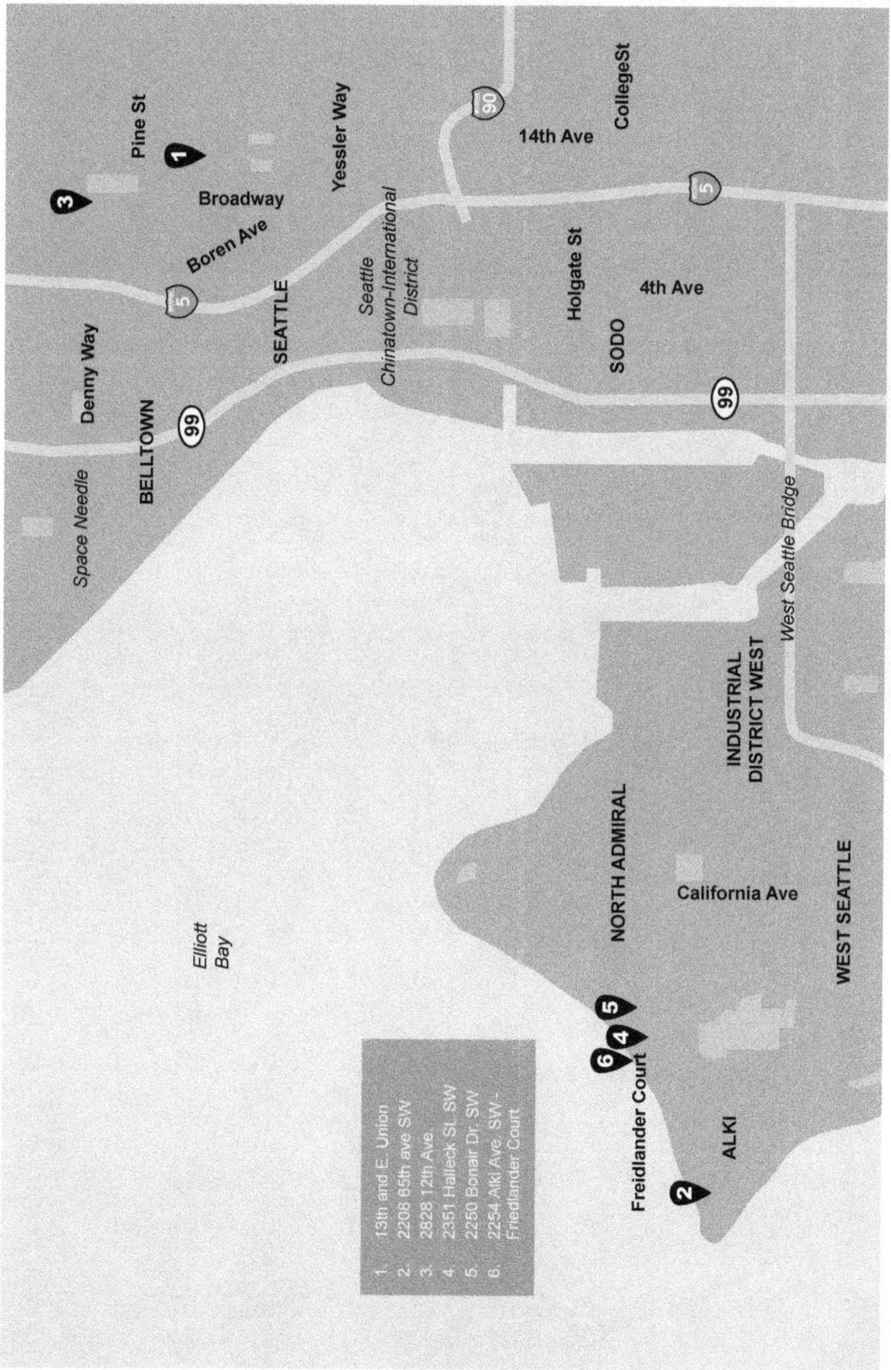

Friedlander Maps - Stores

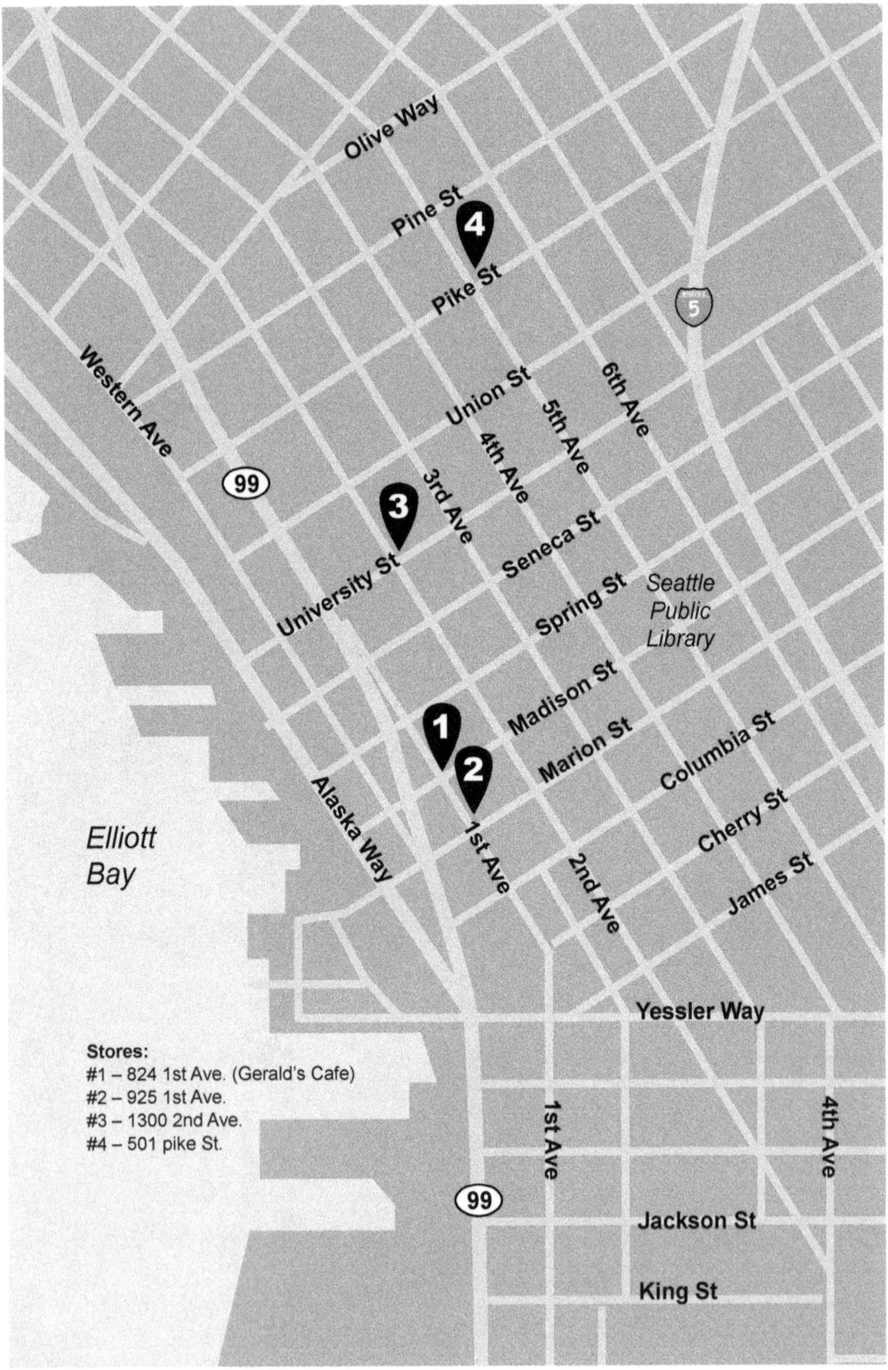

mischievous grandfather. He had a deep, gruff voice, but it sounded melodic to me. He used to send us home from our Sunday afternoon visits with M&M packets tucked in our socks. We would play Candy Land with a one-dollar bill placed squarely in the middle of the board. He would say, "whoever wins gets the dollar" – after all it's important to teach your grandchildren the value of gambling and competition at a young age.

When my brothers and I were roughhousing, our play often involved much laughter; we were having fun. Papa Jack would then intone one of his mantras: "laughing leads to crying." He was of course correct, at some point one of us would get hurt and start crying. That would be the end of the fun.

When I was about nine years old, he took me, together with my older brother Louis and our cousin Susan Goldfarb, on a trip to Harrison Hot Springs, just over the Canadian border. We went together with his girlfriend of the time, Ciccie, and her two sons, Gary and Steve, who were about our age. Our days were spent under sunny skies jumping off the high dive into a crystal blue swimming pool. We dressed up for dinner, and Susan and I would awkwardly dance with Gary and Steve (me with Gary and Susan with Steve) on a large dance floor. I tried to watch Papa Jack and Ciccie dancing to figure out what I was supposed to do.

We grandchildren were instructed to call our grandfather "Jack," not Papa Jack, so he wouldn't sound old in front of his younger girlfriend. We stayed up way past our bedtime. Right before bed, Papa Jack ordered room service. We could have whatever we wanted. I ordered a tuna sandwich and ice cream with hot fudge. Remarkably, I don't recall a late-night stomachache.

On the other side of his character as a caring, indulgent grandfather, Papa Jack drank (scotch), smoked, gambled, and fooled around with women he was not married to. He had three wives, with the first two marriages ending in divorce. He had a limp because of gout, and he loved to bet on Sunday's TV football. He loved to say: "If I didn't drink it away, gamble it away, I pissed it away."

"There was lots of *shtupping*," my mother, his daughter, recalled. "Daddy had lots of women over the years."[329]

As we sat around Aunt Jackie's living room, my mom and Aunt listed the names of women they believed Papa Jack "*shutpped*," some while married to one of his three wives and some while single. I will refrain from listing any of them here for lack of hard evidence. However, it was hilarious to hear them throw around these names and laugh about it.

They told a story of when Papa Jack was married to Corrine, his third wife. Corrine once wore a beautiful suede dress to a party. One of the women that is an alleged mistress, with whom Papa Jack worked at the jewelry store, saw the dress and liked it. Papa Jack went to Nordstrom's and bought the mistress the same suede dress. Corrine saw the bill from Nordstrom's and asked Papa Jack about the dress. He told her straight out that this woman saw her wearing the dress and liked it, so he bought her one.

In February of 1990, Papa Jack died of emphysema in Palm Springs at the age of eighty-five, leaving behind his wife Corrine, two daughters, one step-daughter,[330] six grandchildren, four great-grandchildren, and two landmark divorce cases in Washington State.[331]

When I was a teenager, I had the grand idea that when I got older, I would be a businesswoman and take over the running of Friedlander & Sons. We would, of course, change the name to Friedlander & Sons & Daughters, but that was a detail that could wait. I was ready – after all, I learned the most important marketing lesson of all time working with the Japanese women who sat in the corner of Freidlander's basement wrapping gifts with exquisite tiny roses made of ribbon – if the wrapping is beautiful, the item inside will be received with great joy – no matter what it is. Marketing 101 – packaging and presentation – whether it's a gift or how you present yourself to the world.

Further, I had graduated from my high school gift wrapping job to a job in the "vault." The vault was on the main floor of the store and lay behind a heavy, thick door, secured with three gigantic combination locks, like in old cops and robber movies. The vault felt like a spaceship with its low ceiling and not much room to walk around. I had my own tiny desk and a pair of tweezers, the tool used to pick up diamonds, rubies, sapphires, and other jewels. Carefully laying them out on a flat, black velvet square pad, I recorded the size and cost of each stone and priced them for sale. It was a lot of responsibility and I felt I was moving up the ladder – learning the business from the ground up.

"Papa Jack," I said at the age of 17, "after college, I'll come back and help run the business."

"Women," he intoned, "can't run a business."

And that was the end of that.

I went to law school.

Sam And Augusta Friedlander

The year of my Lenox salt and pepper shaker purchase was 1968. That was eighty-two years after my great-great-grandparents, Samuel[332] and Augusta[333] Friedlander, arrived in America from, as Papa Jack said, "somewhere between Minsk and Pinsk." However, census responses given by Sam and Augusta during the 1930 U.S. Census, shows they were from Latvia, which is near neither Minsk nor Pinsk.[334] Google maps indicates it's north of Lithuania. Sam's parents were Louis and Anne Friedlander. Louis was "a prosperous manufacturer of beverages."[335] Both Sam and Augusta spoke Yiddish in their homes,[336] but in America, they learned to speak, read, and write English.[337]

I've seen photos of Sam – he was short with broad shoulders, like Papa Jack. His bald head accentuated his round face. He exuded confidence.

"My grandfather was afraid of being taken into the [Russian] army," Papa Jack explained in a 1975 interview with the Jewish Archives, when asked why Sam and Augusta left Europe, and "there was no opportunity there." Sam and Augusta married in the old country and traveled across the Atlantic Ocean with tickets bought for them by Augusta's parents, Goldie and Morton Borenstein, also of Latvia.[338]

I've heard the apocryphal Ellis Island arrival story hundreds of times. It goes like this:

It was 1886 when Sam and Augusta arrived by ship to Ellis Island and were sitting for hours waiting for their names to be called. Then a loud voice rang out – "Friedlander." Time went by and no one responded. Sam finally, jumped up and said – "that's me, I'm Friedlander." And that's how our family name became Friedlander.[339]

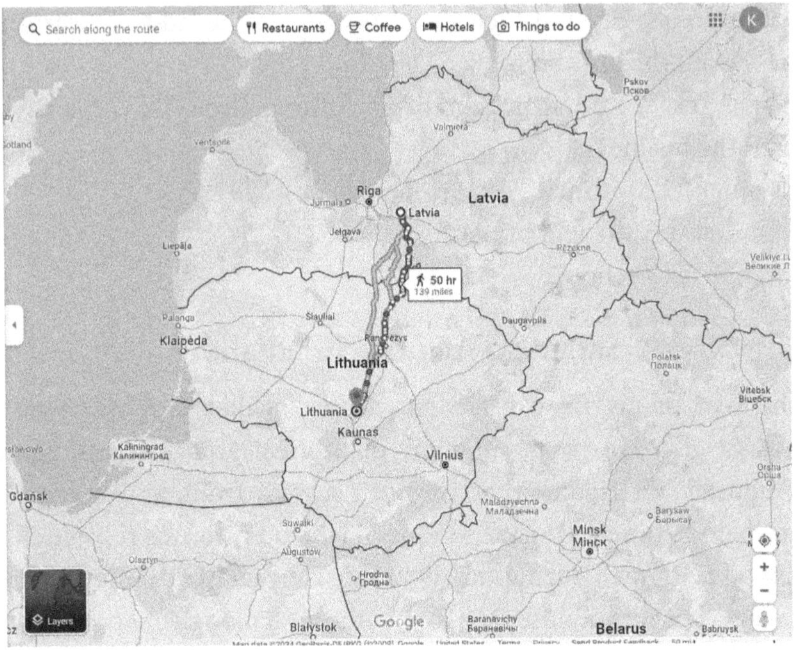

Google map – Latvia

Growing up, this story was absolute gospel. No one questioned its truth. However, a genealogist friend of mine let the air out of the balloon. She told me that at Ellis Island the name on the immigrants' documents had to match the ship manifest. Another fact that raises suspicion is that Sam's brother, who also immigrated to America, had the last name of Friedlander. Papa Jack explained this away by saying that Sam's brother changed his name once in America so their names would match.[340] Unfortunately, I was unable to track down the ship manifest showing their travel across the Atlantic, so this will remain a family mystery.

Did Sam and Augusta see the Statute of Liberty as they arrived in New York Harbor? Lady Liberty was dedicated in October of 1886, so perhaps, but I am not certain of their arrival date. For some context, Grover Cleveland was the President and that the first bottle of Coca Cola was sold in 1886.

The newly minted Friedlander family settled in Rochester, New York, where their sponsoring relatives lived.[341] Rochester was a city with somewhere between 90,000 and 130,000 residents.[342] There was a small

Jewish community, with the first Jewish congregation having formed in 1848.[343] Sam began his career like so many other Jewish emigrants, as a peddler with a cart and some odds and ends to sell.[344]

It was Christmas of 1887 when Augusta gave birth to their first child, Louis, named for Sam's father. Their second child, Anne, named for Sam's mother, was born six years later in 1893.[345]

Believing that greater opportunity lay further to the west, Sam and Augusta traveled 400 miles to Columbus, Ohio in 1894. Sam, having apprenticed with a jeweler in Europe, gave up peddling and found a job working for a jeweler. Soon, he achieved the peddler's dream and opened his own shop. Hugh Harrison, an acquaintance, told Sam he was heading to the Pacific Northwest to strike it rich. Sam gave Mr. Harrison some "diamonds, watches and other expensive articles"[346] to sell in Seattle, agreeing to split the profits.

With no news from Harrison, Sam sent his son, Louis, on a six-day train ride to Seattle. Louis found Mr. Harrison all right, but Harrison didn't want to hear from a Friedlander. Harrison shooed him away, saying, "Get away from me boy, you're bothering me."[347]

Defeated, Louis caught the next train back to Columbus and reported the encounter to his father. Incensed, Sam bought a train ticket himself and headed to Seattle. It wasn't hard to find Harrison in this small town. Harrison admitted that he "sold all the jewelry and spent the money gambling, drinking and on women. He confessed, 'I have no money left at all.'"[348]

"He was a *ganef*" (thief in Yiddish)" Papa Jack told me, as if that explained everything.

Harrison said he'd make it up to Sam if he moved to Seattle.

"I'll introduce you to everyone I know," Harrison assured him, "it'll get you started in business.

"You bet, you will," Sam said, "I'm your new partner."[349]

Sam, seeing an opportunity in this growing town of 80,000+,[350] packed up his family and his inventory and was back on the train. It was 1906 and it was a perfect time for an entrepreneurial businessman to arrive in this growing pioneer town. Seattle had experienced boom times during the

Yukon Gold Rush, from 1896 to 1899, as thousands of men flocked to the city to buy the provisions they needed for the long and difficult journey up north.[351]

The downtown prospered and by 1906 it ran the length of the waterfront, from Jackson Street in the south to Pike Street in the north. The main roads were paved, and electric lights illuminated the stores, homes, and streets. The city sported telegraph, telephone, and automobiles. The main downtown street, 1st Avenue, had been straightened and widened after the Great Fire of 1889. New city building codes required all downtown buildings to be made of brick – no more quick burning wood for this traumatized city. Seattle had enough of that and now handsome brick gave the place a look of a real, solid city.

Sam joined Harrison in his pawn shop called Hugh Harrison, Collateral Banker.[352] The pawn shop was in Gerald's Café, located at the northeast corner of 1st and Marion.[353] The café was a long, narrow restaurant with the customer counter running the length of the space with bar stools to sit on. It was the sort of place where cigarette smoke hung in the air and waitresses served strong black coffee and burnt toast. Given Gerald's central location in Seattle's bustling core, I imagine business was brisk. In 1909, they changed the name to Friedlander, Hugh Harrison, Jeweler and Pawnbroker and moved the business to 925 1st Avenue.[354]

I wondered quite a bit about Augusta. What was she like? All the family stories I have heard are about Sam. I searched my parents' boxes and the internet for a photo, any photo, of Augusta. No luck. But then one day I was speaking to John Louis Friedlander, Sam and Augusta's great-grandson and he said he had some old Friedlander photos in his basement. So I drove across the lake to his home in Bellevue, Washington and looked through his boxes. I found a beautifully framed photos of a woman with very large breats.

"Who is in this photo?" I asked.

"I have no idea," he replied.

I turned it over and on the back it said "Augusta Friedlander, wife of Samuel Friedlander, mother of Louis Friedlander." Jackpot.

I had an image in my mind of a strong, tough woman, but this photo screams – "don't mess with me." I am so grateful to have found this photo.

Augusta (Borenstein) Friedlander. (Treiger Collection)

My internet searching found much more about Sam Friedlander. A 1924 book titled *Seattle and Environs 1852-1924,* by C. H. Hanford, includea a two-page profile of Sam Friedlander.

"There is no more highly respected citizen in Seattle," Hanford opens, "than Samuel Friedlander, one of the city's most prominent businessmen and philanthropists."[355] According to this profile, Sam "disposed of his interest [in Columbus] and in 1906 came to this city."[356]

Clocks & Watches

Hugh and Sam worked the pawn counter together for a few years, but as Papa Jack recalled, Harrison "drank himself to death," and Sam took over the business and changed the name to Friedlander's.[357]

After Louis graduated from college,[358] he joined his father and the name was changed to *S. Friedlander & Son – Jewelers and Silversmiths.* They sold all kinds of merchandise – but watches were especially popular.

Watches were big business in the early 1900's. The transcontinental railroad came to Seattle and trains, boats, and ferries were docking and leaving on specific schedules, so time took on new importance. "Men were carrying watches in increasing numbers," explains Paul Middents, in *Bringing Time to the Public in the Pacific Northwest,* "and the commercial life of cities and towns was being conducted in accordance with the standard time for the whole region. Jewelers were the first to provide reliable accurate local or standard time to the inhabitants of these towns."[359] In 1884, a fifteen-year-old Jewish watchmaker named Joseph Mayer arrived in Seattle and revolutionized watch sales. His business evolved and he began making street and tower clocks.[360]

It seemed that a Mayer-built tower clock outside of your jewelry store was a must. Seven jewelry stores survived the great Seattle fire in 1889 and all seven bought street clocks from Joseph Mayer, placing the clock outside their stores.[361] Not to be outdone, Sam Friedlander bought a Mayer clock in 1908. It was planted in the cement outside the store at 925 1st Avenue. When the store moved to 1300 2nd Avenue (at University) in 1915, Sam brought the clock with him. It was sold and replaced with a larger Mayer clock around 1918.[362] "Friedlander & Son" was written on the face of both clocks.

I couldn't believe my luck when I found a photo of the store on 2nd and University in the collection held by Seattle's Museum of History and Industry (MOHAI). I was, however, puzzled by the name: *Friedlander & Son – Jeweler and Optician.* No one in the family ever spoke of glasses being part of the family business. Asking professor Google, I found that it was common for jewelers in the early 1900's to have an optical department. Since jewelers used small instruments and made minute repairs, they often

(Above) Friedlander and Son - 2nd & Seneca (MOHAI, Austin Seward Photo Collection, 1980.6877.5.46)

(Right) Friedlander tower clock (MOHAI, Austin Seward Photo Collection, 1980.6877.5.53)

used their skill to craft and repair glasses. Perhaps it was a way to attract people into the store. Enter for eyeglasses repair, leave with a new watch.

Watches were always a big part of Friedlander's business. As a girl, I recall walking into Friedlander & Sons on the corner of 5th and Pike and being in awe of the majesty of the place. Friedlanders had moved to the corner of 5th and Pike in 1928, installing a brand new, even larger, Mayer clock outside.[363]

Entering through the heavy double glass doors was to enter a magical fairyland, with crystal chandeliers hanging from high ceilings, marble floors, and sparkling jewels. I felt like a princess every time I walked in. I was almost always greeted by Papa Jack who would be "standing on the crack." He stood, in his tailored suit with a handkerchief sticking out of the breast pocket, just as you entered. Though he was short, he filled the space with his charismatic presence and loud voice. "Hi, hi, hi," he would greet me (and everyone). There were always three "hi's."

The "crack," where he stood, was a literal crack in the marble floor. Papa Jack always said, "you can't sell anything from the back room, you have to stand on the crack." "Standing on the crack" became synonymous in our family with being a successful, hardworking businessman. Just behind the crack were glass-top, dark wood display cases filled with watches. As a girl, I loved the feel of running my hand along the smooth wood and looking at all the different kinds of watches.

In 1979, I was an eighteen-year-old, keen to start my adult life. As I prepared to leave home and head to the Big Apple to study at Barnard College, I needed a new watch. I heard terrible stories about muggings in New York and how people had their watches stolen right off their wrists. My older brother, Louis[364] had been in University in New York for two years already. He hadn't been mugged, but before he left, he bought a Timex watch, so that if his watch was stolen, it wouldn't be so terrible.

"Papa Jack," I began, "can you help me buy a Timex watch?"

"Why do you want a Timex?" he asked.

"Because I am going to college in New York," I respond, "and I'm afraid I'll get mugged. Louis got a Timex before he left two years ago."

"No granddaughter of mine is going to wear a Timex," he growled as he walked me to the watch counter and pulled out a beautiful Seiko with a round face and brown leather strap. He took the tag off and attached it to my bare wrist. Slightly stunned, I gave my grandfather a hug and said thank you. I walked out of the store into a rare sunny Seattle day, wearing my new Seiko. I wore that lucky Seiko for years; I was never mugged.[365]

Friedlanders Settle In

Just three years after Sam, Augusta arrived in Seattle from Ohio, their son, Louis married Belle Singerman. The year was 1909. Lou and Bell had their first child on May 9, 1910. They named him John Morton Friedlander, calling him Jack (Hebrew name – Mordechai). I don't know why they named him John, but Morton must be after Augusta's father Morton Borenstein.

It was 1911 when Belle's father, Paul Singerman, bought an empty lot on 15th Avenue, just a few blocks south of Volunteer Park[366] and built a house for Lou, Belle, and baby Jack. A second child was born on July 12, 1912, in the house on 15th.[367] They named him Paul, after his maternal grandfather.

As a child, Papa Jack attended Lowell Elementary School. Lowell had been enlarged from six to sixteen classrooms in 1904. The location between Aloha and Roy on Federal Avenue made the school 1.8 miles from their home.[368] After elementary school, Papa Jack attended Broadway High School, which opened as Seattle High School in 1902. Located at the corner of Broadway and East Pine, the original building is now the performing arts center on the Seattle Central College campus.[369]

Papa Jack also attended Temple De Hirsch Sunday School. At the age of sixteen, he was confirmed. He had a close relationship with Rabbi Koch and often spoke of him.

Soon after his confirmation, Papa Jack switched to a boarding school in Portland, Oregon. Hill Military Academy, a boarding and day school, was located in a residential area in Northwest Portland. It consisted of two buildings and included a drill hall and workshops. Uniforms were mandatory and students had general high school courses, as well as military classes.[370] I have no idea why Papa Jack was sent to a military boarding school in Portland, but I can fill in the blanks of a rebellious

1925 Temple DeHirsch Confirmation Class, Jack Freidlander is 2nd row, far left (UW Libraries Special Collection, Jewish Archive Collection, UW1145).

teenager, whose immigrant parents felt a strict military education would get him into shape.

After high school, Papa Jack returned to Seattle and attended the University of Washington. He dropped out after two years and joined his father Lou in the jewelry business. As an adult, Papa Jack lived in his father Lou's shadow. Lou, it seems, had a controlling personality and wanted Papa Jack to follow his instructions to the letter on how to run the business. My Aunt Jackie tells of the time that Lou was in Europe on a buying trip. Lou wrote letters home to Papa Jack detailing how to run the store in his absence. Papa Jack was so exasperated with the micromanagement that he told his therapist, Dr. Lemere, that he couldn't take it anymore. Dr. Lemere told him to ignore his father's orders from afar and do what he (Jack) wanted. He suggested writing back to his father with the following – "thanks for the great ideas, keep 'em coming." That phrase turned into a mantra in the Goldfarb family – when people want to ignore someone's ideas they say, "thanks for the great ideas, keep 'em coming."

After Lou's death in 1955, Jack might have moved beyond his father's shadow, but Lou loomed large. When I was in first grade, Lou's ghost showed up. A teacher at my Jewish day school told us that the *Moshiach* (Messiah) will come and, when he does, all the Jews will return to the land of Israel. Not only that, the dead will be resurrected and live happily and peacefully in the land of Israel. Well as a six-year-old, this blew my mind. How could the dead come back to life? I thought this was an amazing piece of information. I had to share it.

Paul, Lou (chef's hat) and Jack, at Glendale Golf and Country Club. (Treiger Collection).

"Papa Jack," I excitedly said, "did you know that when the *Moshiach* comes, all the dead people will come back to life and we'll all go to live in Israel?"

"Oh, no," he exclaimed, "that's terrible – will my father come back? If Lou comes back to life, he'll see what a mess I made of this business. He'll kill me. When's this guy coming?"

Throughout the rest of his life, another twenty-three years, Papa Jack frequently asked me "when's that guy coming? I need to know so that I can get out of town before my father comes back."

In 1938, the house at 709 15th Avenue was gifted to my grandparents, Jack and Elizabeth Friedlander, when my mom, Betty Lou, was a small child. Jack's father, Lou and his mother, Belle moved into the Gainsborough Apartment on Minor and Spring, which still stands just one block away from where my mom lives today. In the early 1940s when the penthouse opened up in the nearby Marlborough Apartment building at 1220 Boren Avenue, they moved in. This is the apartment that my mom and Aunt Jackie remember best.

One spring day in 2021, I met my mom, Betty Lou and her sister,

Jackie, and we went to the house at 709 15th Avenue. We got out of the car and they both stared silently. They looked younger standing there in the shadow of their early lives. My Aunt Jackie was the first to speak – "that was my room, up there," she said pointing to a window at the second floor.

The house has two series of concrete steps to get up to the front door. One set brings you to an iron gate, while the next set brings you to the front door. It's a three-story home and, though not as large as some of the other mansions in the Volunteer Park neighborhood, it's impressive. We knocked on the front door, but no one answered. Our inside look at the Friedlander home would have to wait for another day.

"That was my room," my mom said pointing to a different window. "I liked living here. We moved to Magnolia when I was still very young. I wish we had stayed in this neighborhood. I didn't have many friends in Magnolia. The Jews who belonged to Temple mostly lived in Capitol Hill."

One day my mom and I found ourselves in Magnolia picking up her car.

"Mom," I said, "we're in Magnolia. Let's find the house you grew up in."

"Sure" she said and without hesitation she blurted out the address: "4216 West Barret."

Sometimes, my mom can't remember what she ate for breakfast and yet she threw out the address from her childhood home without a second thought.

We drove through the quiet streets of Magnolia and found the brick house. We went up a few steps and knocked on the door. A teenage girl answered.

"Hi, I'm Karen and this is my mom, Betty Lou. She grew up in this house and we were wondering if we could come in and look around?"

"Sure," she said. "My mom is on a phone call for work right now, but I am sure she wouldn't mind."

We entered the home and walked into a light-filled living room. My mom said that the house was the same as when she grew up. Surprisingly, it was not grand as I had imagined it. I had heard about the cook and the maid, so I imagined a larger home. There was a hallway to the right of the door, with three bedrooms and a bathroom. My mom pointed out the master bedroom as her parents' room at the end of the hall and one on the right, her sister Jackie's. Then we turned to the room on the left.

"That's my room," the teenage girl told us.

"It was my room too," my mom said, "when I was growing up here."

"Could we go in your room?" I asked.

"Sure," she said.

"Yeah, this was my room," my mom said wistfully. "That's the closet."

"That's the closet?" I asked. "It's so small."

My mom and aunt told us the story many times of how the maid locked them in the closet when my grandmother wasn't home. She put a dresser up against the door so that my mom and aunt couldn't get out. They were stuck inside, sometimes for hours. Like the house, the closet was much smaller than I had imagined.

"We hid flashlights, games, and cigarettes in there," my mom explained, "it happened a lot when Mother wasn't home."

"Cigarettes?" I asked. "How did you put them out?"

"I left a glass of water in there," she explained, "to put them out after I was done smoking."

To me, the closet is a metaphor for my mom's life and what she had to overcome to be the remarkable person and mother that she was to me and my two brothers. She was locked in that dark closet for hours at a time, but she and her sister made the best of it. They played games, smoked, and made it a place to have fun. My mom took her challenging experiences as a child and her imperfect family life and found her way. She is one of the most optimistic people that I know, always looking on the bright side.

I have learned many life lessons from my mother, but this one is powerful: if you find yourself stuck in a dark closet (whether real or metaphorical), make the best of it – play games, have a flashlight and glass of water ready (be prepared), and always get along with your siblings.

Standing in the living room of my mom's childhood home, looking out at Puget Sound, the islands across the way, and the majestic Olympic Mountains looming, I felt time collapse. It was some seventy years ago that my mom lived here and looked out at this same view. Now she is eighty-nine and living out the last chapter of her life. The harsh reality that we are merely visitors on this earth slapped me in the face. I wondered, when will my mom's visitor's visa expire? When will mine? Why was I granted the visa in the first place?

Lost in thought with these unanswerable questions, my mom touched my arm and brought me back to the living room. She pointed to houses down the street, telling me who lived there and which friends she played with.

"Our family was the first on the block to have a TV," my mom told me. "All the neighborhood kids came over to watch. It was black and white. We loved it."

We didn't venture down to the basement, where the maid's room was, but I wish we had. It's there in December, the family placed their Christmas tree. As a girl, Nanny celebrated Christmas with presents under the tree, and she wanted one in her own home in Magnolia. Papa Jack wasn't keen on the idea, he didn't want a Christmas tree in his home. They compromised – the tree was in the basement.

"We woke up Christmas morning," my mom said, "and went down to the basement and found lots of presents under the tree. We loved it."

Lifting my eyes again to the bay, I noticed that straight across is Alki beach in West Seattle, where my mom's great-grandparents, Sam and Augusta lived. Augusta died in 1931, before my mom and Aunt were born. But Sam lived until 1943, so I imagine they visited him. Alki is a historic part of Seattle – it's where the first European settlers, called the Denny Party, landed in 1851, finding members of the Duwamish tribe living there.

The white settlers named it Alki-New York. Alki is a word from the Duwamish language, a dialect of Lushootseed, meaning bye and bye – so the message was clear – someday (bye and bye) this town will be the New York of the West Coast. The Denny party did some exploring by canoe and found that across the bay, the water was deep and clear, and it was perfect for docking large ships, not just shallow canoes. There were also plenty of trees to cut for timber to build homes and to sell down the coast to San Francisco. Seattle was named for Chief Sealth, the Chief of the Duwamish Tribe, who was friendly with the white settlers.

As I looked over the bay to the peninsula we now call West Seattle I wondered why Sam and Augusta made it their home. Their friends and social life were centered in Capitol Hill, around Temple De Hirsch. Perhaps they bought the property because it's just so beautiful there. They moved to West Seattle in 1916, ten years after arriving. Their first West Seattle home was located way down at the end of the peninsula, 2208 65th Avenue SW and was half a block from the beach. I imagine that they enjoyed the Sound's wildlife, watching ships and ferries traveling across the bay, and on clear days, the glorious Olympic Mountains. In 1926, Sam and Augusta built an apartment complex right across from the water at 2252 Alki Avenue SW. They named it "Friedlander Court."

In May of 2023, I visited the Friedlander Court apartment. It's a one-story brick building in the shape of U. A gray stone slab over the entrance is engraved: "Friedlander Court." Did Sam and Augusta carve their name into this building in hopes of outliving themselves, dreaming that after they die, their name wouldn't be forgotten?

The outer brick wall has a red shield with the Friedlander coat of arms. I found that super weird. What were they thinking? There's a locked gate

Friedlander Court (Treiger Collection).

with well-manicured gardens, chairs, and tables just inside. My three-year old grandson, Ted, was asleep in my car, so I didn't ring any bells or try to go in.

Friedlander coat of arms (Treiger Collection).

Though they lived in Capitol Hill (12th Avenue North) for a few years around the time the Friedlander Court was built, Sam and Augusta settled back in Alki at 2351 Halleck Avenue SW, just a half block from Friedlander Court. After Augusta's death in 1931, Sam moved across the street to an apartment house called the Playa Vista Apartments, located at 2250 Bonair Place, which was constructed in 1927. The Census report indicates that Sam lived in apartment #5 at this address. The apartment building still stands today just behind Friedlander Court.

Sam Friedlander (Treiger Collection).

Sam and Augusta were part of a small group of Jews who settled in Alki. There is a remarkable plaque on the ground, very close to Sam and Augusta's first home in Alki that provides evidence of a small Jewish community there:

"Fleeing anti-semitism in Russia and Eastern Europe, Jews were among the early pioneers who came to Seattle. A descendant of these early settlers, Lydia Pearl Offman (b.1912) recalls spending summers on Alki Beach playing with American Indian children. She attended Salish ceremonies here at Duwamish Head, and especially liked eating salmon cooked over the fire on a stick, which met with Jewish dietary laws of keeping Kosher.

Later she and her husband established a synagogue in their house, which became the center of a lively community at Alki. Pearl Street is named for her family."[371]

Upon Sam's death in 1943, my great-grandfather, Louis Friedlander inherited Friedlander & Sons, and his sister Anne Friedlander inherited the West Seattle properties. Auntie Anne, as we called her, lived in the home on Hallek Street until her death in 1979. My mom would take us to visit Auntie Anne when I was a child. She was the oldest person I had ever met, and her prune-like face scared me. Auntie Anne went swimming in Puget Sound every day – summer, fall, winter, spring. We were visiting one gray winter's day and I watched wide eyed as she put on a "bathing costume" and a plastic shower cap and marched straight into Puget Sound. She dunked and came back out. How did she do that? The water was freezing.

"It's good for the health," she told me as she passed me by to go inside and shower.

Anne Friedlander

Anne lived alone when I knew her. But she had a colorful life. It wasn't a story shared with the grandchildren, but I found newspaper articles that told the story of a grand double wedding in the summer of 1909. It seems that my great-grandparents, Lou and Belle, had company under their *Chupah* (Jewish wedding canopy). Belle's brother, Louis, and Louis's sister, Anne, got married in the same ceremony. This blew my mind. I asked my mom and Aunt if they knew that Auntie Anne had married their Uncle Louis Singerman. They both said – "Yeah, it's true, but I don't know much about it." All Aunt Jackie knew was Auntie Anne never really wanted to marry Louis Singerman, but she said "yes" to his proposal. When she changed her mind, her parents told her she couldn't back out. After the wedding, Louis and Anne moved to Salt Lake City.

Eight years after the grand double wedding, Anne and Louis went through a bitter divorce. The 1917 court record at the King County Courthouse reveals that Anne was the one who filed the petition for divorce. She claimed that Louis was not supporting her and for the past year she had to rely on her parents for support. In fact, for the last year she explained in her court filing, she had been living with her parents in Seattle.[372] Further, she claimed that there was no love between the two of them and their marriage was "irreparably broken." Louis responded in his court papers that he was supporting Anne just fine, that he had no interest in divorcing, and their marriage was not broken, thank you very much.

The court granted the divorce. Although Anne got no alimony or financial support from Louis, she did get her last name back. She again became known as Anne Friedlander. I can only imagine the strain that this unhappy marriage and divorce put on the relationship between the Singerman and Friedlander families.

A few years later Anne married Sanford Cohen and moved to Providence, Rhode Island. They had two daughters, Joyce and Joan. This marriage lasted until Sanford ditched Anne for his secretary and moved to Florida. After Sanford's unceremonious exit, Anne moved back to Seattle. She lived in the Friedlander home in West Seattle. Anne's daughter Joyce often visited Seattle in the summer with her two children, Kyle and Stacey.

Since Kyle and Stacey were about the same age as my brothers and me, we would go on an annual summer excursion to Victoria, Canada. With tuna sandwiches and potato chips packed in our lunch bags, we boarded the Princess Marguerite for a four-hour ferry ride to Victoria. Once we got there, we went on the Tally Ho – horse-drawn carriage ride with its accompanying manure-perfumed air. Sometimes we would take a bus to Buchard Gardens. But every year at 4 p.m. we went to the Empress Hotel for High Tea. I didn't care for the tea, but I loved the crumpets and jam. I had not seen Kyle or Stacey since I was about eleven.

"I think Kyle lives here in Seattle," my mom told me when I asked her about Auntie Anne. "Your father helped him with some property some years ago. His last name is Henessey."

"Wow," I answered, "I'll see if I can find him."

After some sleuthing, I found a Kyle Hennessey on Linked-In. I wrote him a note. He responded and said that yes, he was son of Joyce and the grandson of Anne Friedlander.

We spoke on the phone and agreed to meet. We caught up on each other's lives and reminisced about the trips to Victoria. The craziest part of the conversation was that Kyle's strongest memory of those ferry rides was my brother Louis leaning over the side of the ship to spit. He leaned too far and his glasses fell into the frothy waves of the Salish Sea. This is

(From left to right) Anne Friedlander, Belle (Singerman) Friedlander, Jack Friedlander holding Louis Treiger and Susan Goldfarb, Jackie Goldfarb on Alvin Goldfarb's lap (Treiger Collection).

one memory that I can recall at a moment's notice because I was gleeful when it happened. Louis shouldn't have been leaning over and spitting over the edge. I've always felt that it served him right to lose his glasses into the depths of the water. It gave me great satisfaction that Kyle's most vivid memory was of the Great Glasses Drop.

Anne married a third time on February 7, 1940 in Yuma, Arizona. This time it was to Leonid Fink, a well-known, Seattle-based photographer. Mr. Fink died in 1960.[373] Anne lived another nineteen years, dying in 1979. I attribute her long life to her daily ice-cold dips into Puget Sound.

Mah-Jongg And More

Based on what I read in the Society Pages of the *Jewish Transcript*, the Friedlanders had more parties than the Mad Hatter had teas.

"Mr. and Mrs. S. Friedlander," the *Transcript* Social Page dated January 23, 1925 noted, "entertained fifteen friends at dinner on Sunday, January 11th at their home, followed by Mah Jangg and bridge."[374] Another entry on Tuesday,

July 1, 1924, notes: "July 1, being the fifteenth wedding anniversary of Mr. and Mrs. Louis Friedlander, they were at home to welcome their many friends."[375]

Louis Friedlander (Treiger Collection).

These posts about dinner parties repeated many times – whether it was Mr. and Mrs. S. Friedlander or Mr. and Mrs. L. Friedlander – so many dinner parties and so much Mah-jongg.

The *Transcript* bubbled with articles mentioning Sam, Louis, and later Jack, as Presidents of the Temple and the Kline Galland Home. Jack and Lou were both very active with the Federated Fund, Glendale Golf & Country Club, and Bnai Brith, a Jewish Fraternal organization.

"Past President Lou Friedlander," the May 1, 1925 Transcript reports, "gave a short talk on his experience in Europe. Brother Friedlander is to be the principal speaker at our next meeting. His topic will be 'Personal Observations of My Trip to Europe.' Brother Friedlander is noted for his oratory and skill in pleasing his audience and will relate many interesting experiences."

Then, two weeks later, the Transcript reported that "Bro Lou Friedlander ... otherwise known as 'Genial and Jovial Lou' told of his trip to Europe."

"Genial and Jovial Lou" – how great is that?

Lou and his wife, Belle, frequently traveled to Europe to buy jewelry and other items for the store. There were some very memorable ones: London in 1937 when King George VI celebrated his coronation; Austria in March of 1938 when Hitler arrived to a cheering crowd in Vienna and incorporated Austria into the Third Reich.[376]

Sam too was involved in Seattle's civic community. He was a member of the Chamber of Commerce and a Mason. In Hanford's 1924 profile, Sam is described as, "a worthy exemplar of the teachings and purpose of the Masonic fraternity, having attained the thirty-second degree of the Scottish Rite and being also a member of the Mystic Shrine."[377]

(Left to Right) Paul Friedlander, Sam Friedlander, Louis Friedlander, Jack Friedlander outside Friedlander Store at 5th and Pike (Treiger Collection).

Sam was described by Hanford as a "self-made man."[378] Papa Jack explained, Sam "had no education at all, and yet he knew everything that was going on, and he was always one step ahead of everybody. He knew what was going on in the basement, in the office, and everyplace."[379]

Sam retired in 1928, when the new jewelry store opened on 5th and Pike. He put the running of the business in the hands of his son Louis. He lived fifteen years longer than Augusta, dying in December of 1943. He died in Loma Linda, California at the age of eighty. [380]

Louis lived only thirteen years after his father's death. He died on January 3, 1955 at the age of sixty-eight. I don't know if he and Belle had a happy marriage, but they never divorced. I am, however, told by my mother and Aunt that Lou was not a faithful husband. One day, my mom recalled, she saw her grandfather Lou walking into the Paramount Hotel in the middle of the day. The Paramount was home to her Aunt Gertrude Singerman, the widow of Lou's deceased brother-in-law, Isidore Singerman.

"He was *shtupping* Aunt Gertrude," my mom explained.

Paul (left) and Jack (right) Friedlander (UW Libraries Special Collection, Irwin and Betty Lou Treiger Photograph Collection, UW41906).

Before Lou left this world, he saw the opening of the remodeled Friedlander & Sons on 5th and Pike. Over two days in 1954, 10,000 people visited the store,[381] which had been enlarged by 5,000 square feet.

"The store ...," the Seattle Times reported, "retains all the dignified charm and grace that walnut paneling and fine fixtures placed there many years ago... yet the ceiling lighting and the handsome new glass doors give it a modern feeling."[382]

After Lou's death, his sons, Jack and Paul, took over. They ran the business, expanding to Southcenter, Everett, Tacoma, and many malls in the Puget Sound area. Some years after Papa Jack retired, the business was sold in 1986 to Sterling, Inc. of Akron, Ohio.[383]

Paul attended Stanford University for college and graduated from the University of Washington Law School. He married Marjorie Strauss in 1937 and had two sons, Paul Jr. and John Lewis. Both of Paul's sons worked for Friedlanders until it was sold in 1986. Uncle Paul was active in raising money for the arts and served as the Port Commissioner for Seattle for eighteen years. During his tenure as Port Commissioner, the city built the unsightly grain terminal that still stands at Pier 86. My mom calls it "Uncle Paul's grain terminal." Paul died on June 30, 1994[384] and his wife Marjorie died ten years later.[385]

Papa Jack married Elizabeth Staadecker on December 27, 1933.[386] This was an arranged match from two prominent Reform Jewish families, a merger of sorts. My Aunt Jackie told me that Papa Jack was in love with Pearl Tipp and wanted to marry her.

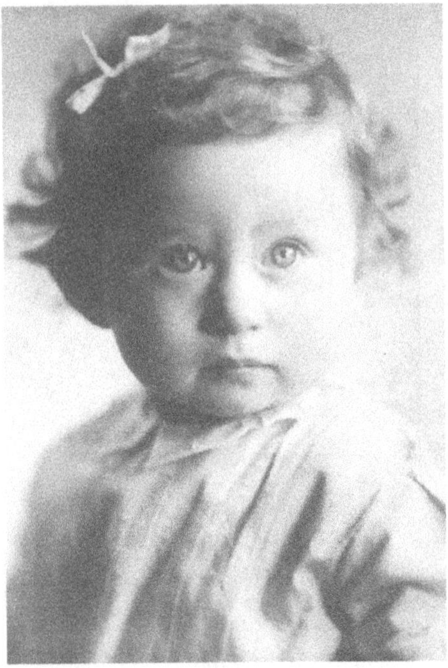

Betty Lou – Baby (Treiger Collection).

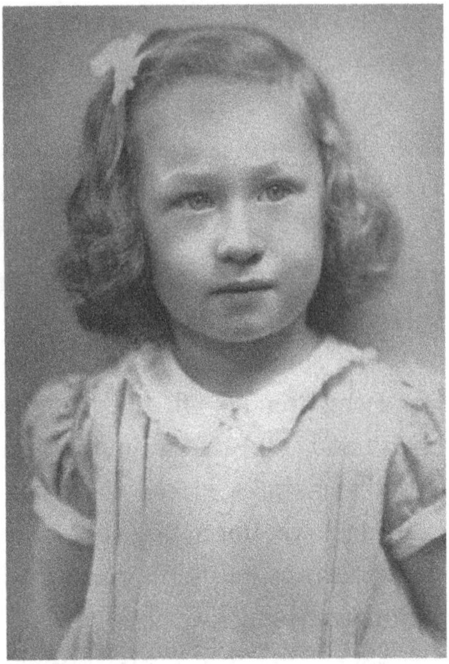

Betty Lou – 4 year old (Treiger Collection).

"No son of mine is going to marry the daughter of Ben Tipp," Jack's father Lou told him.

Ben Tipp owned his own jewelry shop, called Ben Tipp Diamonds on 3rd Avenue, but my aunt was told "it was a shlock joint," meaning that it sold low quality goods. Pearl ended up marrying a man named Polichuck and lived in Magnolia, not far from the Friedlanders.

"Pearl was a lovely woman," Aunt Jackie recalled. "She played piano and when families were told to get their children vaccinated for polio, Pearl picked us up and took us to Dr. Klein to get the shots."[387]

Jack and Elizabeth had an ill-fated marriage. There was a lot of screaming between the two of them. When I asked my mom and my aunt which one of them did the screaming, they responded, "both of them."

"It was hard to grow up in that household," my Aunt Jackie said. "There was so much bitterness between them."[388]

Though their marriage ended in divorce twenty-eight years after it began, something good came from this marriage – two wonderful daughters. My mom, Betty Lou, named for her mother Elizabeth (Betty is a nickname for Elizabeth) and her grandfather Lou, born in 1935 and Jacqueline (Jackie), named for her father, Jack, born in 1937. Between Betty Lou and Jackie, six grandchildren came into the world, of which I am one.

Papa Jack – with Jewelers award (Treiger Collection).

The Friedlander story is the immigrant story, told thousands of times. Families escaped persecution, antisemitism, and economic stagnation to reach the United States and a chance at the golden ticket. The Friedlander family's immigrant story is my story. I learn about myself as I realize that my life is built on a series of intriguing stories, of people who visited and now are gone. What they left behind are lessons of perseverance, talent, and commitment.

Having Papa Jack as a grandfather fills me with mixed emotions. He was playful, funny, caring, and generous. He was a successful jeweler and an active volunteer in Seattle's civic and Jewish community. Such a loved personality and a successful businessman. But it becomes challenging when my spouse, Shlomo and I explain to our son, Jack, why he is named for this complicated character, who was divorced twice and smoked, drank, played around, and gambled too much. Ultimately, for us, the impact of Papa Jack dying on February 12, 1990, just seven days after our son's birth coupled with the tradition of naming children for dead grandparents was so strong that we overlooked his flaws.

I'm proud to have named our son for this man, Jack Friedlander. I hope my son realizes that like his namesake that life is complicated and that our legacy is a delicate balance between the good we do and the less than perfect lives we inevitably lead. We must strive to have the balance tipped with our good deeds. Perhaps we all live in that liminal space, filled with feelings of regret, but also pride for the good that we do.

When I ask myself, why I spend all this time researching these dead relatives, my mind recalls my innocent, first-grade conversations with Papa Jack about the *Moshiach* - the hopeful yet dreaded "guy" who might arrive and bring Lou back to life. Though the Jewish people are always "waiting for *Moshiach*" and for the peace and tranquility that the prophets of old described as the Messianic era, the "guy" has not yet arrived.

Perhaps for me in 2025, there is a different meaning to "bringing back the dead." Perhaps my reading the tiny print of the *Transcript* Society Pages and scrolling through the *Seattle Times* archives is a way to bring them back. Before I began, I knew little about Sam, Augusta, Lou, and Anne Friedlander. By looking into the past and discovering information about these family members, I'm bringing to fruition my first-grade prophecy, that they all will come back to life – if not in body, in my memory and spirit and in the memory of those who read these words.

I read somewhere that we die twice – once when we stop breathing and second, when someone says your name for the last time. Long live "Friedlander Court."

CHAPTER 5

TREIGER FAMILY

Thrifty's

My strongest childhood memory of my grandfather, Sam Treiger, is a Hershey bar, a very large Hershey bar. Visiting Papa Sam, as we called him, at Thrifty's 10¢ store in Seattle's Central District, resulted in walking out with the prize to beat all prizes. It was as if someone handed me a brick of gold. I was afraid to eat it – it seemed of infinite value. Sometimes I just saved it, knowing if I ate it, it would be gone forever.

I don't have many memories of Papa Sam. He died of prostate cancer in 1968, when I was seven years old, but I remember those Hershey bars. Thrifty's candy was a hit with all the grandchildren. There were jars of licorice sticks on the front counter – a penny a piece. When my dad, Irwin Treiger's brother, Ray, came from New York to visit with his three children, "the kids went right to the candy jar," Uncle Ray told me. "A red one and black one. They wanted seconds, my father said 'no – that was enough.'"[389]

Thrifty's, as I have come to appreciate, was a fixture in Seattle's central district neighborhood. It was on the south side of Jackson Street just east of 23rd. Later, it moved to a larger location on the SE corner of 23rd and Jackson. Thrifty's was as mom and pop as they come. Papa Sam and my grandmother Rose, who we called Bobby,[390] were "full partners." Uncle Ray said, "they worked together."[391] A U-shaped counter greeted the customer, upon which sat one of those old-fashioned cash registers, with a pull-down lever that rang out a satisfying "ding" when the drawer opened. Behind

Treiger Family Tree

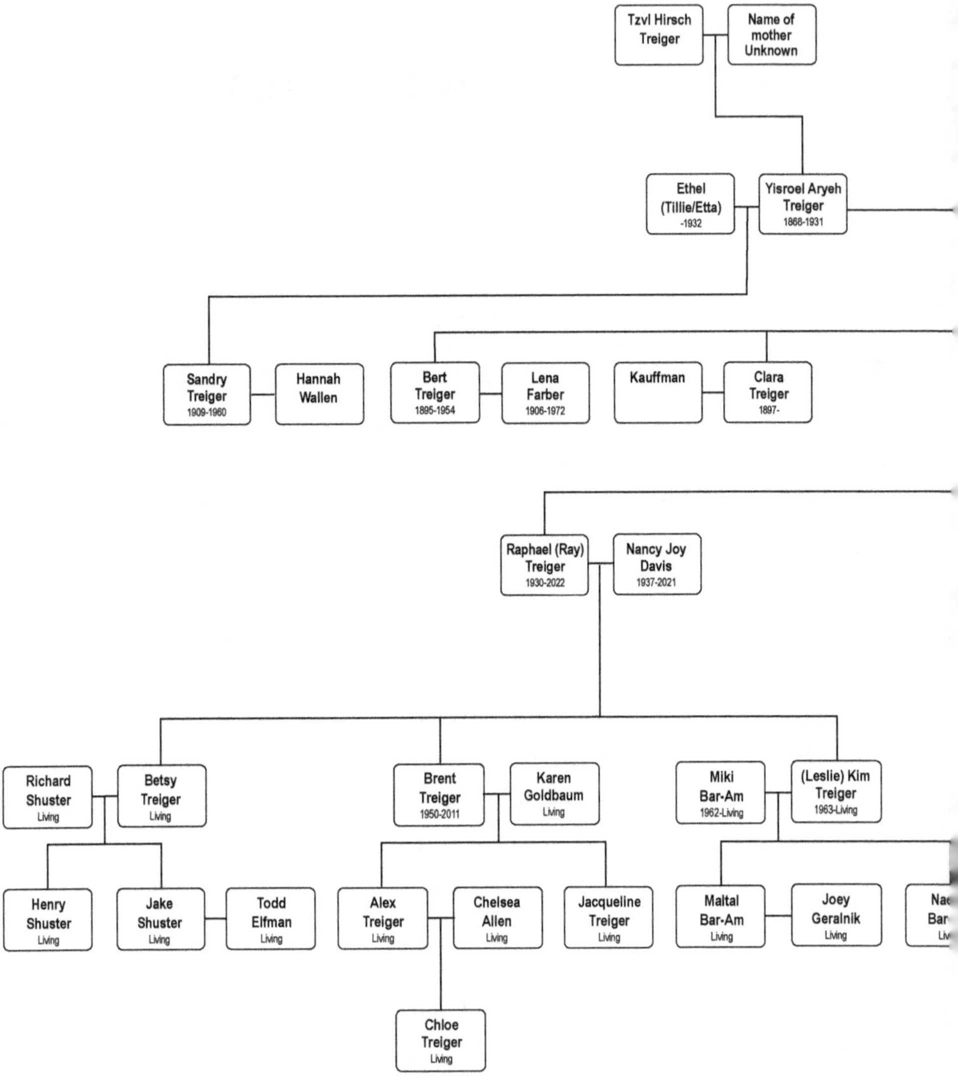
Tzvi Hirsch Treiger
Name of mother Unknown
Ethel (Tillie/Etta) -1932
Yisroel Aryeh Treiger 1868-1931
Sandry Treiger 1909-1960
Hannah Wallen
Bert Treiger 1895-1954
Lena Farber 1906-1972
Kauffman
Clara Treiger 1897-
Raphael (Ray) Treiger 1930-2022
Nancy Joy Davis 1937-2021
Richard Shuster Living
Betsy Treiger Living
Brent Treiger 1950-2011
Karen Goldbaum Living
Miki Bar-Am 1962-Living
(Leslie) Kim Treiger 1963-Living
Henry Shuster Living
Jake Shuster Living
Todd Elfman Living
Alex Treiger Living
Chelsea Allen Living
Jacqueline Treiger Living
Maital Bar-Am Living
Joey Geralnik Living
Chloe Treiger Living

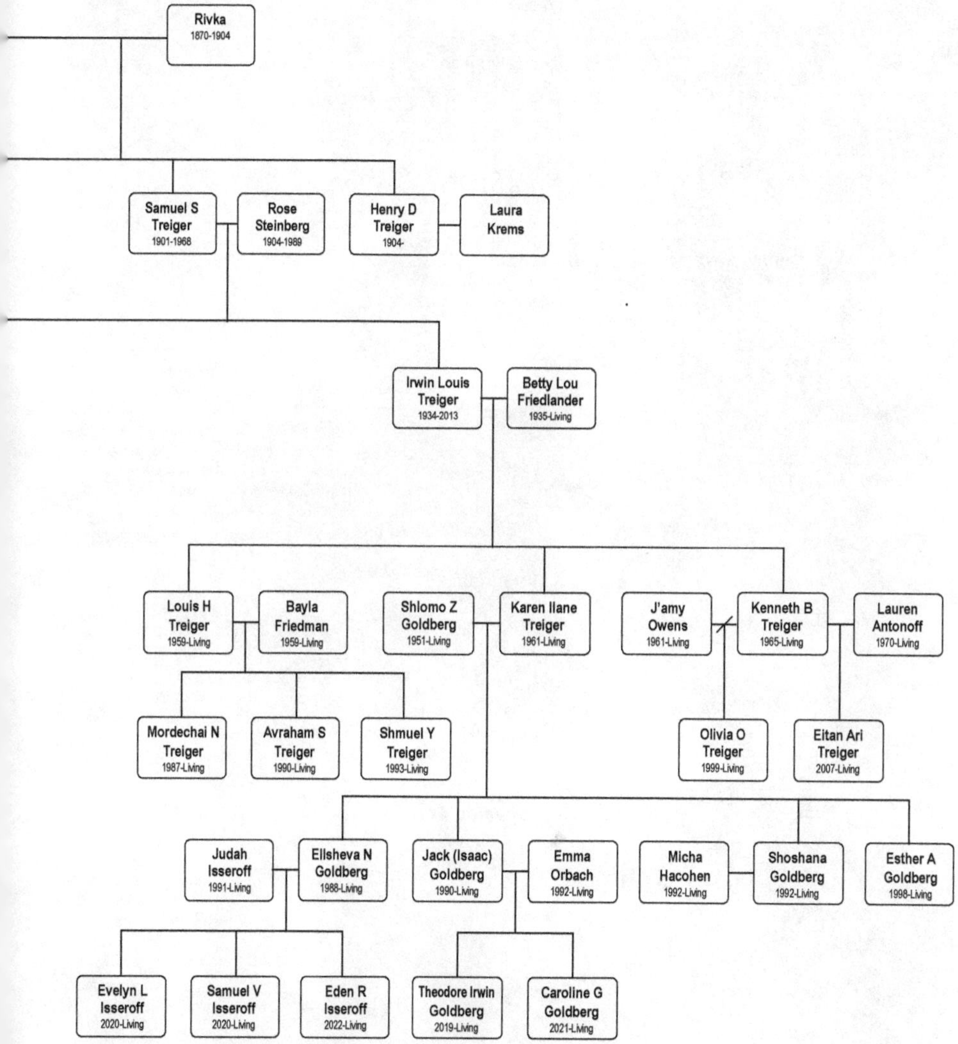
Rivka 1870-1904
Samuel S Treiger 1901-1968
Rose Steinberg 1904-1989
Henry D Treiger 1904-
Laura Krems
Irwin Louis Treiger 1934-2013
Betty Lou Friedlander 1935-Living
Louis H Treiger 1959-Living
Bayla Friedman 1959-Living
Shlomo Z Goldberg 1951-Living
Karen Ilane Treiger 1961-Living
J'amy Owens 1961-Living
Kenneth B Treiger 1965-Living
Lauren Antonoff 1970-Living
Mordechai N Treiger 1987-Living
Avraham S Treiger 1990-Living
Shmuel Y Treiger 1993-Living
Olivia O Treiger 1999-Living
Eitan Ari Treiger 2007-Living
Judah Isseroff 1991-Living
Elisheva N Goldberg 1988-Living
Jack (Isaac) Goldberg 1990-Living
Emma Orbach 1992-Living
Micha Hacohen 1992-Living
Shoshana Goldberg 1992-Living
Esther A Goldberg 1998-Living
Evelyn L Isseroff 2020-Living
Samuel V Isseroff 2020-Living
Eden R Isseroff 2022-Living
Theodore Irwin Goldberg 2019-Living
Caroline G Goldberg 2021-Living

Treiger Map - Homes and Stores

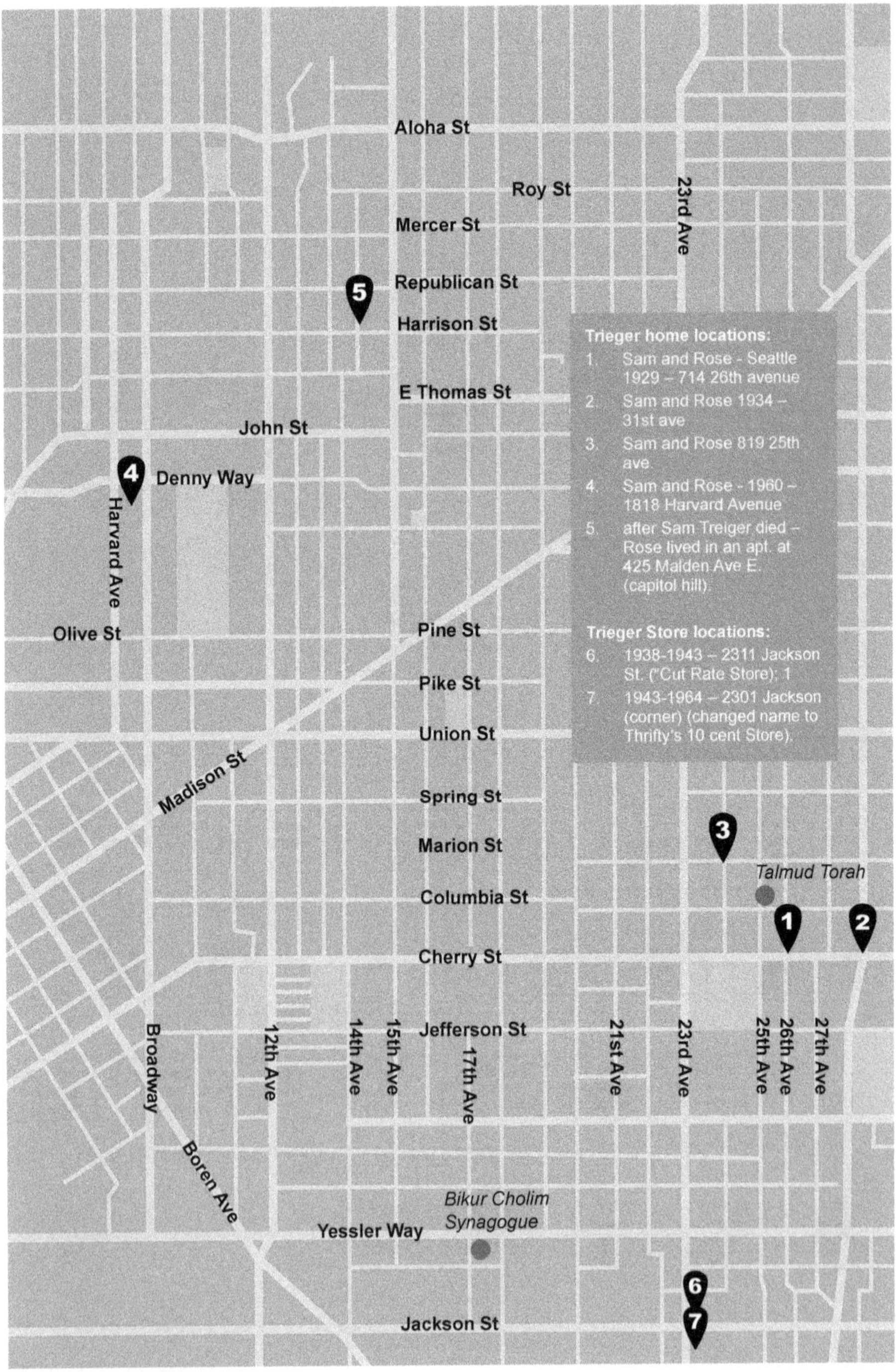
Aloha St
Roy St
23rd Ave
Mercer St
Republican St
Harrison St
E Thomas St
John St
Denny Way
Harvard Ave
Olive St
Pine St
Pike St
Union St
Madison St
Spring St
Marion St
Columbia St
Cherry St
Jefferson St
Broadway
12th Ave
14th Ave
15th Ave
17th Ave
21st Ave
23rd Ave
25th Ave
26th Ave
27th Ave
Boren Ave
Yessler Way
Jackson St
Bikur Cholim Synagogue
Talmud Torah
1
2
3
4
5
6
7
Trieger home locations:
1. Sam and Rose - Seattle 1929 – 714 26th avenue
2. Sam and Rose 1934 – 31st ave
3. Sam and Rose 819 25th ave.
4. Sam and Rose - 1960 – 1818 Harvard Avenue
5. after Sam Treiger died – Rose lived in an apt. at 425 Malden Ave E. (capitol hill).
Trieger Store locations:
6. 1938-1943 – 2311 Jackson St. ("Cut Rate Store); 1
7. 1943-1964 – 2301 Jackson (corner) (changed name to Thrifty's 10 cent Store).

the U, Papa Sam cloistered the cigarettes, fingernail polish, and lip stick – stuff easy to stick in your pocket and walk out the door.[392]

Sam and Rose purchased the store in 1938 from Rose's sister Ettie and her husband Mitchell Ketzlach. Sam had just been summarily fired from Steinberg & brothers by his borther-in-law, Rueben Steinberg. Sam was looking for a new opportunity. The store had "everything," my cousin Shim Elyn[393] told me. Shims mother, Goldie, (Rose's older sister), would send him down to the store to pick up "a few things." It sold hardware, toothpaste, clothing, underwear and socks, Dutch Boy paint, men's work boots, slippers, shoe polish, soap, toiletries, and of course, candy.[394]

"We had no parking," Uncle Ray explained, "Thrifty's was across from Safeway and [there was a] furniture store on the corner, Volotin and Schreiber. Across from Volotin and Schreiber was the barber shop where my father and I both got our hair cut – Fred. Kitty corner was Fuchsin – drapery man - drapes and linens. Next to him was Selig. Manfred Selig was a refugee. He sold cloth and his son was younger than I was."[395]

I think my father, Irwin Treiger, described Thifty's in a poem he wrote as a boy: "Come Buy at Thrifty's."

Come Buy at Thrifty's.
If it's the best
You're looking for
You can always get it
At Thrifty's 10¢ store.

They have all your needs
And even more
The magnificent and great
Thrifty 10¢ store.

The candy and shoes
And union suits
To little toys dolls
And rubber boots.

They have good clerks
But they could use more
To work in the magnificent
Thrifty 10¢ store.[396]

Thrifty's wasn't just the way the family put bread on the table, it was a family project and this poem wasn't the only ink my father spilled about Thrifty's. When he was in his last year at Washington Jr. High School,[397] my dad remarkably wrote a one time "newspaper" as a school assignment, called *My Ambition*. My dad saved a copy in the dusty files he kept for so many years (thank you, Dad). This article about a "small variety store, owned by the father of the author, Irwin Treiger," sheds light on the essence of what Thrifty's meant to the Trieger family.

Life At Thrifities[398]

By Irwin Treiger

I can still remember the day just ten years ago this August, when Thrifties opened its doors. Ever since that day, affairs at Thrifties have ruled the lives of our family.

Growth from our first little cramped quarters at 2311 Jackson, to our larger, more spacious store, down the block at 2301 Jackson took, five years of downright hard work.

Back in 1938 it was called 'Cut Rate Store'. From then to 1943 we gave Thrifties almost every name conceivable under the sun. The present title which in full reads 'Thrifties 10¢ Store,' was chosen in 1943 when we moved.

Moving day was very important and very back breaking. I still don't see how our entire stock was transferred in one day.

Christmas is our busiest part of the year. During that season our family practically camps at the Thrifties.

Perhaps the most interesting part of life at Thrifties is [sic] the characters who frequent the place. The most comical is an old chimney sweep who lives in a cottage between a garage and a beer tavern.

With his stovepipe hat covered with grime, short stubby whiskers, corn cob pipe and the shorts he wears in the summer, the old dutch gent looks quite like a man escaped from [the prison at] Sedro Wooley. His vocabulary is equivolant [sic] to that of a sea cook and he loves to be the center of attraction.

Thievery is prevalent at Thrifties as in most stores. Several years ago my brother found a five dollar bill on the floor, 'Look,' he yelled, 'I found five dollars.' A woman standing near looked into her purse and wiled 'Oh, I lost five dollars. That must be mine you found.' We gave her the money. An hour later the owner of the bill came in and inquired about it. What could we do? The dishonest woman never came in again.

This year, one of Thrifties most fabulous eras was brought to a close. The four year long Hurst Era came to a close when Lorraine, 'Rena' Hurst quit work to be married. It seems like years ago when a scared high school girl began working after school for us. But by the end of her first year she'd changed our opinions.

Rena was a mechanic, expert clerk, cashier, gift wrapper, authority on store cats and good worker. For four long years we shared our problems and our joys with her and she in turn with us. The manager of Thrifties quit just this winter to be married.

Despite all the heart rending experiences, troubles and disappointments we've had, at Thrifties, we know now we'd never give it up and we'd do it all over again if we had to.

I can't look into the crystal ball and foretell the fate of Thrifties, but I do know that if I'm not successful anywhere else I can always look for a job at good old Thrifties 10¢ Store."[399]

Papa Sam, the proprietor of Thrifty's, was a handsome, short (5'7"), bald, slim, outgoing man, with a confident walk that messaged, "I may be short, but don't mess with me." What remained of his hair in the 1960s was brown and his eyes were a penetrating hazel. Except for the Jewish Sabbath, (*Shabbes*),[400] Papa Sam had a pipe hanging from his mouth. If I close my eyes, I can smell the pipe smoke – sweet and sticky – as it floats in the air for a few seconds before dissipating. Papa Sam's personal warmth led to strong relationships with his customers. On Saturday nights in the winter, Papa Sam and Bobby opened the store after *Shabbes*, from 6 to 10 p.m. When they arrived, there were often customers waiting outside the door.[401]

"Sam," my cousin Shim told me, "was a humorous guy. He appreciated a joke. He was a really nice guy. He could do a lot – he could build a Succah[402] blindfolded. Much better than my dad. He used to corn beef and make root beer. He was very independent."[403]

The census report for 1940 states that Sam was a sole proprietor of a business and worked seventy-two hours per week, fifty-two weeks per year.[404] With those hours, it's no wonder Ray and Irwin didn't see him much.

"He would go to work at seven and come home at seven," my father said, "and [then he would] sit down and do the books. I always marveled how he had enough stamina to do all this. He loved working with his hands, contrary to any other Treiger I have ever known, except maybe Kenneth [my brother]. He loved building things. He would do carpentry work, electric work – and he enjoyed it. He should have been a carpenter. He never got wealthy, but he made a decent living."[405]

Left: Irwin Treiger; Right Sam Treiger (Treiger Collection).

By the end of the work week, when *Shabbes* arrived, Papa Sam was exhausted. He'd come home from *Shul*[406] on Friday night and allow his muscles and his mind to relax. The *Shabbes* candles glowed, spreading shadows on the wall as Papa Sam entered the small dining room. He gathered with Rose and his two sons Ray and Irwin at the table. He smiled as the well-worn, stained, brown-paper-covered *Siddur* fell open, as if by memory, to the page with *Shalom*

Eliechem, a song to welcome the *Shabbes*. Their singing, though somewhat off-key, was enthusiastic. Then Papa Sam recited the *Kiddush*, the prayer to sanctify the day, in the singsong chant he learned from his father, Yisroel Aryeh Treiger. As the red, sweet, syrupy wine ran down Sam's throat, he felt *Shabbes* enter his soul.

With a scrape on the floor and a sigh, Papa Sam would push back his chair and walk to the kitchen sink for the ritual washing of the hands. Pouring water over each hand, once, twice, three times, he dried his hands on the towel and said the blessing under his breath. As the family sat back down, two loaves of *Challah*, were revealed from under the embroidered cover, and the *Hamotzi* (blessing on bread) was recited, slices cut, sprinkled with salt, and shared all around.

The meal that followed was spectacular, though pretty much the same every week. Chicken soup, corn flake crusted chicken (once in a while lamb chops), *lukshen kugel (*a noodle dish*)*, sometimes my father's favorite *-pcha (*jellied calf's feet*)*, and a vegetable, usually green beans (sometimes from a can). Finally, there was dessert, perhaps *mandel broit* (similar to a biscotti*)* or, my favorite, chocolate Rice Krispy cookies.

After the meal, the brown paper covered *Siddur* would re-emerge, falling open to the Grace After Meal – the "*benchin*" – and the family would recite blessings of thanks for a delicious dinner.

"Promptly upon completion of the dinner, Friday night," Uncle Ray said, "my father fell asleep at the dining room table. He started out by reading the paper. Never got past one or two pages. Fell asleep with his head on his arms, on the table and when it was time to go to bed, my mother woke him and he said, 'I'm not sleeping.' Always the same routine."[407]

"Many Friday nights," my dad said, "he didn't even make it to page one; he sometimes fell asleep during the *Benchin*."[408]

Back To The Beginning – Demydivka

This seventy-two hour work week, with a family to support in Seattle, is not how my grandfather, Sam Treiger's story begins. He was born in 1901, in the *Shtetl* of Demydivka, in the Vohlynia region, in today's Ukraine, some eighty miles east of Lviv. The name of his hometown was

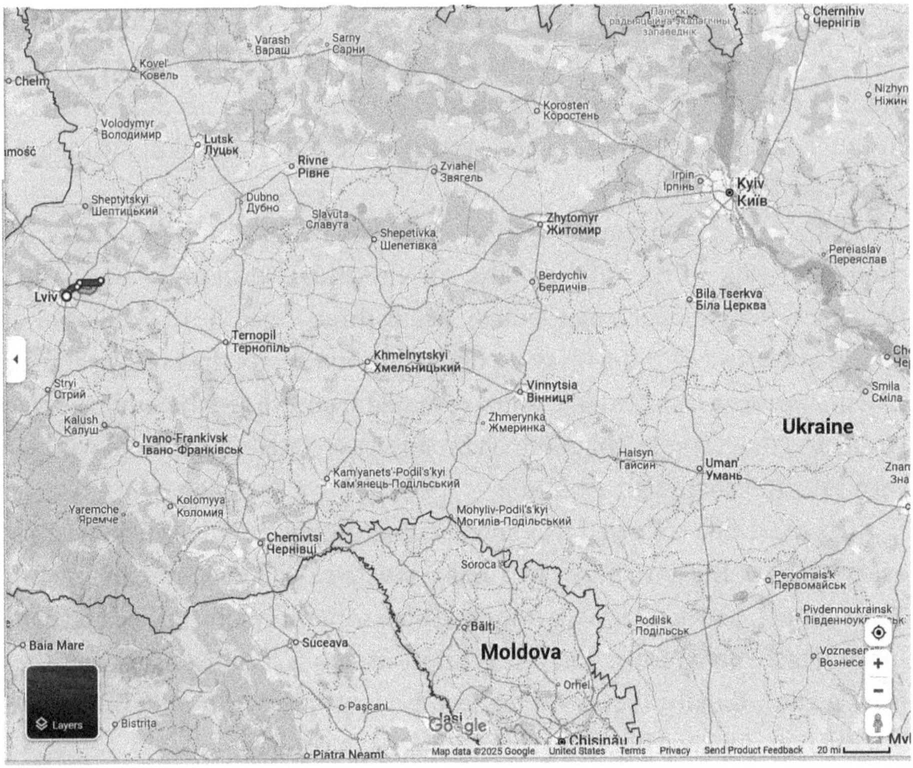

google map – The line shows 82 miles from Lviv to Demydivka.

conveyed from my father, but how to spell it and find it on a map were a different story. I found three different small towns with similar names. With the help of Google maps and my nephew Shmuel Treiger, I found what I believe to be the correct town.

Google maps provides a tremendous resource when searching for towns in Europe since you can see what region they are in and what other towns they are geographically related to. There may be stories of family members going to certain towns for school, trade, travel, or for other opportunities. Using this simple tool, cities can be located on a map. Once I had the correct city, a wealth of information flowed from JewishGen, a website that provides tools to research one's Jewish family history.

I learned through JewishGen that the first Jewish community records of Demydivka date back to the end of the eighteenth century. The 1897 census shows that Jews were the majority at 679 people. Three Synagogues filled each week with men sporting *Talleisim* (Prayer Shawls) and the *Cheder* (Jewish school) was packed each day with boys of the town. Most Jews in Demydivka produced handcrafted items and were involved in small-scale trade.[409]

Tzvi Hirsch Treiger, Sam's grandfather, was born in Radzville, and, according to my father in a videotaped interview with my nephew Avraham Treiger, he was a matza baker.[410] That sounds like a recipe for poverty, but somehow, the Treiger family survived. They moved to Demydivka where Yisroel Aryeh was born. He grew into a bearded, devoutly religious man, who had a goose feather shop. My father mused that perhaps this was a good business in the old country, as goose feathers were "a big commodity then – blankets, pillows, and other things were stuffed with goose feathers."[411] Some of these geese ended up served for dinner, especially during Chanukah time. Papa Sam told my dad that Chanukah was his favorite holiday in Demydivka because they ate goose for dinner.[412]

Yisroel Aryeh married Rivka, and together they brought four children into the world – Baruch (Bert – 1895), Claire (1897), Shimon Shlomo (Sam – 1901), and Chayim (Henry – 1904). Leaving the family bereft and motherless, Rivka died in childbirth when Henry was born on March 8, 1904.

Yisroel Aryeh remarried. His new wife, Tillie (Ethel), gave birth to a son, Zindel (Sandry – 1909). Tillie was neither warm nor loving to her four stepchildren. As adults, the four Treiger siblings had nothing nice to say about Tillie. Both my father and Uncle Ray reported that whenever Tillie came up in conversation, there was no love expressed. Mostly, they heard Papa Sam and his siblings say: "Sandry got all the *schmaltz* (chicken fat)."[413] The four stepchildren, it seems, were treated like chopped liver.

The Goldene Medina - Portland, Oregon

Why did Yisroel (Israel) Aryeh leave Russia? With the economic stagnation in the region, he felt there was no future for his children. He was also afraid, like so many others, that his sons would be taken into the Czar's army. Word on the street was that America was a "*Goldene Medina,*" a "Golden Country." They risked it all to cash in on the dream of a better future than Demydivka could provide.

The Treigers had lots of company. Between 1881 and 1924, 2.5 million Jews emigrated from Eastern Europe to America.[414] The Treigers were seven among a huge mass of people dreaming of a better life.

The Shank family of Portland, somehow related to the Treigers, was their sponsor.[415] Yisroel Aryeh went first, crossing the Atlantic and the North American continent in 1910. He arrived in Portland with a bit of cash and less English. He got himself a horse and wagon and began to peddle. He saved up enough money to bring Tillie and the five children to Portland.

The Portland that welcomed Yisroel Aryeh in 1910 had experienced rapid growth. While the 1900 census count was 90,426, it swelled to 207,214 by 1910.[416] This was, in part, thanks to publicity and renown generated by Portland's 1905 world's fair – the Lewis & Clark Centennial Exposition.[417]

Ancestry.com led me through the trip taken by the rest of the family. Tillie, Bert, Claire, Sam, Henry, and Sandry crossed the Atlantic in 1914, traveling first from Demydivka to England and then by ship to Montreal, Canada. From there, they boarded the Canadian Pacific Railway for a week-long trip ending in Vancouver, B.C. They changed trains and entered the United States, heading south to Portland, Oregon. The Shanks provided the family with a small house, just next to their own home. The address, found in the 1920 Census Report, was 543 2nd Avenue.

A photo of Yisroel Aryeh in America shows a man lifted out of the *Shtetl* and awkwardly dropped into a new reality. He wore a *Chasid*-like long black coat with a vest and tie and a hat that perched on his head like a cantor's *Kippah*. He had a bushy, rabbi-like beard and a smile that reminds me of my grandfather, Papa Sam. Tillie, a stern, matronly-looking woman, is shown wearing a necklace, a modest dress, and a hair covering typical of devout Eastern European women – no hair poking out. Both Yisroel Aryeh and Tillie learned a bit of English, just enough to talk to the non-Jewish shop owners.

South Portland, where they settled, must have felt like a warm blanket in an arctic winter. The "immigrant neighborhood" was one-third Jewish with Yiddish was spoken on the street and in many of the shops. The

Yisroel Aryeh and Tillie Treiger – portraits (Treiger Collection).

neighborhood was on the "west side of the Willamette River, between the river and 5th Avenue and between Harrison and Curry Street."[418]

Within these few blocks, *The Jews of Oregon: 1850-1950* explains, there were "synagogues, a mikvah, public schools and a Hebrew schools, the Neighborhood House with its myriad activities, and many small shops that served the community."[419] The shops were especially busy on Thursday and Friday as people prepared for *Shabbes*. After *Shabbes*, on Saturday night "most of the neighborhood could be found strolling along 1st Avenue, just enjoying themselves or shopping for the coming week."[420] The Jewish influence was so pervasive that some called it the Lower East Side of Portland.

Peddling was a common trade among South Portland's Eastern European Jewish immigrants. For Yisroel Aryeh, it was a hard life. Day in and day out, he hitched his horse to a wagon and went collecting. At the end of the day, tired and dirty, he sold the collected scraps to junk dealers. His profit was insufficient to care for his family of seven.

"Everyone remembers South Portland's ubiquitous junk peddlers," states Polina Olsen in *Stories from Jewish Portland*. "Newcomers often

Peddler with buggy– (Oregon Jewish Museum and Center for Holocaust Education, OJM01199).

borrowed money for a horse and wagon and went into business for themselves. They picked up scrap, bottles, whatever they could find, and sold them to the junk dealers who lined Front Avenue. They eventually organized into the Oregon Junk Peddlers Association and held regular meetings at the Neighborhood House on Southwest 2nd Avenue."[421]

The horses that drew the wagons were kept in people's barns next to their homes. One barn on Southwest Mead Street was owned by the Reihardt family. They charged one dollar a month as rent.

"There were about twenty horses," recalled Gussie Reinhardt, "and it was a big help."[422]

The Treigers settled into their small home which was at the northern edge of the neighborhood. They walked to the local Jewish owned shops and found "everything Jewish immigrants might need. There were kosher butchers, bagel makers, a fish market, and even a barbershop where 'Dr. Wolfe' applied leeches.[423] The Neighborhood House gave citizenship and English classes. After work, men sat on apple boxes outside the grocer and discussed 'Bintel Brief,' an advice column in the Yiddish press."[424]

Visiting Portland in March of 2023 with two of my adult children, Shoshana and Esther, I checked out the old neighborhood. My first stop was the Neighborhood House, which, thanks to Landmark status, is preserved (mostly) as it was in the early 1900s. It's currently occupied by a school and, after I explained my presence, they graciously took me on a tour. Its sturdy red brick exterior gives way inside to warm and inviting dark wood doors, exposed pipes in the ceiling and a wide wooden staircase that leads up three flights. I climbed the stairs, imagining these hallways and rooms filled with school children, packed with Yiddish speaking immigrants learning English, learning to cook, playing basketball in the gym, studying Hebrew and other Jewish subjects, and enjoying a night out with friends – a true community center.

Besides the Neighborhood House, there wasn't much left of the old neighborhood. Walking down the block filled with small, well-kept homes, I stumbled onto an old Synagogue, paint peeling and worn, that now serves the community as a church. Another block down, I noticed a small one-story wooden apartment house that looked old, but well kept.

Karen outside Neighborhood House, now a school (Treiger Collection).

Neighborhood House Plaque (Treiger Collection).

It has a plaque indicating that it was built in 1890 and is now preserved by Landmark status.

The colorful old neighborhood of South Portland was brutally dissected by highways and swallowed by Portland's expanding downtown. The landscape was so different that I was left speechless when I found 543 2nd Avenue and saw a FedEx office where the Treiger home used to sit.

There were many synagogues to choose from in old South Portland. The largest was Shaarie Torah, commonly known as the First Street *Shul* (1st and Hall). The rabbi at the First Street Shul was a charismatic Eastern European rabbi, Rabbi Fiavusovich, who later changed his name to Fain. Rabbi Fain was known as the "*Royta Rov*" because he had a red beard (Royta means red in Yiddish). This may have been the Treiger family's *Shul* of choice, as it was the closest to their home, but I don't know. Two other smaller Synagogue options were Linath Hazedek, established in 1914, which was known as the Kazatzker *Shul* (SW Front and Arthur) and Kesser Israel, founded in 1916.[425]

Papa Sam was thirteen years old when he arrived in Portland. He knew no English but learned quickly. As an adult, he spoke without an Eastern European accent, except according to my father Irwin, pronouncing his "v's" as a "w's" – "as in wegetables."[426] When they first arrived, both Sam and his younger brother Henry were newspaper boys (Newsies). With their small earnings, they helped the family put food on the table.[427] I imagine my grandfather as a teenager with a cap on his head, his arms full of newspapers, standing on a corner hawking them for a nickel a piece.

Indeed, there were hundreds of Newsies, jostling each day for the best corner and the most business. These South Portland boys, *The Jews of Oregon* states, were all Jewish or Italian.

"When I first came to Portland in 1911 [at age nine]," Scotty Cohen recalls in an interview, "[t]he first thing I did was I sold newspapers at 1st and Alder Street. In them days, I got the papers at three for a nickel. When I sold them, I made a dime... When I made a dime, I'd go to 1st and Madison where there was a cook; he used to sell a big sack of brown mashed potatoes for a nickel. The other nickel I took home to mother... We had very hard times in them days, very, very, hard times. I really had to help the family and how!"[428]

Another interviewee, Boris Geller, recalled that "[w]e were all immigrants at the turn of the century. My father worked for five dollars a week. There were three hundred to four hundred newsboys on the streets of Portland. For every quarter that came in, the boys could buy food for their parents. There were seven in our family, and someone had to help. Ours wasn't the only family in that situation. Meat was ten cents a pound in those days. If you had fifty cents, you could feed a family of six."[429]

A Newsie in Portland, Oregon (Oregon Jewish Museum and Center for Holocaust Education, OJM01602).

The 1920 US Census Report that I accessed through Ancestry.com paints a picture of the Treiger family some six years after Tillie's arrival with the children. Israel Treiger is listed as a fifty-two year old peddler of junk, Ethel (Tillie) was fifty with no job; Bert (twenty-four) was a Hebrew School principal and Sam (nineteen) and Henry (sixteen) were newsboys. Sandry was listed as eleven years old. Claire (twenty-two) was noted as Claire Kaufman and her one-and-a-half-year-old daughter, Lina. Claire's spouse isn't present in this entry.[430]

The census states the place of birth (except for little Lina) as Russia and their language as "Hebrew." Was this an error on the part of the census taker? Is it possible that the Treiger family spoke Hebrew at home? Bert emphasized the importance of Hebrew language as the Principal of the Hebrew School in Portland and later in his career as a rabbi. But it's hard to believe that Yisroel (Israel) Aryeh and Tillie spoke Hebrew to their children. It's more likely that they spoke Yiddish, the language of Eastern European Jews and that they told the census taker that their language was "Jewish," which was translated as Hebrew.

Back Row: Sam Treiger, Sonny Treiger, Henry Treiger. Front Row: Bert Treiger, Lina Kaufman, Claire (Treiger) Kaufman (Treiger Collection).

Below: TREIGER FAMILY – Approx. 1925. Back Row: Henry, Sonny, Bert, Sam. Front Row: Ethel, Mr. Kaufman holding son Harold, Claire, Lina, Yisroel Aryeh (Treiger Collection)

Bert & Lena Make Their Mark

Searching Genealogybank.com for the name Treiger turned up a 1917 newspaper profile of Bert Treiger in the Oregon Journal. At the age of twenty-two, Bert explained that his family immigrated to the United States because their father wanted to "give his children greater freedoms and equality than could be obtained in Russia."[431] Bert zipped through elementary education at Failing School[432] in two years. Bert was placed in "ungraded rooms," or "Opportunity Rooms," which were usually reserved for the benefit of "sub-normal children." But in 1917 these rooms were filled with "foreign boys and girls who are older and capable of going faster as they learn the language more perfectly."[433]

On my 2023 trip to Portland, I located the Failing School, named for a former Portland Mayor, Josiah Failing. It's a sprawling, unattractive brick building from 1912, built to replace an 1882 wood schoolhouse. Josiah Failing's name remains engraved in stone above the entrance of the building that hasn't changed since then. Sitting on the bank of the Willamette River, with a stunning view of Mount Hood, it was great spot for a school until the highway isolated it from the rest of the neighborhood.

The building is currently owned by the National University of Natural Medicine. There wasn't much security so I slipped in. I meandered through the halls and up the two sets of worn-down stairs, encountering mostly empty halls and classrooms. It's well kept for an old building, and like the Neighborhood House has exposed ceiling pipes and original solid wooden doors. Walking the halls, I imagined Bert, Claire, Sam, Henry, and Sandry rushing to class, breaking their teeth on a new language, and absorbing a new culture.

At the time of the newspaper profile in 1917, Bert was twenty-one years old and attending Lincoln High School. Surprisingly, he was enrolled in honors courses. "This," the article explains, "is the story of a Russian boy who found his eagerly sought chance in the Portland schools."[434]

Bert explained that he intended to go to college after graduating high school. "My only regret," he said, "is that we didn't come to America sooner, so I could have been farther ahead now. I must work just that much harder to catch up. When I finish high school, I mean to work my way through college. I cannot receive assistance from my parents, who are poor, but I know I will succeed."[435]

Bert Treiger, graduation from High School (Treiger Collection)

Bert attended Reed College, majoring in Ancient History. He earned money for tuition and books by teaching and later serving as the Principal of the Portland Hebrew School, which children attended in the afternoon, after public school. The Airbnb that I rented in Portland was a short walk to Reed College. The picturesque campus is a mash up of New England Tudor-Gothic style architecture with monumental red brick buildings and the Pacific Crest Trail, with its hiking path through dense woods and a large stream called Crystal Creek Springs. Reed is on the eastern side of the Willamette River, just a ten-minute drive from the Treiger's home. Bert likely took a streetcar to get to school and it probably took longer than ten minutes.

The Portland Hebrew School moved to the Neighborhood House[436] in 1916, and a new board of directors was installed, including its main funder, Joseph Shemanski. The new board, *The Jews of Oregon* states, "wanted to retain Jewish tradition and culture, but within a revitalized American context."[437]

"Bert Treiger," The Jews of Oregon continues, "a young man with strong ideas about 'modern' Hebrew education, was hired in 1918. He immediately instituted the *Ivrith B'Ivrith*, or direct method of teaching, which replaced the old *Heder* with its system of davening. Hebrew was the language of the school, and English was rarely spoken. Students were trained and tested on the Bible in its original language, Jewish history,

Jewish law and custom and the Hebrew language. The fundamental purpose of the school, according to Mr. Treiger, was 'the perpetuation of Judaism.' In the powerful, secular environment of America, effective Jewish education was essential if Jewish culture, language, and moral precepts were to be instilled in its youth."[438]

Bert served as Principal of the Hebrew School until 1930, when he left for New York City to obtain rabbinic ordination at the Jewish Theological Seminary. Two years earlier, in 1928, Bert married Lena Farber, who was born in New Jersey, but later moved to Tacoma, Washington with her family.[439] Lena was a remarkable woman, who by the age of twenty-two, when she married into the Treiger family, was an honors graduate from the University of Washington and a member of Phi Beta Kappa. She moved to Portland with Bert and became the director of "girls' activities" at the Neighborhood House and served as the Portland Chapter Hadassah President.

When Bert and Lena left Portland in 1930, the Oregonian published an article stating that Bert left behind "one of the few big Hebrew schools in the country. The work has been of such high standard that a year ago the colleges and universities of the Pacific Coast agreed to recognize a diploma from it and to grant two years' credit for foreign language work to graduates, to be counted toward a Bachelor of Arts degree."[440]

After graduation from the Jewish Theological Seminary, Rabbi Bert Treiger's first pulpit was in Lena's hometown of Tacoma at a synagogue called the Talmud Torah. Upon his arrival, Bert found strained relationships between the leaders of the town's synagogues. He decided to form a Junior League, inviting the youth of all the synagogues to join.

"'Rabbi Treiger brought the youth of the entire community together,' said Josephine Kleiner Heiman, whose father had long been a respected member of both the temple and the synagogue. 'We met every Sunday night in the vestry of the Talmud Torah.' 'We started out with only nine members,' said Rhoda Sussman Lewis, first president of the organization, 'and by the end of the year we were up to twenty-five members.' The friendships made between the youth of the synagogue and the youth of the temple through the Junior League, as well as the AZA boys' group and B'nai B'rith girls' groups which followed, provided much of the strength for the merger, said Heiman."[441]

Bert and Lena strengthened the Tacoma Jewish community by forming a Hadassah council. This council, established in 1938, brought "together women from several organizations, including Talmud Torah Synagogue and Temple Beth Israel. The group pledged to save at least one European child."[442] Lena served as Secretary of the first Tacoma Jewish Fund, while Bert served as a board member.[443]

Bert had a number of positions during his career – Toronto, Reno, and finally Altoona, PA. It was in Altoona that Bert died on November 12, 1954. He and Lena had no children. Lena moved to New York and began working for the Women's League of United Synagogue of America. She served as the Executive Director of the League from 1962 to 1969.[444]

"Aunt Lena always went out of her way to be nice to Irwin and me," my mom told me when I asked her about her relationship with Aunt Lena. "I never knew Uncle Bert; he died before I joined the family. But

Bert and Lena Treiger in Nevada (Treiger Collection).

Lena was a lovely lady. When we lived in New York during that first year we were married, Lena was the only family member that would talk to me."

"Why wouldn't other family members talk to you?" I asked.

"Because I wasn't Jewish enough," my mom replied with some bitterness lingering in her voice as she enunciated "Jewish enough."[445]

Back To Portland

Papa Sam took my dad on a trip to Portland around 1946. They visited the Shank family. He showed my dad the old neighborhood, including the small wooden home where his family lived.

"It wasn't much of a house," my dad said, "but it was home."[446]

As a young man, Papa Sam was drawn to business. He attended the Failing School, but unlike Bert, who attended the large Lincoln High School, Sam chose the smaller High School of Commerce. Started in 1916 and located at the site of today's Portland State University, it was an independent high school with a focus on business.[447] He graduated, with thirty-eight other seniors, in June of 1921, at the age of twenty.

The High School of Commerce seniors, including "Sam S. Treiger," the Oregonian reported, "received diplomas in graduation exercises last night in the Lincoln High School auditorium. The address to the class was made by B.F. Mulkey, who told the students that at this time, more than any other period in history, the nation looked to the younger generation to furnish leaders in all worthwhile fields of work. The presentation of diplomas was made by J.F. Elton, principal of the school. The girls' glee club presented several songs and Ruth Agnew sang 'Hayfields and Butterflies' and 'Your Eyes Have Told Me So.'"[448]

As a student, Papa Sam developed a stunning style of penmanship. I've seen his script on the back of old photos. It's like something out of a Victorian novel or an example of fine calligraphy. My father, whose penmanship was atrocious, always marveled at his father's ability.

"His handwriting was beautiful," my dad said. "Those were the days when they taught penmanship in school."[449]

Papa Sam also learned to spell, and he didn't shy away from competition.

Just a month before graduation, he participated in a unique event – a spelling bee between High School of Commerce students and prominent businessmen of Portland. It was a tough competition.

"Twelve pupils from the high school of commerce will attempt to spell down twelve prominent businessmen of the city at the noon meeting of the Progressive Business Men's Club today," reported the Oregonian in May of 1921. "Of the dozens of pupils, five were born outside of the United States: of their parents all but two were born in foreign lands, Russia taking the lead... The pupils who will take part, their birthplace and the birthplace of their parents follows: ... Sam Treiger: Russia."[450]

With his high school diploma in hand, Papa Sam enrolled in the ROTC and became a "Duck," attending the University of Oregon, where he studied business. A small photo of Papa Sam outside a small, wooden home shows him wearing an ROTC uniform. It looks like one of those proud photos we take of our children when they are about to leave home.

Getting out into the mountains, lakes, and the Pacific Ocean during these years was part of life for Papa Sam. There are photos, most dated 1922, that I found in my father's file, showing him among stands of timber or at a viewpoint. Lots of smiling young people went on some summer-time outings on the "South Parkway Excursion Boat 'Blue Bird,'"[451] and the Rambler Excursion on Boat "Swan".[452] They seemed to be having a great time.

In one photo Papa Sam can be seen with a group of friends, huddled together – a typical college shot. The back of the photo says "Hill Villa, on a hike, May 3, 1925." This was the end of the academic year, and it marked a sad moment for Papa Sam. It was the end of his college career. He never returned to the University and didn't graduate. My father believes that Papa Sam dropped out of college because his father Yisroel Aryeh, couldn't support the family. I can only imagine his disappointment at not completing his degree. After moving back home, he took various jobs and opened a business with a friend, the Peerless Packing Co. of Portland.

"Sam and a friend," my dad said, "pickled meats and things like that and sold them to delicatessens and restaurants – not kosher. He made great corned beef and great pickles – like the Lower East Side in big barrels."[453]

Rose Steinberg And Sam Treiger Marry

Papa Sam and his friends were interested in meeting eligible Jewish women. So, the summer of 1927 a few young Jewish men from Portland drove up to Seattle to attend a "mixer." It was here that Sam met Rose Steinberg. They were married a year later on June 10, 1928, in the backyard of the Steinberg home. Sam moved up to Seattle.[454]

In 1928, Calvin Coolidge was President of the United States and Seattle's first woman mayor, Bertha Knight Landes, led the crusade to quash the illegal bootlegging and smuggling of alcohol during Prohibition.[455] Though alcohol was illegal, Seattle was prospering. The Paramount Theater and the Seattle Civic Center[456] were established in 1928, as was a new highway from Seattle to Tacoma and a south-side airstrip, named Boeing field.[457] By 1930, the U.S. Census Report counted 365,000 residents of Seattle.[458]

Rose and Sam settled into life as a married couple in Seattle's Orthodox Jewish community, which was made up of two distinct groups – Ashkenazic and Sephardic Jews. These two communities lived separately and "rarely mixed socially."[459] Besides cultural differences, there were

Sam Treiger and Rose (Steinberg) Treiger (Treiger Collection)

Sam Treiger (Treiger Collection).

language barriers: the Ashkenazim spoke Yiddish while the Sephardim spoke Ladino. *A Family of Strangers: Building a Jewish Community in Washington States*, first published in 2003, gives the rich history of this era.

"The Ashkenazim," *A Family of Strangers* states, "looked down on [the Sephardim] as any group looks down on the next wave. They were ... greenhorns. They talked funny. They cooked different." [460]

This is of course, ironic because the 1st wave of Reform Jews, most of them of German origin, lived in the Capitol Hill area, felt "American", and wouldn't dream of socializing with these new traditionally religious Jews – whether they be Ashkenzik or Sephardic.

"Little social contact existed," *Family of Strangers* states, "between the Capitol Hill Jews and the Eastern European and Sephardic immigrants who arrived later. The acculturated and financially comfortable temple Jews saw the need to aid their co-religionists and to quickly educate them to American ways, but not to include them in their social circles."[461]

It's important to note that the feelings were mutual. The Orthodox Jews living in this tight-knit community, "regarded the temple Jews with a wariness that bordered on suspicion."[462] I suppose it's just a sad commentary on human nature that we look down on others who are different from us, even those with the same religious faith.

Moving from South Portland, Sam may have felt at home in Seattle's Orthodox Jewish neighborhood. It had many of the hallmarks of South Portland, though the non-Jewish population was more Scandinavian than Italian.

"Seattle's distinctive neighborhood," *A Family of Strangers* explains, "lay between Twelfth and Twentieth Avenues, bounded on the south by Yesler Way and on the north by Cherry street... The Yesler Way-Cherry Street neighborhood contained a mixture of ethnic groups which included Jews, Scandinavians, African Americans, and Asians... During the decade after World War I, a visitor to Yesler Way would have encountered the impressive Bikur Cholim sanctuary looming at Seventeenth Avenue. Three more synagogues lay to the north within a block or two of Yesler Way: Herzl, Ezra Bessaroth, and Sephardic Bikur

Holim. By 1930, Machzikay Hadath's little sanctuary appeared at 26th Avenue and Spruce Street."[463]

With all these synagogues clustered together, it was quite the sight on *Shabbes* and holidays as Jews from various synagogues walked the streets. People paraded on Yesler Way, greeting each other in Yiddish, Ladino, and English.

"'You might have lived on 25th and Fir,' Elazar Behar, a member of Ezra Bessaroth described, 'but you would not walk straight up Fir Street. You would go to Yesler Way and then you would walk up to 25th or 29th ... and then you would walk back to your block... Yesler Way was the parade route ... On Yom Kippur night it would be unbelievable. It looked like a never-ending procession for a good hour... They'd walk three steps forward, stop and talk a little bit more, take a couple more steps and talk. As we said in Spanish, they would be saludando ... greeting each other. You'd have to stop and wish everybody a happy holiday.'"[464]

Jewish shops lined Yesler Street with Hebrew lettering, including the word "Kosher" written in Hebrew. There was the New York Restaurant, L. Hoffman's Grocery and Delicatessen, and Ziegman's butcher shop – all just across the street from the Bikur Cholim Synagogue which had moved to 17th and Yesler.[465] Intermingled among the butcher shops, restaurants and grocery stores were kosher bakeries, such as Brenner's and Lippman's, and from which wafted "the enticing smell of freshly-baked challah, pumpernickel, and rye breads."[466]

"Dozens of other businesses, Jewish and Gentile," *A Family of Strangers* explains, "could be scattered along or near Yesler Way. Favorites included Condiotty's candy shop and the Yesler Theater, where children paid a nickel for movies. Funes's and Oziels' Yesler Furniture Company, jewelers and watchmakers, laundries, barber shops and hardware stores, plumbers, and shoe repair shops provided goods and services to a close-knit community."[467]

Sam moved to Seattle in 1928, but within five years the center of the Jewish neighborhood shifted as Jewish families moved six blocks north, making Cherry Street, rather than Yesler, the center. Though the synagogues remained on or near Yesler, "Kosher groceries, bakeries, and butcher shops followed the migration of the Jewish community as it fanned north and east from its anchor at Seventeenth and Yesler."[468]

The small geographic area where the Jews lived made for a cohesive neighborhood and a tight-knit community, but we must recognize that it was due to racially restrictive policies known as redlining.

"The 1920s in Seattle," writes Ron Judd in a 2020 article for Pacific NW Magazine, "saw the continuation of long-established ethnic segregation, with sizable populations of native, Black, Asian, Latin and Jewish residents shoehorned into established neighborhoods such as the International and Central districts. The city, notes University of Washington historian James Gregory, for most of its history has been 'as committed to white supremacy as any location in America.'"[469]

Banks would not make loans to Jews for homes in other neighborhoods and many properties outside of this restricted area had racially restrictive land covenants.[470] While the practice of exclusion, referred to as redlining, was reprehensible, by forcing the Jews into a specific geographic location, this discriminatory practice created an insular, uniquely tight-knit community.

Sam married the youngest of five Steinberg children and joined a large family. Each *Shabbes* after *Shul,* the laughter and chatter of the five Steinberg siblings and their spouses rose from the dining room of the grand house on 28th and Washington, floating up through the vents to the "attic" where the grandchildren played. Before the kids climbed the steep steps to play, they ate their fill of their grandmother, Chaya Tsivia's *lokshen kugel*[471] and chicken.

Beyond the immediate family, there was a large network of Steinberg and Lawson cousins, all of whom immigrated from Samke and lived within walking distance of the Synagogue. The closeness of the family was typical of immigrant families in the 1930s.

"For many," describes the *Family of Strangers*, "the extended family served as the focus of social life. Grandparents, aunts, uncles, and cousins gathered not only for religious celebrations but also for entertainment and mutual support."[472]

And what of Treiger relatives left behind in Europe? There is evidence that Sam stayed in touch with some of his kin. Receipts evidencing money orders for five dollars, sent by Sam S. Treiger to S.A. Brezner at M. Demidowka, Poland on March 12, 1929. Again on Sept. 25, 1930, Sam sent money orders for ten dollars to Mojsze Trejger in Radzwilow, Poland and five dollars to S.A. Brezner in Demidowka. These receipts suggest that Sam was in contact with relatives in the old country and knew that five or ten dollars would make their lives more comfortable. Those who didn't leave were murdered in 1941 by the Nazis – shot into open pits.[473]

The Family Grows

It was April 29, 1930 when Papa Sam and Bobby (Rose) brought their first child, Rafael Levi (Ray), into the world. Naming the baby for Sam's mother Rivka must have raised bitter-sweet memories for Sam. He was only three years old when his mother died. My father, Irwin Louis came along four years later, on September 10, 1934, the first night of Rosh Hashanah, the Jewish New Year.[474] He was named in Hebrew, for Sam's father, Yisroel Aryeh, who died on July 17, 1931.[475]

Yisroel Aryeh and Tillie had moved from Portland to Seattle not long before his death, either in 1930 or early 1931. They left Portland after Bert and Lena moved to New York, as they had no more children living there.[476] Yisroel Aryeh's grave is in the old Bikur Cholim cemetery, just across the street from the more recent graves where my dad is buried. It was surreal to visit my father's grave with his name, Yisroel Aryeh, and then cross the street to where the older graves are located and see an aging tombstone with the same name: Yisroel Aryeh. As I left the cemetery, tears welled in my eyes as I thought about the hardships of Yisroel Aryeh's life in Portland and how my father, bearing his name, succeeded to be a leader of both civic and Jewish Seattle and one of the top attorneys in the city and the United States. Then the tears really erupted as I thought about my grandson, Theodore ("Teddy") Irwin - Yisroel Aryeh in Hebrew - named to honor my father. The passing of this name creates a direct link from Demydivka to Portland to Seattle that spans five generations. Names are powerful vehicles of memory.

Looking around in the old section of the cemetery, I stumbled onto Tillie Treiger's grave. Oddly, it wasn't next to Yisroel Aryeh's. The gravestone

Irwin Treiger (UW Library Special Collection, Irwin and Betty Lou Treiger Photo Collection, UW41904).

Ray Treiger with baby brother Irwin (Treiger Collection).

read, "Ethel Treiger, passed to Eternal Rest, March 27, 1932, Age 65 Years." In Hebrew it stated, "Eshet Yirat Elokim, Eitel Bat R. Yosef Zindle," (A G-d fearing woman, Eital the daughter of R. Yosef Zindle) with her date of birth and death inscribed as well. This explains Zindle's (Sandry) name – after her father. I imagine it was challenging for my grandfather, Papa Sam, who had mixed feelings (to be kind) for his stepmother, to decide what to put on her gravestone.

Though neither Aunt Claire,[477] Uncle Bert, nor Uncle Sandry,[478] lived in Seattle, Uncle Henry did. He moved in with Papa Sam and Bobby after graduating from pharmacology school in Philadelphia, living there until he married Laura Krems in 1940. In 1933, Henry opened a drug store in the heart of the Jewish neighborhood, at 2726 E. Cherry Street.[479]

"Henry and I," my dad said, "had a very good relationship. He raised me when he was living at my parents' home. My mother and father were busy with the store, and he was like a third parent. We went places together."[480]

Life in the Treiger home was full of energy and sibling rivalry. Ray, the older brother by four years didn't have much patience for his younger brother, Irwin. The way Ray tells the story, Irwin was spoiled and "never" helped with any chores. "I," Ray said, "always had to wash the car, but Irwin never had to; I helped in the store all the time, but Irwin never had to."[481]

Yisroel Aryeh gravestone (Treiger Collection).

The brothers shared a bedroom and sometimes this caused friction. Like the time Ray got angry and put a piece of tape down the middle of their room. Ray told Irwin, "'you can't cross the middle line.' The door, of course, was on Ray's side of the room."[482]

"There was another time," Ray explained, "I just came from a movie – I went to Madrona movie a lot – it was ten cents every week. Ten cents for the movie and a few cents for an ice cream or comic book. It was *The Mark of Zoro* and I showed Irwin how to fight with a sword. I put a paper bag on his head... I was getting lower and lower on the head and at one point I hit him in the head [with a knife], just above his eyebrow. Luckily, it wasn't lower. [As a punishment] my mother rolled the kitchen towel, she rolled it and snapped it. She had a very sharp snap in the wrist."[483]

Ray tried his best to get Irwin in trouble. One oft-discussed technique was to give Irwin a nickel to start a fight. One time, the nickel was paid, and Ray chased Irwin around the coffee table in the living room while their mother Rose was having a card game with friends. Irwin fell on the coffee table and broke it. Papa Sam and Bobby were furious with Ray because they had to buy a new coffee table.

"Why are you getting mad at me?" Ray asked. "It was Irwin that fell into the table. It was unfair. I gave him the nickel to start a fight so he would get in trouble. I gave him the nickel, but I got in trouble."[484] My father wasn't alive when these allegations were made by Uncle Ray. Consequently, he can't proffer his rebuttal. However, as adults, Ray and Irwin were close friends and spoke often by phone and visited when they could.

By 1935, the Treiger family lived at 819 25th Avenue. This was the home that Ray and Irwin remembered best. One spring day I drove down a tree-lined street in the central district neighborhood of Seattle, parked my car outside the home, and uncharacteristically didn't knock on the door. I didn't knock, but I did look around. The door to this humble home is reached by walking up three cement steps. It's not large, but it's a sweet house. Peering into a fenced-in yard in the back, I imagined Ray and Irwin playing ball. The house was a short half-block to the Talmud Torah building, where, each day after school, Ray and Irwin studied Jewish texts and learned to read and write Hebrew.

Their elementary school, Horace Mann, was also just a short, five-minute walk from their home. Located at 2410 East Cherry Street, this school was named Horace Mann in 1921 to honor the "Father of Free Schools," who was a "lifelong proponent of universal public education."[485] In 1933, Jews made up 50% of the student body.[486] This photos shows my dad with a group of boys who served as the traffic patrol. He looks to be around eight or nine years old. Most of the boys look serious with a few of them sporting straps across their torsos, while others hold traffic flags that say "STOP." My dad is one of the few boys with a smile on his face.

While a student at Horace Mann, my dad wrote poetry. One of his earliest poems was written at the age of eight:

SPRING (1942)
Spring is here, and this will be a happy year.
The flowers are blooming.
The little birds are singing.

Horace Mann Crossing Guard - Irwin is in the back row, third from end (on right) (Treiger Collection).

The sky is blue.
The sun is golden.
A cheerful song is in the air.
Old man winter has gone away.
And will let us children play.

His mother, Rose, sent another poem to the Seattle PI. It was published on October 5, 1946.

A Child's Prayer
By Irvin [sic] L. Treiger

"The lines below were received with a letter from Mrs. Rose Treiger, 819

25th Avenue, who wrote: 'My little son, who is just 12 years old, tries to write poetry in his spare time. He just wrote the enclosed poem for our Yom Kippur, day of Atonement ... It expresses the prayers of all of our people. Would it be possible to print this prayer in your paper this coming Saturday, when we observe our Holy Day.'

Our Father, Who are in heaven,
Who decrees all fate,
Look down upon Thy children.
We stand at mercy's gate.

Too long we've stood there
Bleeding and dying;
Life has compelled us to live in hate.
And out of fear and hunger we are crying.

Our little land of Judea
Stands ready across the sea.
Help us! Please help us!
Make it free.

Time is so short
We can no longer wait, Help us, O Lord,
To open the gate."[487]

Washington Junior High School was their next educational stop. This school, between 18th and 19th on Washington and Main streets was a fifteen-minute walk. The twenty-two room schoolhouse was erected in 1906. When it became a junior high school in 1938, it had 706 students. Originally, junior high school was seventh and eighth grades only, but it was expanded to include ninth grade in 1946 – exactly the time my dad was a student there (1945-1948).[488]

It was during his ninth grade year that the single and only edition of *My Ambition,* was published. It was a class assignment. The "Book Review" about Thrifties was just one of many articles. This one-time publication included articles, a sports page, trivia, and three photos: two of my dad, (age 5 and age 7) and one photo of his cousin Harold (Sonny) Kaufman. The sports page is prominent and focuses on two local Jewish baseball teams, one of which my dad was the manager of.

The trivia section of *My Ambition* noted: "Did you know that... Washington School had bathtubs in the hall several years ago? The school nurse would round up the dirty students and scrub them clean."

The staff of the paper is listed as follows:

Editor – Irwin Treiger
Layout – Irwin Treiger
Sports – Irwin Treiger
Copyreader – Eleanor Snodgrass [teacher]
Typist – Rose Treiger

Prominently feature led on the front page of *My Ambition* was: "Police Still Hunt for Abductor."

Irwin Treiger, five, son of Mr. and Mrs. S. Treiger, 819 – 25th ave. was returned to his home last night, after a strange four-hour disappearance. An alleged kidnapper, who is still at large, lured the child into his Dodge shortly after seven p.m., while his car was being serviced at a local gas station.

The child's first comment to his worried mother upon his return was, 'Look Mamma, the man gave me four ice cream cones and some pop corn and candy.' The boy later told reporters he had taken a drive with the man along the beach (Lake Washington).

Irwin gave no description of the man or his car but did say the man told him he had helped design the local Hebrew School.

Police cars that were called out at nine p.m. are still searching for the abductor.[489]

Did this really happen? Was my dad abducted at the age of 5? I asked my Uncle Ray – he didn't remember. I asked my dad's first cousin, Shim Elyn – he didn't remember. I asked my mom if my dad ever mentioned this abduction – she couldn't remember. Sadly, there was no one else to ask.

Calling this newspaper *My Ambition* says so much about who my dad was at the age of fourteen and the adult he became. The budding journalist introduced himself to his readers.

My Ambition.

Dear reader,

Allow me to explain my idea in writing this paper. First I will tell you something of myself, which will help you to better understand my actions.

I am of Russian-Jewish stock. I was born here in Seattle on September 10, 1934. My full name is Irwin Louis Treiger. Living in Seattle all my life, with only short vacations here and there, my greatest desire, for the present, is to travel.

II

I can do little with my hands, having poor handwriting and worse craftsmanship, so I must depend on my poor brain for everything.

All small children have cravings to do the unusual. Mine was to be a showman. I don't recall how many 'carnivals' were held in my back yard. The most successful had about twenty customers, and seven participants. I don't remember how much money we coined.

Ever since third grade I've wanted to enter the field of Journalism, which is wide, and has few really successful members. When I was about eight, I 'published' a neighborhood newspaper. My brother was the reporter and I was forced to pay him two cents for lesser news events and five cents for big breaks.

The one and only copy of Seattle's smallest and most short-lived news sheet was sold for five cents, (with a four cents loss due to the high price of my reporter), to a girl who lived up the block.

III

My ambition is still to edit a newspaper, and with the proper aid from Ray, my brother who is majoring in journalism in the U of W., I shall achieve this dream.

When six compositions had to be written for composition, I determined what could be a better theme than my ambition. All the stories on these pages have something to do with my life, past and present.

I hope you enjoy, 'My Ambition.'

Sincerely yours,
The Editor

No more need be said – this article foreshadows my dad's whole life. He was of "Russian-Jewish stock," which he wore proudly, his handwriting was truly horrible, and he depended on his "poor brain." His ambition led him not to journalism school, but to law school and to a career filled with successes.

My grandmother Rose, who we called Bobby, was the typist of *My Ambition* and of all the poems. By all accounts, she was extremely involved in the lives of her sons. Both Ray and Irwin described her as "the best mother on the planet."

"She was an excellent mother," Ray said, "warm and perfect. She graded my papers – read them and made corrections in high school and college. She was serious. She was good. Her suggestions were always terrific. She was valedictorian of her high school... I remember the food she made – soup, chicken. Once in a while we splurged and had lamb chops. My mother made *-pcha*... frozen feet-calf feet, with loads of pepper. There is only one place in New York, 2nd Avenue deli, that has *-pcha*."[490]

"She loved Mah-jongg," my dad said of his mother.

"She got together with the girls. She was very American. Her English was impeccable. She was active in the Talmud Torah, the Sisterhood at Bikur Cholim and she became the Regional President of Hadassah. She went to the Hadassah Regional Convention once. One of the great things – she was an avid reader and she loved to tell about books she read. She was in popular demand to give book reviews. She probably gave 20 book reviews a year."[491]

Hadassah was Bobby's favorite organization. She served as political chairman in 1948, then the following a year as chapter Treasurer and Regional Financial Officer. She served as chairman of the 1958, 13th Annual Northern Pacific Coast Conference of Hadassah.[492] Later that same year, she was elected President of the Seattle Chapter. In my parents' storeroom, I stumbled upon a framed "Hadassah Service Award."[493] My grandmother proudly displayed this Service Award on the wall of her small apartment in Capitol Hill.

The Treiger family's social life centered around family and the Orthodox Jewish community. They created their own fun and often raised a bit of money too.

"Synagogue and Talmud Torah fund-raising events" states *Family of Strangers*, "provided some of the most memorable festivities. Picknickers rode the cable car to the Leschi neighborhood, then the ferry to Fortuna Park on Mercer Island, a favored spot. There the various Jewish organizations held daylong events that included raffles, races, contests, games, and prizes. They would end with dancing before everyone embarked back to Seattle."[494]

Papa Sam and Bobby bought their first car together in 1946. My grandmother was slim and short (under five feet) and never drove unless she had to. Periodically, she drove me and my two brothers somewhere, mostly when our parents were out of town. Nervously grasping the wheel, she would boost herself up so she could see out the front window.

By contrast, it seems that Sam couldn't wait to get on the road. In 1946, Papa Sam took his two sons, Ray (age sixteen) and Irwin (age twelve) and drove down to Reno, Nevada. Sam's brother, Bert, lived there with his wife Lena.

"We drove to Reno then to LA where we had other relatives," my dad said, "Steinberg relatives and then back up the coast to Seattle. We were gone several weeks. I remember that trip very well – it was fun."[495]

Naches From The Kinder
(Pride and Joy from the Children)

Ray and Irwin both attended Garfield High school. They both excelled and gave their parents *Naches.*[496] Following his mother's footsteps, my father was the valedictorian of his high school class.[497] Though Irwin didn't play sports, he loved baseball. He was the Garfield High School baseball team manager.

In 1951, Irwin entered a State-wide American History essay contest.[498]

"Five boys won top scores in the regional examination of the eight annual American History Awards," writes the PI, "to become Washington finalists in the national competition sponsored by The Post-Intelligencer

Irwin Treiger, Head Manager of the Garfield High School Baseball Team, 1950 (UW Library Special Collection, Irwin and Betty Lou Treiger Photo Collection, UW41900).

and the Hearst Newspapers from coast to coast... . Irwin Treiger, 16, a senior at Garfield High School, first prize, $200 in United State Savings Bonds... 'Oh my gosh,' he exclaimed when he heard the news, 'I didn't think I'd win.'"[499]

The essay went on to place second in the national contest. My father received more positive press:

"Irwin Treiger, [high school] senior," wrote the PI on February 16, 1951, "received the national second place history award from Superior Judge William J. Wilkins at the County-City Building at noon, February 1. The ceremony took place in the presence of eleven Superior Court Judges sitting en banc in the court room of the Presiding Superior Judge.

Jude Wilkens presented each winner with his respective award after being introduced to the judges by Mr. Samuel E. Fleming, Superintendent of Seattle Public School.

Dr. Charles Le Cugna of Seattle University, chairman of the local judges in the history awards, was also introduced as were Mr. E.E. Hanselman, Principal of Garfield and Miss Mary Knight, head of the History Department who coached Irwin... .

Irwin said that he was very nervous, but recovered when the judge handed him the $1,000 savings bond.

'It was an experience that I will always remember,' Irwin declared."[500]

Both Ray and Irwin attended the University of Washington. They joined a Jewish fraternity since the non-Jewish fraternities did not accept Jews. After college, Ray was drafted into the Army during the Korean War and served as the assistant to the Jewish chaplain at Fort Lewis. After completing his service, he moved to Washington, DC and began a career in real estate, ultimately moving to New York, marrying Nancy Davis and raising three children in Queens – Brent, Betsy, and Kim. He had a long and successful career with Macy's as the VP of Real Estate.[501] Irwin went to law school at the University of Washington, becoming Editor in Chief of the Law Review and graduating first in his class.

In 1964, Papa Sam closed Thrifty's, after he was robbed one too many times. I found reference to three robberies in the local papers. The first was on December 13, 1950. The robber took forty dollars and tried to make a quick escape. But Papa Sam "grabbed a claw hammer and struck the robber on the head twice."[502] During the struggle, the robber ran off, it seems with the cash in his hand. The second was in 1960 when Papa Sam was assaulted by "bandits." The bandits asked to see some merchandise and '[w]hen Treiger turned to show one of the men some gloves, the other struck him on the head with a gun."[503] The bandits ran out the back and got away. "Treiger," the article concludes, "was treated at Group Health Hospital for head lacerations."[504]

In the third violent encounter, Papa Sam was robbed at gunpoint and clobbered on the head with the gun butt. It happened at 6:30 in the evening on January 15, 1964. The robbers demanded his wallet, "and then hit him over the head and the two fled without taking the wallet."[505] The robbers forced the eighteen year old clerk, Shizue Okada, to hand over forty dollars.[506] This attack sent Papa Sam back to the hospital for more stiches. His family pleaded with him to close the store. He agreed and retired.[507]

The cancer came just a couple of years after retirement – it was prostate cancer. Before he died from this disease, Papa Sam saw both his sons married and became a grandfather of six.

Sam died on October 15, 1968, which on the Hebrew calendar was the same date of his birth, the Jewish holiday of *Simchat Torah*.

"He was," my father wrote to my cousin Henry Shuster, Uncle Ray's grandson, "a good, honest, and upright man, very pious in the practice of Judaism."[508]

Bobby was a widow for twenty-one years until her death in 1989. For those twenty-one years, she remained active in Jewish organizations, going to meetings, and giving book reviews. We continued to go to her house each Friday night for dinner – same menu, but now my dad recited the *Kiddush* that his father used to say.

When I wonder where I come from, the Treiger family's unprivileged beginnings give me a foothold to answer the question and fill me with pride. Yisroel Aryeh, as a middle-aged father of five, moved his entire family halfway around the world in the hopes that it would provide a better life for his children. He, himself, had a hard life, peddling in Portland. He was never successful enough to support his family. But his children succeeded, becoming a Rabbi, a pharmacist, and a small business owner. Though Yisroel Aryeh's children and grandchildren faced antisemitism in their lives, they didn't suffer as Jews did in Eastern Europe and by coming to America in the early 1900s, he saved his family from Hitler's genocidal massacre.

Sam and Rose Treiger (Treiger Collection).

I'm deeply humbled as I learn of the Treiger family's start in America. From the dream of a goose feather merchant, out came a cascade of families who succeeded in this country. I am especially humbled when I reflect on the life of his grandson, my father, Irwin Louis Treiger. He was as honest as his father and as intelligent as his mother, and he made his way in a profession and a city that was not open to Jews in the 1950s. Pride and honor are feelings that well up inside me as I carry the Treiger name.

CHAPTER 6

STEINBERG FAMILY

It was freezing in this empty, old house with its guts ripped out. There was dust and dirt everywhere. I drew my heavy coat around my body and closed my eyes. Behind my eyelids, I saw my great grandmother, Chaya Tsivia Steinberg, standing five feet tall, wearing a simple dress with snaps down the front, with her black hair pulled up in a bun. She was here, in the kitchen, baking *Challah* for *Shabbes* (Jewish Sabbath).The aromas emanating from the old stove are a smell that was sweet, yeasty, and lovely, like walking into a bakery in the old city of Jerusalem on a Friday morning. The stove burned hot, warming the room. I didn't feel cold anymore. Absorbing the warmth and the love of the woman who spent countless hours in this room baking Eastern European delicacies for her large family connected me to the past. I carry her Jewish name, Chaya Tsivia, and I feel her presence in my soul.

I opened my eyes, the cold and dust slapped me in the face. I was so lost in the imaginary warmth and smell it took a minute to reorient myself. It was 2018 and I was standing in a room that was the kitchen of a home on 28th and Washington in Seattle. The house, built in 1904 by wealthy German-Jewish immigrants David and Hulda Kaufman, was being restored by its current owner.

My Yiddish-speaking great grandparents, who came to America from a *Shtetl* called Samke, near Minsk, Russia (currently, Belarus), bought the house from the Kaufmans in 1920. My great-grandfather, Chayim Leib, died in 1940 and Chaya Tsivia died in 1944. After her death the home was sold to Dade Nursing Home, then to a Buddhist center and yet later, to investors who turned it into a boarding house with individual rooms

Steinberg Family Tree

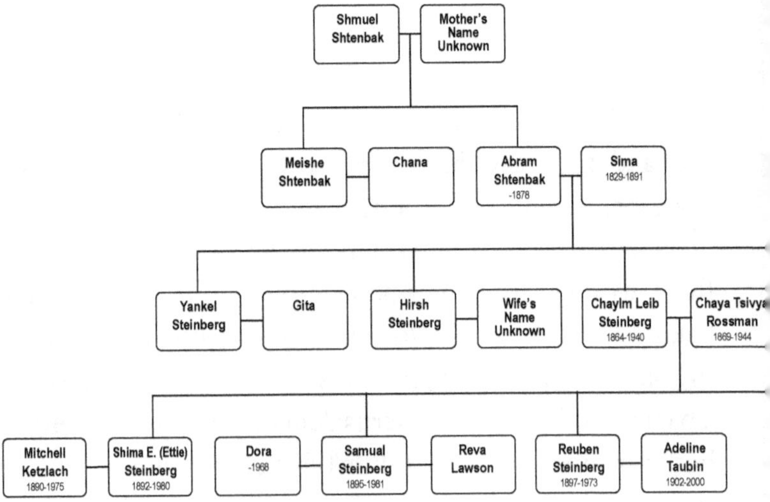
Shmuel Shtenbak
Mother's Name Unknown
Meishe Shtenbak
Chana
Abram Shtenbak -1878
Sima 1829-1891
Yankel Steinberg
Gita
Hirsh Steinberg
Wife's Name Unknown
Chaylm Leib Steinberg 1864-1940
Chaya Tsivya Rossman 1869-1944
Mitchell Ketzlach 1890-1975
Shima E. (Ettie) Steinberg 1892-1980
Dora -1968
Samual Steinberg 1895-1981
Reva Lawson
Reuben Steinberg 1897-1973
Adeline Taubin 1902-2000

Zalman R
Steinberg
1870-
Soreh Mere
Rashell
Isadore
Elyn
1896-1983
Goldie
Steinberg
1902-1962
Samuel S
Treiger
1901-1968
Rose
Steinberg
1904-1989

Steinberg Family Tree, continued

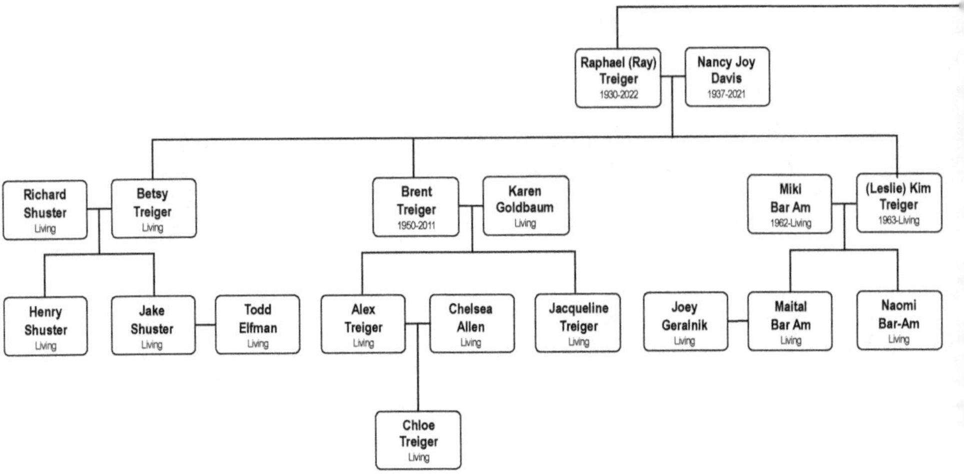

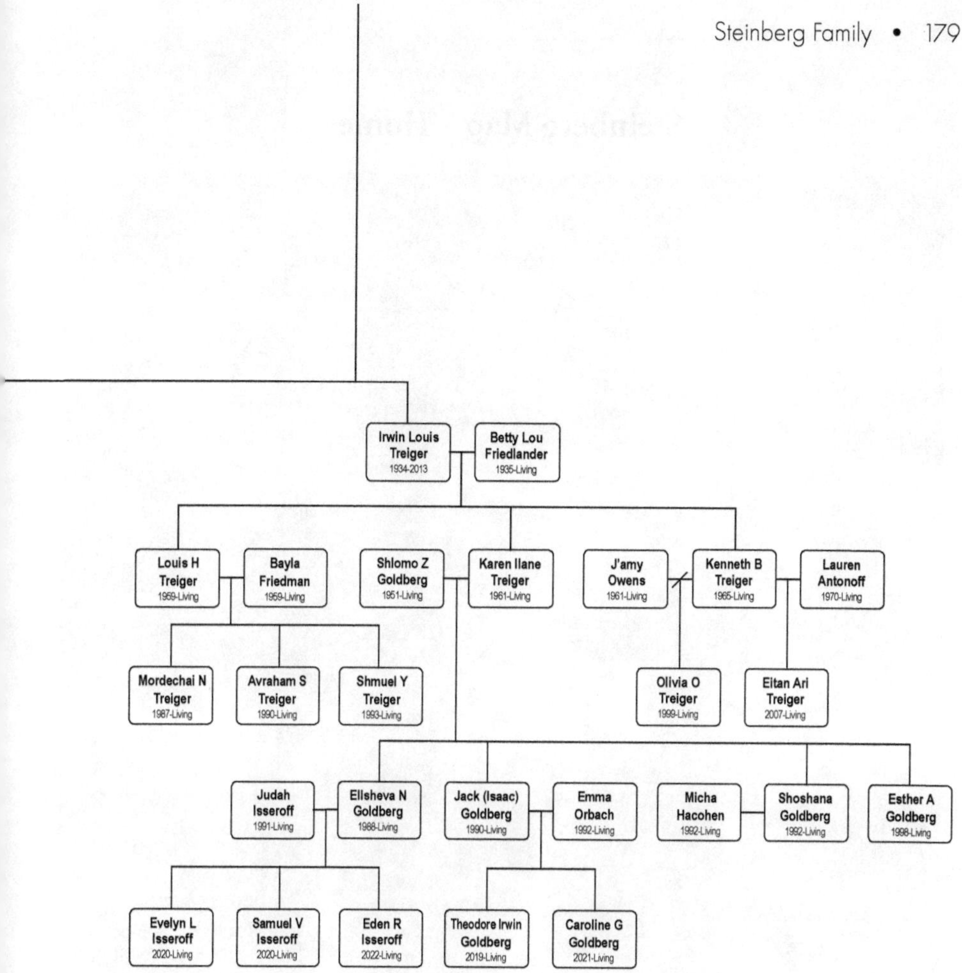

Irwin Louis Treiger 1934-2013
Betty Lou Friedlander 1935-Living
Louis H Treiger 1959-Living
Bayla Friedman 1959-Living
Shlomo Z Goldberg 1951-Living
Karen Ilane Treiger 1961-Living
J'amy Owens 1961-Living
Kenneth B Treiger 1965-Living
Lauren Antonoff 1970-Living
Mordechai N Treiger 1987-Living
Avraham S Treiger 1990-Living
Shmuel Y Treiger 1993-Living
Olivia O Treiger 1999-Living
Eitan Ari Treiger 2007-Living
Judah Isseroff 1991-Living
Elisheva N Goldberg 1988-Living
Jack (Isaac) Goldberg 1990-Living
Emma Orbach 1992-Living
Micha Hacohen 1992-Living
Shoshana Goldberg 1992-Living
Esther A Goldberg 1998-Living
Evelyn L Isseroff 2020-Living
Samuel V Isseroff 2020-Living
Eden R Isseroff 2022-Living
Theodore Irwin Goldberg 2019-Living
Caroline G Goldberg 2021-Living

Steinberg Map – Homes

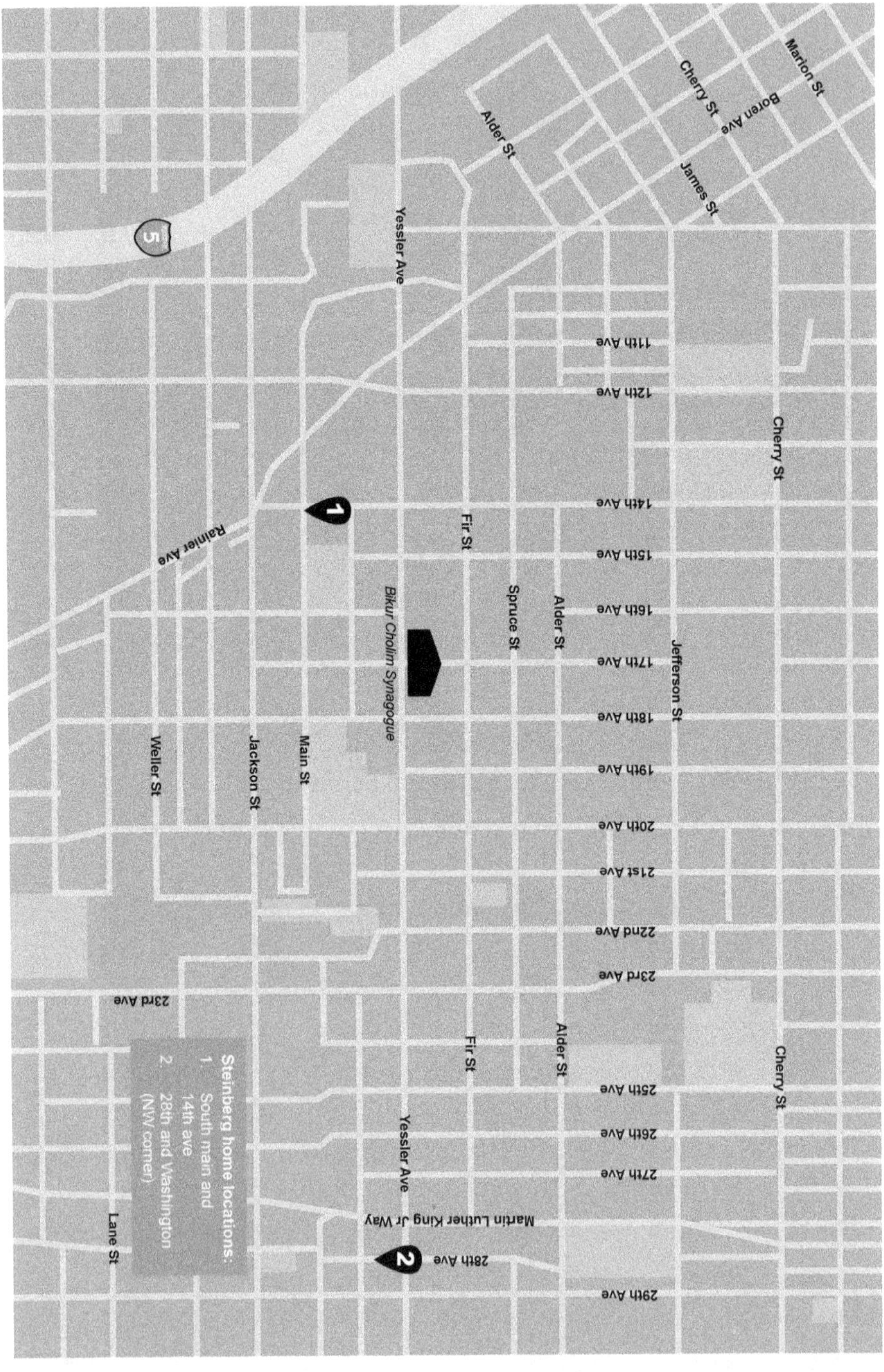

Steinberg Map – Business

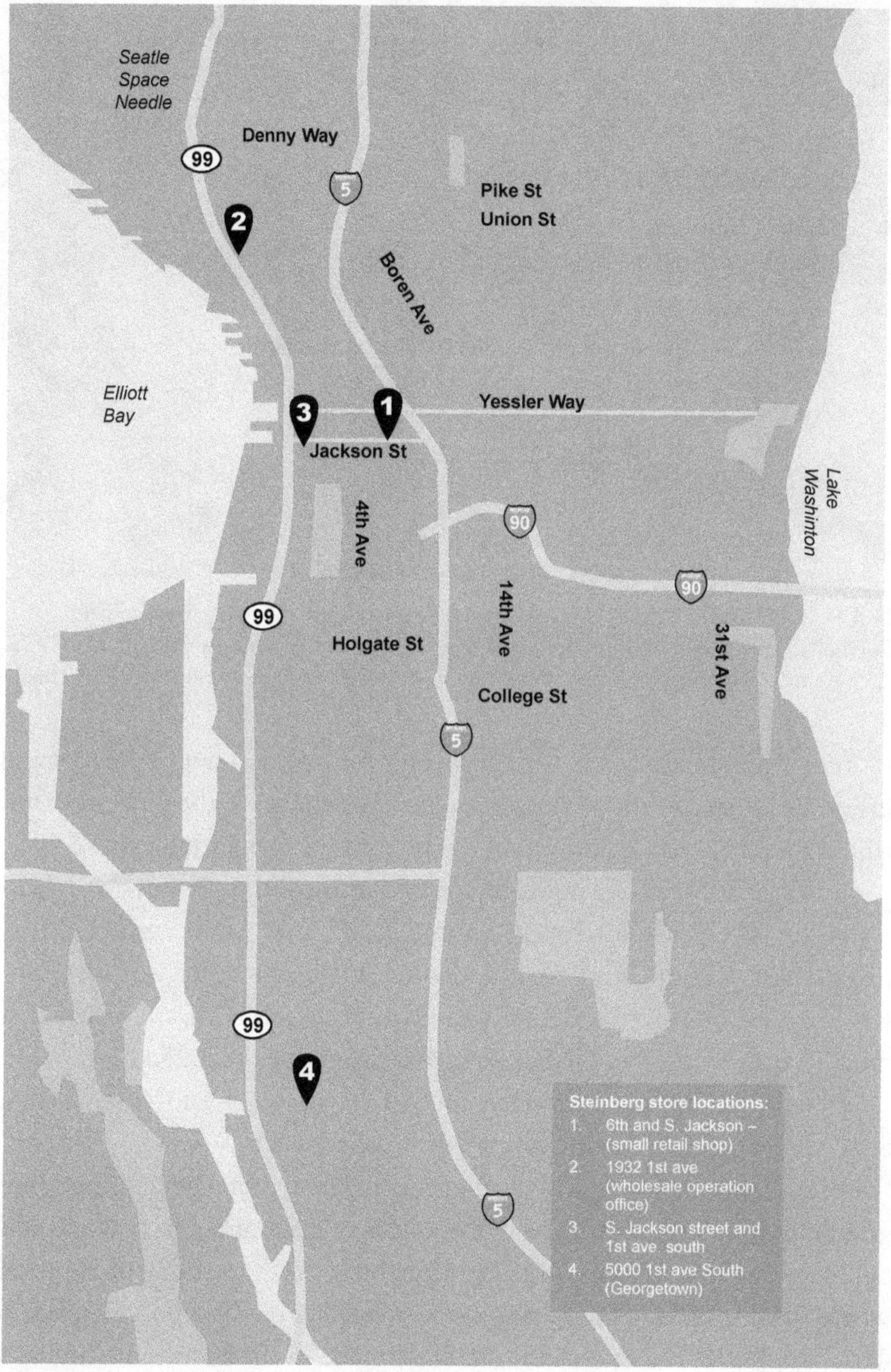
Seatle Space Needle
Denny Way
99
5
Pike St
Union St
2
Boren Ave
Elliott Bay
3
1
Yessler Way
Jackson St
4th Ave
90
Lake Washinton
14th Ave
90
99
Holgate St
31st Ave
College St
5
99
4
5
Steinberg store locations:
1. 6th and S. Jackson – (small retail shop)
2. 1932 1st ave (wholesale operation office)
3. S. Jackson street and 1st ave. south
4. 5000 1st ave South (Georgetown)

Back Row: Norman Ketzlach. Middle Row: Ettie (Steinberg) Ketzlach, Chaya Tsivia Steinberg, Rose (Steinberg) Treiger. Front Row: Evie Ketzlach, Irwin Treiger, approx. 1938 (UW Libraries, Special Collection, WA State Jewish Archives Photo Collection, JEW1140).

for rent. This stately house with large airy rooms was chopped into small, insignificant spaces to maximize profit. I'm grateful to the current owner who undertook major renovations to recreate its former majesty.

I was at the Steinberg home on the invitation of the current owner with my eighty-five year-old cousin, Shim (Mark) Elyn. Shim was one of the two Steinberg grandchildren still alive in 2018. The other was my Uncle Ray Treiger, who lived in New York. I interviewed both and learned so much. Sadly, Uncle Ray died in 2022 and Shim died in 2023.

I've heard legends and tales about Chayim Leib and Chaya Tsivia Steinberg and the "grand home" that filled each *Shabbes* with their five children, spouses, and ten grandchildren. All the children and grandchildren lived within walking distance and came each week after *Shul* for lunch. The home was especially busy on the holiday of Passover, where the dining room table was set with a white cloth; round, handmade *Matzas*; bitter herbs; and sweet red wine made in the basement. The table expanded and spilled out to the entryway. Each grandchild recited their own *Kiddush* and the Four Questions.[509]

The youngest of the grandchildren was my father, Irwin Treiger. His mother, Rache (Rose) was the baby of the Steinberg family. Sima Esther (Ettie) was the oldest, followed by Sam, Reuben, and Goldie. Rose was seven years old when her family illegally crossed the White Russian border to Germany and made their way to Glasgow. From Glasgow they traveled by ship, the Scotia, to Montreal. "Ettie, the oldest," my cousin Shim Elyn (Goldie's son) told me, "wanted to walk around the see the town [of Glasgow] a bit. Off she went by herself. The other kids were afraid and said '*Oy, meshuga* (Yiddish for crazy) something bad will happen to her.' But she was fine. They had enough money for boat tickets, enough to have their own cabin and kosher food. From Montreal, the family took the railroad westward to Vancouver and then south to Seattle."[510]

Chayim Leib Steinberg, a slender man with a full black beard, was even shorter than his five-foot tall wife. By the time the rest of the family arrived in Seattle, Chayim Leib had crossed the Atlantic three times. First in 1907, making his way to Seattle where his brother Zalman Reuben Steinberg had settled in 1904. Zalman Reuben arrived to Seattle via Harbin and Nagasaki.[511] He was hired by the observant Seattle Jewish community to serve as a *Shoichet* (ritual slaughterer).[512] According to my cousin Reva Twersky (Ettie's daughter), Chayim Leib's first trip was to fulfill his brother, Zalman Reuben's request to accompany his wife and son "on the long journey to the new home."[513] After completing his mission, Chayim Leib crossed back over the continent and the Atlantic Ocean, returning to Samke. He informed his wife that he didn't want to live in Seattle because "it would be difficult for a Sabbath observing Jew to get a job in Seattle."[514]

Chaya Tsivia packed some sandwiches and sent Chayim Leib back across the pond in 1910. This time accompanied by their eldest son Sam, who was fifteen years old. Ancestry.com gave me access to the ship manifest that showed that they left from Bremen, Germany on March 27, 1910, on the ship Rhein, arriving in New York harbor on April 7, 1910. According to Sam and Reuben, the family left because there was not enough land to split up among the many children; the small parcels of land would be insufficient to make a living.[515] As the story came down to my generation, it included the mantra of Chaya Tsivia not wanting her sons to be taken into the Czar's army.[516]

Like so many other Eastern European Jewish immigrants, Chayim Leib bought a horse and buggy and "peddled." He and Sam spent their days collecting rags, old clothes, and metal and reselling it to make a few pennies. The horse was kept at a stable in the middle of the block between 12th and 14th on Main.[517]

Between what Chayim Leib saved and the proceeds from the sale of the farm in Samke, there was enough money to bring the rest of the family over in 1911. The family settled in a duplex on 14th, in the heart of the Orthodox Jewish community. The Steinberg's journey to Seattle took them far from the small farming village where they lived in a three-room log house that had no indoor plumbing.

Samke, Russia

At nineteen, Chaya Tsivia Rossman and Chayim Leib Steinberg, both children of Samke, married. The wedding was held in the beautiful Synagogue, made of logs that stood at the highest point of the town. Moving into their own home, they farmed the piece of land given to Chayim Leib by his parents and raised geese, for their own table and for sale in nearby towns.

Though the toilet was outdoors, there was a massive wood burning stove in the center of the Steinberg's Samke home. It was of epic importance. Here, the women would bake *Challah* for *Shabbes,* honey cake for *Rosh Hashanah*, *Blintzes* for *Shavuos,* and *Latkes* for *Chanuka.* But it was much more than the tool to produce these delicious, mouth-watering foods, the mention of which makes me ravenous. The stove was the only source of heat for the home and its flat top served as the most sought-after sleeping spot during the deep freeze of Belarusian winters.

"The stove was the center of their life," explained Shim Elyn.

"In the kitchen, there was a wood burning stove, floor to ceiling. They had plenty of wood, I don't think they used coal. It provided the heating for the house. It had an area that was lower that they all slept on in the winter – parents and all kids – seven people. They knew how to do it – they all did that because of the terribly cold winters. There was probably a way to dampen down the stove so there was not an active flame but just cinders, but it was pretty warm. They would put a heavy quilt or a thin mattress for padding and sleep on it. I would hear about that from my mother. It must have been a pretty terrific stove for a rural people. ... All the [things they baked] - *Heir kichlech* and *tzuchen kichlech* and other cookies... required an oven of 500, at least 450 degrees. The *Heir Kichlech* were flat and thin, and they would have curly cues and a big bubble. When I was a kid and I got a bubble in the bite, it was really fun."[518]

There are other Samke stories passed down – told over and over – mostly while one family member or another was "sitting *Shiva*" – the seven days of mourning after a close relative dies. One of the favorite stories that always brought gales of laughter from the aunts and uncles is how Uncle Sam ran four kilometers (2.8 miles) to get the mail at the post office in Kholopenichi (pronounced Chaloponitch).

"One time," his second wife, Aunt Riva Steinberg, explained, "when [Sam did] not remove his hat before the picture of the Czar in the Post Office, he [was] nearly arrested."[519]

Uncle Sam only spoke Yiddish and the post office official was speaking to him in Russian. The official finally pointed to the portrait of the Czar on the wall and motioned to Sam to remove his hat. Once he understood he must remove his hat, he did so quickly and with great trepidation. This was a very funny story to all who heard it. To me, it's terrifying because Sam could have been shot on the spot for not removing his hat before the picture of the Czar. The stories informed me how life was precarious.

Uncle Sam was a great storyteller and one time my father, Irwin Treiger, got him going while secretly recording his stories – three hours of tape. But, alas, the tape was lost in one of our family moves. My father never got over the loss of Uncle Sam's recordings.

Other stories survived. For example, when someone in Samke was very ill, they sent word to Kholopenichi to fetch a doctor. Once when my great-grandfather was ill, he went to see a Lubavitch Rebbe, who was known to cure people with his blessings.

"[The Zeide's] name was Leib," Shim explained, "and the Rebbe added Chayim to his name to give him a *bracha* (blessing) of long life."[520]

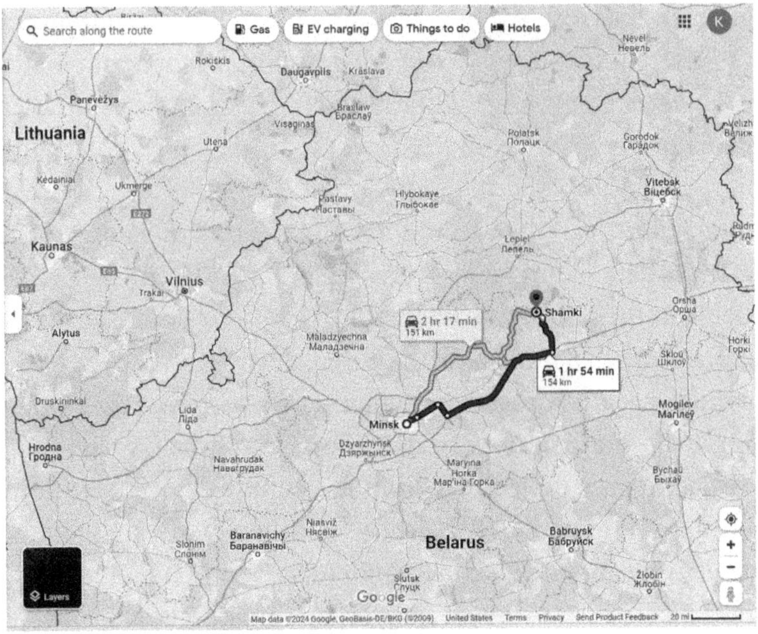

Google map Samke (Shamki)

Another favorite *Shiva* story was about Mordche – the town fool. Mordche, my father retold, "built a house without a chimney. Inside it was so smoky. When asked why he did that, he answered in Yiddish: "*Ich Zol Varmen de Malachim d'fees*?" ("I should warm the angel's feet?")[521] This story too would bring deep belly laughs from all who heard it, even if it was the 100th telling.

"My mom told me," my father recalled, "when fruit came to the village, they cut it up into very small pieces so that everyone could get a taste."[522]

Aunt Riva helped me place Samke on the map. She told of the town of Borisov, sixty kilometers away. "It has paved roads," she explained and "is the place to find a train to travel to the 'big city' of Minsk." [523]

This location, places Samke smack in the middle of the Pale of Settlement, the 472,590 square miles of land where Catherine II of Russia, forced the Jews to live in 1791. At its height, the Pale had over five million Jews living there, representing the largest segment of the Jewish population at the time.[524]

Land ownership was restricted, and it was rare that Jews owned large farms. How did the Jews of Samke come to own their farms?

"[In Samke,] a certain Jew had done a favor for one of the czars," my grandmother Rose who we called Bobby, told me, "and that's how the Jews of Samke became landowners."

Four generations before my grandmother was born, eight Jewish families received a land grant from the Czar, which became the *Shtetl* of Samke. The crops grown in Samke were stored for the winter in the cold cellars or sold in nearby towns. Wheat was turned to flour in Samke's own mill.

The aunts and uncles described a carefree, idyllic summer life of swimming in the stream and picking berries. Chaya Tsivia "used to swim in the river," Shim said. "They loved to swim in the river. At least a part of it was wider and it was like a lake so she could swim across very easily."[525]

There was a one-room school for the children with a non-Jewish teacher who was paid by Samke's families to teach their children math and to read Russian. The boys, including Sam and Reuben, attended *Cheder* (Jewish school) in the afternoons, taught by the *Melamed*, Yisroel Pesach Lawson, who had studied in the Yeshiva of the Lubavitcher Rebbe. Yisroel Pesach married Chaya Tsivia's sister, Seema Esther Rossman.

"The families of Samke were close," my Aunt Riva, the daughter of the *Melamed*, Yisroel Pesach, recalls, "united by mutual feelings of love and respect, all living a traditional Jewish life."[526] The children play together, "picking berries in the spring and summer and swimming in the nearby stream."[527]

"My mother Goldie told me," Shim said, "in the winter, the Steinbergs had plenty of [goose] meat because they had big barrels outside of their house and they put the geese in the barrels with some water and it would freeze. She told me that she would go out and chop one out – not a whole goose, but part of it, probably cut up and cleaned earlier. They didn't freeze the goose in one piece. She did the wood chopping, my *Bubbe*. But he – Chayim Leib – had two horses and he took care of the horses. That was his whole duties. Chaya Tsivia did everything."[528]

The families that lived in Samke spoke a Litvishe Yiddish. This dialect substitutes the "S" sound for a "Sh" sound. For example, they would say "*gut Sabbes*" instead of "*gut Shabbes*." This, Shim explained, is why the family called the town "Samke" rather than its Bellarussian name "Shamki." However, Shim remembers that his grandparents, Chayim Leib and Chaya Tsivia said "*Shabbes*" – not "*Sabbes*."

"They," Shim explained, "didn't take the Litvish accent to the extreme."[529]

Shim was able to mimic the Litvish accent for me. He recalled a few words in particular, the way they would pronounce them in Hebrew. For example, the prayer of *Borchu* was pronounced: "*Borchu es hashem hameveiroch L'eilom voed*"; *Torah* (Word for Hebrew Bible) was pronounced "*Tereh*"; and the beginning of the prayer *Ashrei* was pronounced: "*Ashrei Yeshvei Vesecha Ed Yeahlelucha Sela*."[530]

By 1911, when the family left for America, there were five children, aged seven through nineteen: Ettie, Sam, Reuben, Goldie, and Rose. I am one of the few family members who has stepped foot on the holy Samke soil – this place of memories and stories. As I worked on the book I wrote about my in-laws, Sam and Esther Goldberg, my spouse Shlomo Goldberg suggested that I make a stop in Samke on my way to Warsaw.

"You'll be so close," he said.

I looked at a map and realized he was right. I added three days to my trip and co-opted my youngest child Esther to come along. It was the summer of 2016 and Esther had just graduated high school.

A Visit To The *Shtetl*

As I planned our Samke visit, I struggled to visualize the Steinberg family living in a log cabin with some sixty other families in this small town. Then I found Aunt Riva Steinberg's interview with the Jewish Historical Society.

"Two large, unpaved streets make up the entirety of the *Shtetl* of Samke," Aunt Riva said. "In front of the log cabin homes that line the streets, one could have found a hardened dirt path measuring 3-4 feet, serves as a makeshift sidewalk. No cars traverse these roads — only horses, wagons, bicycles and human feet. There was no 'town center,' the few stores, such as grocery, shoemaker, blacksmith, tailor, and butcher shop, were located inside the homes. Cellars with walls made of earth or stone store potatoes, carrots, cabbages, apples, and pears for the winter. These cellars remained very cold, but never froze."[531]

As Aunt Riva explained, there was no town square, though there was a central gathering place – the *shul* (synagogue). The *shul* was "a beautiful structure," recalled Aunt Riva. It was "built of logs also, and [stood] up on a hill surrounded by plants."[532] The *shul* also had a *mikve*, a ritual bath, in it.[533]

I would soon see for myself. It was June 16, 2016, when Esther and I landed in the Minsk airport. We stayed at one of the nicer hotels in Minsk and the Soviet influence was everywhere. Nothing to write home about. Most of the buildings were unromantic, rectangular boxes and even in the spring, it felt dour.

Esther Goldberg and Karen Treiger on plane to Belarus (Treiger Collection)

Our translator, Lucy, arranged for a car and driver to take us to Samke. It was a two-hour ride through the countryside. I was so pre-occupied with what we might see in the *shtetl*, I have no memory of the countryside. We drove through the town of Kolopenichi, stopping just long enough to pick up the mayor of the town, Andrei. Lucy had contacted him about our visit, and he wanted to escort us to Shamki.

Chayim Leib Steinberg and Chaya Tsivia (Rossman) Steinberg (Treiger Collection).

My anticipation grew and I could feel the excitement building as we drove out of Kolopenichi – after all, Uncle Sam told us it was just four kilometers away (it's really seven kilometers). Then I saw it – a slightly bent and dirty green sign that stood at the corner of the nondescript street – the sign read: "Shamki." We turned off the main road and the reality of what had become of this *shtetl* was right there for me to see and feel.

I felt as if I was on my way to a hike deep in the Olympic Mountains on an uncared for trail. The road was uneven and covered with rough gravel. The weeds and grass were so overgrown that it felt more like jungle than a *shtetl*. Lush green trees grew on either side of the narrow road where the log houses of my ancestors used to stand. In their place, we saw remnants of wood structures overtaken by nature – wood pieces hanging here and there, many of them gone completely. Where there were once houses, a school, a water mill, there is nothing but rot and decay. I peered into the brush to see the decaying wood structures, which were unrecognizable as buildings. They were now part of the forest that overtook this small town. Though there was no moss on the trees, the thickness of the brush reminded me of the Ho Rain Forest on the Olympic Peninsula.

The only intact home was Raisa's – she was the only human still living in Shamki. Raisa, born in Shamki in 1943, is not a Jew. In fact, Raisa was born two years after all remaining Jews of Samke were shot into a pit a few kilometers away by the murderous Nazi Einsaztgruppen in 1941. After that – no Jews remained in Samke.

Mayor Andrei, the mayor of Kalopenitch, took us to the murder site, just a few kilometers away. There's a small memorial there that according to Andrei, no one ever visits. As I stood at the murder site, I knew that hundreds of Jews, some of them from Samke lay beneath my feet. I felt my stomach tighten as I realized that this horrific death would certainly have been my grandmother and her family's fate if they had stayed in Samke. In 1941, my grandmother was 36 years old.

I never heard the uncles or aunts talk about the Holocaust or discuss how their remaining relatives and friends in Samke were murdered. Shim told me, however, that at one of the *Shivas*, Uncle Rueben said that all their relatives from Samke were dead – killed by the Nazis – no one left.[534]

Raisa was told in advance by Mayor Andrei, that a granddaughter of someone who had lived in Shamki, from the United States, would be coming to visit. Well, I might as well have been royalty. Raisa face lit up like the sun as we stepped out of the van with our translator, Lucy and Mayor Andrei. Raisa grabbed me, called me "sister," and began to cry. She wrapped me in a bear hug from which there was no escape. Finally, released, I looked around and as we began walking down the overgrown, gravel road, Raisa transformed into a tour guide.

Raisa and Karen in Samke (Treiger Collection).

"Over here were homes," she explained, "many of them had a shop in them – like the butcher, the baker, or the blacksmith." We ascended a hill, just on the other side of Raisa's home, she pointed to a plot of earth overtaken by more grass and weeds – "this," she said, "is where the synagogue stood."

I nearly cried as I imagined it – instead of weeds and clumps of earth, a beautiful *shul* made of logs where the people gathered daily, on *Shabbes* and holidays. The *shul* was more than just a place for religious gatherings, it served as the meeting place, a place to discuss matters of the day, to gossip, and to share joys and sorrows. We continued up and to the left just a bit.

"Here is the cemetery," Raisa announced.

It looked nothing like a cemetery, it was on overgrown field. As we searched between the weeds and overgrown grass, we saw a few gray, dirty cement stones. These must be the remnants of tombstones, I thought. I wondered how many of my ancestors were buried here. I wish I had said the *Kaddish*, a prayer for the dead, but I didn't think of it.

"Where's the river," I asked Raisa. "My grandmother, her siblings and cousins swam there in the summers."

"The stream is dried up – you can see the dry riverbed just over there," Raisa said pointing through the thorn bushes. "The water was diverted years ago for a governmental project. No more stream."

Raisa was anxious to welcome us into her ramshackle home, that looked like a many-colored Lego project. She prepared a feast for us – we were the only guests she had in years. How in the world was I going to explain to Raisa, the lone-resident of Samke, the birthplace of my grandmother, that Esther and I can't eat the feast she so lovingly prepared – fried pork and eggs, bread with pig schmaltz (fat), baked goat cheese, goat cottage cheese, boiled potatoes, goat milk, moonshine vodka, from potatoes and well water. She had probably spent hours on these dishes.

"Lucy," I said, "please explain to Raisa that for religious reasons we can't eat the food she prepared."

"None of it?" she asked worried.

"Nothing that's been cooked in her home," I said. "Pork is forbidden to Jews and the other things she cooked in her non-kosher kitchen we cannot partake."

We sat in her cramped indoor/outdoor deck with the pork and eggs before us, Esther and I sipped the fresh goat milk that the goats, Masha and Dasha, had lovingly provided. I was brave enough to try the cottage cheese made from Masha's goat milk. When it came to the homemade moonshine potato vodka, Esther and I both tried it – 50 Proof. One small sip was all I could drink. I poured the rest into my water glass so it would look like I drank it all. But, by the time the meal was over, Raisa and Mayor Andrei had both downed four shots and were singing old Russian songs. When Mayor Andrei asked for a second helping, Raisa didn't seem upset that Esther and I weren't eating the food.

Conflicting emotions settled in my heart as I sat at Raisa's table and turned down the feast she prepared. It was difficult to confront the fact that pork was the main offering left in the *shtetl* of Samke. There are no traces of the vibrant Jewish life, culture, and food that had once coursed through this village. Pork would never have been allowed in Samke. On the other hand, I so didn't want to hurt Raisa, who lovingly prepared this feast and wanted to be a hospitable and welcoming hostess. Nonetheless, my Jewish tradition and values are so much a part of me, of who I am, that I turned down this lonely woman's pork offering.

As I made this decision, I felt the "Who Am I" question arising sharply. To keep Kosher is, to me, a bedrock part of living a vibrant Jewish life. Not accepting Raisa's pork meal helped me understand why I continue to keep Kosher. Being careful of what I ingest allows me to walk through the world with more mindfulness. I'm proud of the Jewish legacy and traditions that were transported to Seattle from this forsaken place.

As we completed our visit and prepared to say goodbye, I marveled at this hearty seventy-three years old woman who is a relic of the harsh, but good life that my family must have had here. I thanked her for her hospitality and for telling us what she knew of Samke's history. As we drove back down the sole long, overgrown road, I was filled with gratitude for my great-grandmother.

"Thank God Chaya Tsivia insisted on leaving this place," I sighed and glanced sideways at Esther in the back seat of the car. Neither of us would be alive without this fateful decision.

The Seattle Home

The Steinberg's 1920s Seattle kitchen was probably nothing like their kitchen in Samke, but it was the place where Chaya Tsivia produced the same delicacies. "I was only five when my grandmother died," my father said. "I don't remember her much, but I have a very strong memory of walking into her house on 28th and Washington on Friday afternoon and the whole house smelling like challah baking. It was heavenly and made my mouth water... She was a wonderful cook. Everything was made from scratch. The bread smell was always there. She made such wonderful things such as *-pcha* [Jellied Calf's feet] – you never see that anymore."[535]

Unlike Samke, the stove was not the only source of heat for the Seattle home. The Steinberg home had a big oil burning furnace in the basement and floor registers that brought the heat up into the house. Shim has a strong memory of his *Zeidy*, Chayim Leib, having terrible migraines. He would, “take a raw potato and make very thin slices almost like great chefs would do... My grandfather would sit over one of [heat] registers, right near the grand staircase. It was very warm, and he would slice this potato very thinly and stick the slices on his forehead. After a while he was so feverish it seems, the potato dried out and would fall off. Then he would slice more and put more on his head. He told Dr. Garhart, ‘the only thing that helps me are the potatoes on my head.’ Dr. Garhart said, ‘Mr. Steinberg, by all means, if they help you, slice the potato.’ He had no idea how to deal with the incapacity and weakness of old age. He was an active guy.”[536]

Shim’s family moved into the home for a few years after Chayim Leib died in 1940. Our visit to the home under renovation in 2018 brought long-stored memories into the open. The owner was beside himself with delight to meet someone who had been in the house in the 1930s and 40s.

“The fireplace in the living room was spectacular,” Shim told me as we stood together in the cold empty space in 2018. There were “dark wood pillars on each side with carvings of Indian heads, not Native Americans, but from India,” Shim explained.

Shim (Mark) Elyn and Karen Treiger outside Steinberg home, 2018 (Treiger Collection).

“The place to burn was surrounded by beautiful tiles and just in front of the fireplace was a brass box, with etchings of boys and girls. It weighed a ton. I don’t ever remember a fire burning, except in the dining room. I actually lived here with my family for a few years in the early 1940’s. I shared one of the upstairs rooms with my brother Irv.”[537]

In Shim’s memory, the front door loomed large. The original door remains; it’s thick and made of

Shim and Karen standing outside Steinberg home (Treiger Collection).

dark wood. Shim described his childhood memories of the sound made by the thick, solid oak door as it closed. "It went 'thunk,'" he said, "it never stuck and was impervious to weather. The lock was a long thing – push down with a thumb and open it or from the outside with a key."[538]

When they were kids, the Steinberg cousins spent hours playing in the "attic" – the third floor – built as servant quarters. The Steinbergs had no servants, just lots of grandchildren who loved to romp in these rooms. Shim and I walked up the narrow stairwell and he showed me how the shoes used to be lined up "like soldiers." Up in the "attic" there are a number of rooms, with low slanted ceilings and one window facing east. I smiled as I imagined the grandchildren playing here, wrestling, giggling.

Shim also smiled as he stood in this construction site remembering his grandmother, his *Bubbe.* Chaya Tsivia was the Matriarch with a capital M and had what seemed to him to be boundless energy.

"My *Bubbe* was a character," he explained.

"She never learned enough English to make a phone call. She would call the operator and say 'I vant Prospect 6175.' That was Rose...

One operator said to her, 'Mrs. Steinberg why don't you dial the numbers yourself?'

'I can't see' she said. She just didn't want to bother dialing."[539]

Shim, a retired opera singer and voice teacher described himself as having "one of those oral photographic minds." He recited other phone numbers his *Bubbe* would ask the operator to dial:

"Adele's number was Prospect 3293 and Ettie's was Prospect 0541. I also remember the Bubbe's phone number," Shim said, "East 4741."[540]

Shim also recited the address of Samke in Russian in the singsong voice his mother used to use when she would nostalgically recite it:

"*Minsk Gebernia Barisava Uyez Mitchtechke Chalponitz Colonia Shamki*," he sang, explaining that "*Mitchetchke* means Town."[541]

Steinberg & Sons

Chayim Leib learned enough English to knock on doors and ask for junk to peddle. Sometimes his peddling led to funny stories.

"He junked with a man named Gardinsky," Shim said. "They had made an arrangement with a woman to pick up an old stove. They were both little Jewish men and they carried this heavy stove out the door and dropped it and they lost control and it tumbled down the stairs and cracked the sidewalk. They didn't know what to do, so they just left it there and got on their buggy and drove off. As they were leaving, the woman screamed at them – 'what is your name?'

Gardinksy said: 'Gamliel ben Pedohtzer.'

She screamed, "where do you live?"

He screamed back, "some place on Madison."[542]

Shim chuckled when he told me this story because neither of these men lived on Madison and Gamliel Ben Pedohtzer is the Prince of the ancient Tribe of Menashe, mentioned in the Hebrew Bible's Book of *Bamidbar* (Numbers).[543]

United States citizenship was granted to Chayim Leib Steinberg in 1916. I found his naturalization document on Ancestry.com. The rest of the family became citizens on his coattails. Shim was told by his mother Goldie that she remembers the year was 1916 because there was a record-breaking snowstorm in Seattle and Chayim Leib couldn't drive his junk wagon in the snow. So, he studied for the citizenship test.

"He learned the material," Shim said, "but his English was non-existent. If he didn't understand, he would ask his son Ruben what it meant. My mother told me, on the test – they asked how many voters in the state of WA? He was floored – '*tzu mein kup* –how am I supposed to know how many voters?' But they meant electoral voters – so he caught on and answered the question correctly – there were six."[544]

Upon attaining citizenship, he decided to take on an English name. He chose Hiram because Seattle's mayor at the time was Hiram Gill. This choice gives me pause. While it's true that Hiram Gill was elected in 1914 on a platform of reform and law and order by a large majority of Seattle citizens, this was Gill's second time as mayor. In 1910 Gill, was elected Mayor of Seattle on a platform of "open town," meaning allowing free reign to bootleggers, gambling, and prostitution. However, after the reality of these policies hit, the people of Seattle didn't "like the sight of brothels and gaming resorts which arose over night in the 'restricted district' south of Yesler Way. Charges of police graft and corruption became prevalent."[545] These actions and the corruption in the police force led directly to Gill's recall in January of 1911.

In an extraordinary political comeback, three years later the people of Seattle gave Gill another chance. They took him at his word when he emphatically stated that he had changed and was now in favor of "a closed town," and "[a]ll I want is a chance to make good on the mistakes of a former year.'"[546] Ultimately, Chayim Leib grew to dislike the name Hiram. He took to signing his name as H. Steinberg, using just the first initial.

Chayim Leib noticed that other immigrants moved on from peddling by buying a small store. Following this example, Chayim Leib opened his first store on the corner of 6th and Jackson in 1916. With $600 in capital, Chayim Leib and his two sons, Sam and Reuben, and his son-in-law Mitchell Ketzlach, stocked the store with men's furnishings, primarily surplus army goods and work clothes.[547] While Sam helped in the business from the beginning, Rueben joined after spending a few years in school. He began his American education at the Pacific School. At fifteen years

Chayim Leib and Mitchell Ketzlach at Steinberg store on 6th & Jackson (UW Libraries, Special Collections, Burton Steinberg Photographic Collection, JEW2156).

of age, he was placed in first grade., but he learned English quickly and moved up through the grades.

"Reuben didn't graduate high school," his son Sheldon Steinberg said, "but he could add up figures in a long column in his head. No adding machine."[548]

Ettie married Mitchell Ketzlach in 1918, so the 1920 Census shows them as a married couple, living right next door to the rest of the family. The University of Washington Jewish archives has a stunning photo of Mitchel and Chayim Leib standing in this first, tiny store. This photo (see above) speaks volumes about the early years of Steinberg's retail stores. Chayim Leib, stands under five feet tall with his beard and his long coat amidst a sea of merchandise – pants, suspenders, belts, and so much more – in this small, crowded space. I love this photo because it provides a glimpse of those early years when Chayim Leib started out, selling one piece of merchandise at a time.

As is evidenced by the hand-written leather-bound logbook I found in the University of Washington Jewish archives, most of the people Chayim Leib purchased from and sold to in Seattle were Jews. The people he hired were Orthodox Jews, many of them relatives, like his son-in-law Mitchel.

The next store the Steinbergs opened was in Port Angeles, Washington. Port Angeles was a small port city, in the shadow of the Olympic Peninsula. In the 1920s its primary industries were timber and paper/pulp mills. The Steinberg store sold men's clothing and shoes. They opened this store in Port Angeles because it was the only place they could find a good location for a retail store that they could afford. They worked long hours with the store being open from 7 am to 9 pm.

"It was actually a big tavern with a pool hall," Uncle Sam said, "but at that time it was Prohibition. This fellow wouldn't allow us even to take out the pool table and the fixtures because he said pretty soon Prohibition would be over and we'll open the saloon again. We used the tavern furniture for fixtures."[549]

Sam and his new wife, Dora, moved to Port Angeles to run the store, living there for six years. At first, they stayed in a hotel for one dollar a day. Reuben, who wasn't married yet, came to help set the store up. He didn't want to spend a dollar a day for a hotel room, so he slept on the pool table.[550] Their father Chayim Leib stayed in Seattle and ran the Store on 6th and Jackson.[551] After graduating from high school, my grandmother Rose lived in Port Angeles and help with the store.

Port Angeles had a tiny Jewish community, and they created a club and gathered together on Saturday nights and Sundays to play cards. For the High Holidays, they rented a hall for three dollars and had services together. Sam helped lead the services.[552]

Retail was a very hard business for an observant Jew. The store had to be closed on Saturday. This sometimes made for awkward encounters.

"You know," Sam said, "nothing to do all day Saturday. I used to walk on the street and people would say – 'oh it's a good thing I saw you. I need this and that.' I had to hide myself. Finally, my wife said, best for us is wholesale business. Then we'll move back, and Saturday won't be in the way."[553]

In 1923, they opened a wholesale business selling men's furnishings. Sam and Reuben traveled all over Washington, Oregon, Montana, Nevada, and Alaska selling men's furnishings to mostly small retail stores. After Sam and Reuben retired, the wholesale business was run by Sheldon

Steinberg, Rueben's son, who joined the firm in the 1940s after completing a degree in marketing from the University of Washington. The wholesale business was liquidated in 1985 when Sheldon, Irene, and their daughter Shana moved to Israel.[554]

Though they sold the Port Angeles retail store in 1930, they opened a number of other retail stores. The usual scenario was that when one of their wholesale customers went out of business and owed Steinberg & Sons money, the Steinbergs bought the store at a bargain price.[555] They ended up with retail stores in Kent, Grand Coulee, Aberdeen, Anacortes, Fairbanks, Butte, and Ketchikan. The stores kept their original names and local identities but now had the increased buying power of a multiple-store group.[556]

Steve Steinberg, Sheldon's son, joined the firm in the mid-1970s and ran the retail division in the 1980s and 1990s. The closing of the wholesale company, Steinberg Brothers, helped fund the growth of the retail stores. By the early 1990s the retail company, Tri-North Department Stores, grew to more than $40 million in annual revenue, with large-branded apparel and show stores (15-20,000 square feet, called HUB Clothing) in small towns in six western states. As Wal-Mart entered these markets in the 1990s, the profitability of the company declined. Ultimately, the retail operation was bought by Stage Stores of Texas in 1998. Stage bought all the retail stores except the largest one, in Ketchikan, Alaska, which Steve continued to operate for a few more years, before shutting it down.[557]

Steinberg Brothers had their first corporate offices in the Terminal Sales Building, located at 1932 1st Avenue, which today has Landmark status. Later, the company purchased a building in Pioneer Square, which became known as the Steinberg building and moved their operations. The Steinberg building was sold and they bought a large warehouse in Georgetown – 5000 1st Avenue (1st and S. Hudson). That 50,000 square foot building is still owned by the Steinberg family, as is the Fox Plumbing building in South Park.[558]

Making A Life In Seattle

The rhythm of life in the Steinberg home followed the music of the Jewish calendar. The weekly *Shabbes*, the holidays in the fall with *Rosh Hashanah* and *Yom Kippur*, which were followed by the festive holiday of *Sukkos*. The Steinbergs built a small *Sukkah* in the yard of their home on 28th & Washington. It was built very close to the kitchen and as Shim described: "You could pass the food from the kitchen window into the *Sukkah*."[559]

The Synagogue was central to their lives. It was the place they gathered on *Shabbes* and holidays. Their social lives revolved around the people who were part of this Ashkenazik Orthodox Jewish community. By the time Chayim Leib settled in Seattle in 1910, *Chevra Bikur Cholim* had been incorporated for nineteen years and had been gathering in their own building (13th and Washington) for twelve years. The whole Steinberg family watched as the synagogue built a magnificent new structure on 17th and Yesler. The architect of the building was one of the foremost theater designers, Bernard Marcus Priteca.[560]

This is the synagogue that my father, Irwin Treiger, grew up in and took me and my brothers to until the mid-1970s when the synagogue moved to its current location in the Seward Park neighborhood. The building was sold to the city of Seattle and currently serves the community as the Langston Hughes Performing Arts Institute.

The Synagogue was especially busy for the spring holidays of *Purim* and *Pesach* (Passover). In the Steinberg home, Pesach was a huge deal.

"Bubbe did *Pesach* cooking in the basement," Shim said. "Big cask of wine. She had a big wash tub. She filled it with hot water and koshered all the silverware. She took rocks from the garden – boulders – big ones. She put them in the wood stove – got them red hot – took them with tongs and one rock at a time, dropped them in the water. It would sizzle – then she would dip the silverware in the water – *three times*. She could go out from the basement door to the back yard directly and that is where the *kashering* tub was."[561]

This statement was made in a joint interview with my father and cousins, Sheldon Steinberg (Reuben's son) and Shim Elyn (Goldie's son).

As Shim was telling this story and he got to the part about dipping the silverware in the water – all three of them said in unison – "three times." This was something that all the grandchildren must have been present for and the memory of it stuck like glue.

The summer brought the festival of *Shavuos* and vacations. Most summers, Shim recalled, his family and Ettie's family (the Ketzlach family) and Chayim Leib and Chaya Tsivia rented "shacks" at Alki beach in West Seattle. They would move into the "shacks" and stay for the whole summer. These vacation homes were right across from the sound – along the main Alki strip.

"It was great fun," Shim said.

"There was a great swimming pool/rec center where there were four pools of water – warm, kiddie pool, average temperature, and freezing cold sound water. We would spend all day there. My father and Uncle Mitchell [Ketzlach] would walk on Saturday afternoon into town and time the walk so that they would reach their stores at sunset – so they could open the store for a few hours on Saturday night. Mitchell's store was 23rd and Jackson, my father's store was in Columbia City. Both stores sold clothing, boots, and small items."[562]

Chayim Leib and Chaya Tsivia periodically went on vacation to Soap Lake in Eastern Washington. The waters of the lake were thought to have healing powers.

"The *Bubbe*," Shim told me, "would swim all across Soap Lake. She was a terrific swimmer."[563]

Chaya Tsivia did a lot of walking – she didn't know how to drive. Her granddaughter Reva (Ketzlach) Twersky recalls that she would "visit her ten grandchildren once or twice a day. She had boundless energy ... [and] was fast in everything she did. She joined every charitable Jewish Women's organization and attended all the meetings. She was always early – didn't want to miss anything."[564]

"*Bubbe* used to walk ... to the Steinberg store on 6th and Jackson," Shim recalled. "She would bring soup to the men working there. There were two *goyim* [non-Jews] who sat on a bench outside the store. She brought soup and gave them some. One of them said: 'For $100 you can't get such soup.' The other said: 'For $100 President Wilson will come and serve the soup to you!'"[565]

As Shim shared memories of his grandmother, Chaya Tsivia, his voice was full of pride and admiration. He described his *Bubbe* as someone who never turned away a guest, whether an out-of-town visitor or a niece or nephew who needed a place to live. A nephew, Jack Steinberg lived in their home for years after his parents died.

As I hear these descriptions – high energy, love of family, involvement in the Synagogue and Jewish community, swimming, welcoming guests – I'm floored. This could be written about me. I'm aware that my energy level is high, and I get things done quickly – sometimes too quickly. I hate being late, my home too flows with the rhythm of the Jewish calendar, I am deeply involved in my synagogue and organizations throughout Seattle's Jewish community, I can't say no to a guest, and I love to swim. I wonder how is it that I am so alike the woman for whom I am named? I feel a deep kinship as I learn more about her life.

Chayim Leib died in 1940 at the age of seventy-five. The cause of death was unclear, but in those days, "seventy-five was old," Shim said. Shim's family – his mother Goldie, father Itzche, brother Irv, and sister Merke moved into the house to live with Chaya Tsivia. Sadly, in 1941 Chaya Tsivia was hit by a produce truck, just outside her home on 28th and Washington.

"She was buying stuff from the back of the truck," Shim said, "and she was back there where the tailgate comes down and [the driver] didn't see her and he backed up and knocked her down. Didn't run her over, but she fell – didn't break anything, but painful. It's stuff like that starts a downward spin. She never really recovered. She was confined to a wheelchair and she used to sit in her bedroom and read *Tzena Urena* and *Techina*... She died in 1944."[566]

Chaya Tsivia was seventy-five years old when she died – poetically, the same age as her husband Chayim Leib when he died a few years earlier. My grandmother Rose was her youngest child, and according to my dad, Rose adored her mother. I imagine that Chaya Tsivia's death in 1944 was devastating.

My grandmother, Rose (Steinberg) Treiger was a slender woman who was as short as her mother. She had a head of black hair that never went gray. She was a brilliant, energetic woman with a smile that welcomed all into her world. She was seven when she arrived in Seattle, so, unlike her siblings, she spoke unaccented English.

She went to elementary school at Washington Grade School and then attended Franklin High School, graduating as valedictorian. I imagine that she would have loved to go to college, but the family needed her to help in the business. She did what she was told and worked in the Port Angeles store.

Rose Steinberg (Treiger Collection).

Rose got involved in the community early on. [567] By her early 20s, she had already become the "secretary" of the Talmud Torah, the afternoon school where the Orthodox children would go to learn Hebrew and Jewish studies. Rose also taught "beginners classes" to the 160 students who attended in the mid-1920s. On June 3, 1924, the Jewish Transcript reported that the Seattle Talmud Torah, "was divided into six academic classes and one music class conducted by Professor Friedland. The academic classes were led by the following young men and women: Rose Steinberg, Sadie Steinberg, Louis Fine, Harold Lawson, David Laurie and Joe Cohen. Mr. H. Chiaken acted as assistant principal to Rabbi Winograd. The curriculum included courses in Jewish history, Religion and prayers, reading and writing Hebrew and Hebrew and American National Songs."[568]

Rose didn't teach Hebrew because as a girl she was not taught to read or write Hebrew. She taught herself at the age of sixty. I remember it well; she wanted to keep up with her grandchildren. We reviewed the Hebrew alphabet together.

Rose met Sam Treiger in 1927 and they were married one year later in the backyard of the Steinberg home. They made their home in Seattle's Orthodox Jewish neighborhood and centered their lives on Uncle Ray and my father Irwin, their business and the Jewish community.[569]

Rose Steinberg at her wedding in 1928 (Treiger Collection).

Rose Steinberg and Sam Treiger at their wedding, 1928 (Treiger Collection).

The other children of Chaya Tsivia and Chayim Leib Steinberg married and settled in Seattle's Orthodox neighborhood. Ettie, the eldest, married Mitchel Ketzlach, and together they had three children, Norman, Reva, and Evie. During my childhood, Rose and Ettie were very close and lived down the hall from each other in their small apartments on Malden Avenue East. On Friday nights, when we had dinner at my grandmother's apartment, my brothers and I would go over to say hello to Ettie. Ettie died at the age of eighty-eight on September 19, 1980.[570]

The second child, Sam, who we called Uncle Sam, married Dora, who died in 1968 on a visit to Israel.[571] She was buried in the Jerusalem cemetery, *Har Hamenuchot*. Uncle Sam later married his first cousin Riva (Lawson) Brodkin, who had been living in Montreal. They lived many years together in Seattle and I knew them both well. Sam, who had no children, died on March 13, 1982[572] and was buried in Jerusalem next to his first wife Dora.

I was studying at Hebrew University in Jerusalem during my junior year of college then, and I had the honor of meeting Uncle Sam's body and being present at his burial. I was the only person there who knew him. Tears fell from my eyes as Sam's body was lowered into his grave. Though he had no children to say *Kaddish* (prayer for the dead),[573] my cousin, Sheldon Steinberg said *Kaddish* every day for eleven months and again on his *Yartzheit*, the anniversary of his death.[574]

Ettie (Steinberg) Ketzlach and Rose (Steinberg) Treiger (Treiger Collection).

Reuben married Adele Taubin and they had two children, Sheldon and Rosyln. Reuben died in July of 1973.[575] Goldie married Isidore (Itze) Elyn and raised three children, Irving, Merke, and Shim. Shim's English name at birth was Alvin. He changed it as an adult to Mark, as he was told that Alvin was not a good first name for an opera singer. Goldie died at the age of sixty-one on June 2, 1962.[576]

The youngest of the Steinberg children, my grandmother Rose, who we called Bobby, died on December 11, 1989.[577] The day Bobby died is as clear a memory as any that I have. I was pregnant with my second child and hormones made me especially emotional. When I heard she had died, I couldn't control my tears. I sat at home and cried until the tears dried up. I spoke at her funeral at the old Jewish Chapel on 12th. I slowed my breathing and directed my words directly to her. I thanked her for all the things she taught me – from baking and cooking to gin rummy, to business savvy, to public speaking, to the importance of Jewish traditions and family, to being an active volunteer in the Jewish community. I told her she will always be with me and my love for her will never cease. Then I sat down and again burst into tears.

Grandparents and grandchildren have unique relationships. From Bobby I received messages of unconditional love, of what is important in the world, of the joy of reading, of just having fun and laughing. Bobby was a bridge between Samke and the new world of the United States. She showed me how to navigate the passage and to be a smart, confident, traditional woman. When I came home from college for a visit, one of the first things I would do was visit Bobby. We sat in her living room discussing school, politics, family, Hadassah, and indeed anything. Iconic photos of her sons, Ray and Irwin (my uncle and my father) in their caps and gowns stared down at us from the wall. Bobby was a great listener and advisor.

When I think of Bobby, my heart fills up with warm feelings. I miss her and wish that my children could have known her because they would have felt the waves of love from her. I bask in her warmth – each time I think of her. She came from Samke at the age of seven and became a child of Seattle, raising her own family and helping to create a vibrant Jewish life, and running Thrifty's with her husband, Sam.

I have such joy in my heart when I think that in 1992, Shlomo and I named our third child after Bobby. We named our daughter Shoshana, which is Hebrew for Rose. Shoshana shares so many character traits with Bobby, to name a few: intuitive understanding, thoughtfulness, intelligence, empathy, and kindness. My father was the only one that called her Rose – usually Rosie – but it felt right that he called her that name. He too felt the continuity as his mother's name and memory are carried forward in the next generation.

Looking back at her impact on my life, I stand in trepidation and excitement in my role as grandmother. Now I am that connector, the one that loves unconditionally, the one that makes great food, the one whose home smells like challah on Friday afternoon. I'm now the one who has the obligation and the privilege to teach by word, but even more by deed how to live as a proud, observant Jew, how to be a good, kind person, and how to be a leader in our community. I want my grandchildren to fall in love with life, because we each have to fall in love with life on our own. We have to find our own path and then shout it out to the world – or at least to our grandchildren.

Rose (Steinberg) Treiger, Karen Treiger, Sam Treiger, Louis Treiger at Karen's family home on Mercer Island, approx. 1965 (Treiger Collection).

From Left to Right: Karen Treiger, holding Eden Isseroff, Evelyn (Evie) Isseroff, Theodore (Teddy) Irwin Goldberg, Samuel (Sammy) Isseroff, Shlomo Goldberg. Sitting in front row - Caroline (Coco) Goldberg.

CHAPTER 7

BETTY LOU AND IRWIN

An Introduction

Irwin Louis Treiger and Betty Lou Friedlander were an unlikely pair. Not exactly a West Side Story mismatch, but not what their parents were hoping for. Betty Lou, a fourth-generation rich girl from a Reform Jewish family, was not supposed to marry a poor boy from an immigrant Orthodox Jewish family. Meanwhile, Irwin's family dreamed of a *shidduch* (match) with a nice Orthodox girl from down the block.

"It's a long story," my grandfather Jack Friedlander, who we called Papa Jack, said in a 1975 interview.

"Betty Lou and Irwin found each other at the University of Washington, and Irwin was in Law School. He came from a very, very, very Orthodox family (the Steinberg family) and we were very, very Reformed. We were as far apart as the North and South Poles. When they elected to get engaged, everybody in the family was opposed to it."[578]

Parents are well known to be unhappy with their children's choice of life partner, often making their opinions crystal clear. But there's a twist to this Jewish love story.

"It was very peculiar," Papa Jack continued, "because nobody knew that Mrs. Staadecker wasn't Jewish, Betty Lou's grandmother. One night Ben Bridge says, 'Isn't it wonderful,' to the rabbi ... that Betty Lou is going to marry Irwin, and her grandmother isn't even Jewish.' With this I get a phone call from Irwin's folks I think, or it could have been the rabbi, I don't remember. They would like to see the papers where Mrs. Staadecker converted to

Betty Lou And Irwin Family Tree

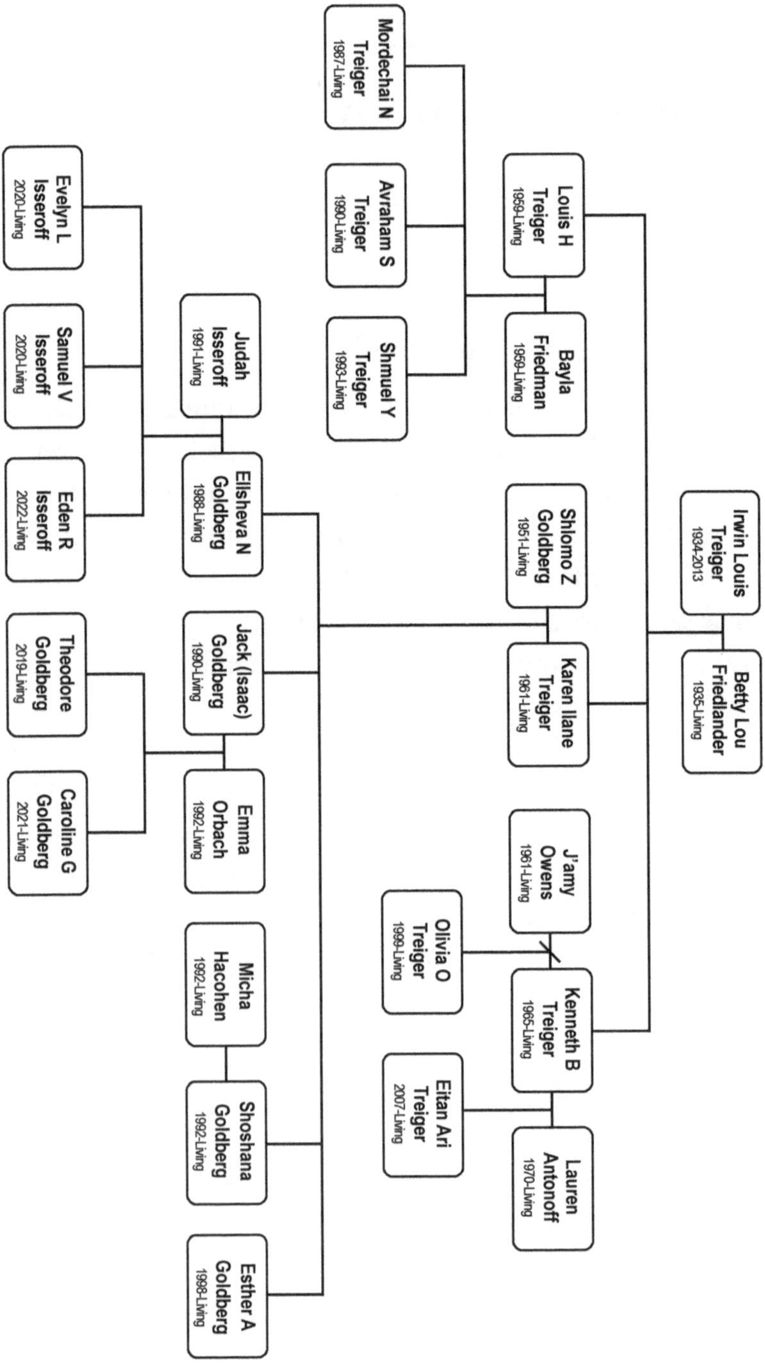

Judaism. Well, there were no papers... So, they came to me, and the rabbi says Betty Lou has to be converted to Judaism. This got my mother [Belle (Singerman) Friedlander] furious and everybody else in the family furious. They didn't want her to be converted to Judaism because she'd already been through Sunday School and confirmed and taught at the Sunday school and everything else. Well, to make a long story short we finally, with meetings and everything else, and her studying, they were ready to convert her."[579]

In my grandfather's retelling, he's the hero of the story. My grandmother, Elizabeth, who we called Nanny, and everyone else on my mom's side of the family, were screaming mad and didn't want my mom to convert and didn't want her to marry Irwin.

"I," Papa Jack said, "was the only one supporting Betty Lou. She desperately wanted to marry Irwin and was willing to convert, so I supported her... The only one [in the family] who stuck by me was my brother, [Paul]. My brother's wife didn't want it, my mother didn't want it. I remember the day of the wedding, my mother [Belle] said to me: 'This is all your fault.'"[580]

Betty Lou Friedlander, Engagement Photo (1957) (Treiger Collection).

Irwin Treiger and Betty Lou Friedlander, Engagement photo (1957) (Treiger Collection).

As I imagine my mother at this moment in 1957, I feel her strength of character. She had to stand up to her family and say – "well, this is what I want and I'm going to do it." Strong-willed is an adjective that fits my mother like a glove.

My mom agreed to "convert" to the religion into which she was born and raised. To convert, she had to go before a *Beit Din* (Jewish Court). There was no *Beit Din* in Seattle in 1957, so my parents flew to Los Angeles.

My mother stood before the tribunal of three bearded rabbis, with her fabulous, just styled hair, sprayed with polyvinylpyrrolidone, creating a tower of hair. She answered all the questions exhibiting her knowledge of Judaism and Jewish traditions, she agreed to keep a Kosher home and send the kids to Jewish day school. She passed.

"All done," she thought.

Well, not yet. She was instructed to go to the *Mikve* (ritual bath), remove all her clothes, shower and wash her hair and then immerse – all the way. My father "neglected" to inform her of this piece of the conversion puzzle.

Now my mom was furious; her hairdo was ruined. She took the plunge, but on top of the deflated, flattened hairdo, my mother felt humiliated.

"Those rabbis watched me go in!" my mom said. "I was naked. I hope they enjoyed themselves!"[581]

According to Papa Jack, my mom went to the home of his friend, Gil Laken, and burst into tears. She cried and cried and then took a warm bath and felt a bit better.[582]

Flying back home, they both hoped that this would be the end of the pre-wedding troubles. But alas, it was not. With the conversion behind them, the families argued over where to hold the wedding ceremony.

"Betty Lou," Papa Jack said, "wouldn't be married at Bikur Cholim and [the Treigers] wouldn't be married at Temple. Finally, my brother came through, it was in summer – 'we'll have a wedding in my yard!' by brother said. We all agreed on that wedding venue. Then it came down to the rabbi – who was going to be the rabbi? We had an argument. Then we finally agreed on both rabbis, Rabbi Levine and Rabbi Appel. We met up in the office before the wedding and laid down the ground rules and they lived up to them ever since. Betty Lou goes to Temple, he can go to Bikur

Cholim. The house is strictly Kosher, when Betty Lou goes out, she can eat anything she wants."[583]

My grandfather, who treated his son-in-law, Irwin, like a son, concluded this story with telling the interviewer: "Irwin is one of the greatest men in Seattle."[584]

The wedding, set on the sprawling lawn of the waterfront home of Uncle Paul and Aunt Marjorie Friedlander, just south of Interstate-90, was straight out of a fairy tale. Looking at the photos and the home movie, one would never know there was strife. Bride and groom smiling, dancing, feeding each other cake, cigarettes in hand. Bridesmaids with gorgeous dresses and huge hats. The fathers of the bride and the groom share a drink. No clue of the trials and tribulations that came before the event. The photos don't even hint at the stress at the beginning of the wedding.

"The rabbi was late," my dad explained to my nephew Avraham Treiger. "He had a funeral; that is why he was late."

"I was going to kill him," my mom said. "We had to ask Shim to sing."

"I got my cousin Shim Elyn to sing," my dad explained. "Mr. Goldfarb[585] accompanied him on the piano."

"Once the rabbi showed up and the wedding began," my mom said, "boats on Lake Washington watched the wedding."

"Yes," my dad chuckled, "a lot of uninvited spectators watched the wedding."

"After all the guests were assembled," my dad added, "my father-in-law shared his little secret about his eldest daughter: 'I have to tell you something – Betty Lou likes to spend money.'"[586]

The Society Page of the Seattle Times covered the wedding. "The gardens of Mr. and Mrs. Paul Friedlander were the setting for the wedding and reception yesterday afternoon of his niece, Miss Betty Lou Friedlander and Mr. Irwin Louis Treiger," wrote the Seattle Times.

"The bride wore a gown of white chiffon and a draped neckline. A floating panel extended down the back from the shoulders and over the bouffant skirt, which extended into a court train. Her should-length veil was caught to a cloche of satin and tulle trimmed in pearlized orange blossoms." The bridesmaids' wore, "ballerina gowns of silk organza

Betty Lou Friedlander, August 18, 1957 (Treiger Collection)

Betty Lou (Friedlander) Treiger and Irwin Treiger at wedding reception, August 18, 1957 (Treiger Collection).

Ray & Nancy Treiger, Irwin & Betty Lou (Friedlander) Treiger at wedding reception, August 18, 1957 (Treiger Collection).

over yellow taffeta and matching picture hats. Their flowers were yellow daisies."[587]

Thus began a love story and life partnership of two dynamic, charismatic, hard-working people. They supported each other in all aspects of life – career, volunteerism, family, and fun.

As I contemplate the role of my parents in my life, I emerge with a deep sense of self. My place in time takes on a new flavor. I carry with me, in my soul, in my cells, the journey from the old country; the long boat trip; the cross-continent wagon or train ride; the long days; the sleepless nights; the elementary, high school, and university educations; the joys; the sorrows; the ups and down that forged the path for me to be born on January 10, 1961, in Seattle, Washington to Betty Lou and Irwin Treiger. This was a golden ticket – we don't get to choose our parents, so I will attribute my good luck to cosmic forces beyond my control.

As this story gets closer to my lived experience, it becomes increasingly hard to zoom out and paint a picture. How do I share something about my parents that captures their essence? I feel very vulnerable to share stories about their lives and my life growing up in their home. Though my dad died in 2013, my mom is alive and well at the age of eighty-nine. This section about Betty Lou and Irwin isn't intended as a complete biography, but rather to provide snapshots of their lives. As I recall these stories, I see myself emerge from childhood to adulthood under their tutelage. I wonder what to say, how to honor them and be honest at the same time. As you read these short pieces, I invite you to think about your own parents, if you knew them, and how they impacted your life.

New York Kickstart

Betty Lou and Irwin were twenty-two when they got married; barely old enough to drink. My mom finished three years at the University of Washington, leaving with her Mrs. Degree,[588] but no university degree. After graduating from the University of Washington Law School, where he served as the Editor-in-Chief of the Law Review, my dad's future as a tax lawyer was not yet written.

"A brilliant student who graduated first in his class at the University of Washington's law school in 1957," writes Max Kvidera in a 2007 article titled, *The Tax Man Cometh.*

"Treiger would not have become a tax attorney at all, except for a twist of fate and Uncle Sam.

After graduation, Treiger's deferment from military service was ending and the draft board told him to get packed. At the same time, then-U.S. Supreme Court Justice and Washington native William O. Douglas wanted Treiger to clerk for him. The UW law school brass pleaded with the draft board to give Treiger a one-year deferment so he could pursue the opportunity, but the board wouldn't budge.

'I thought to myself, I'll show you,' Treiger remembers. 'I knew there was a nice federal tax program at New York University, so I signed up for that and my deferral continued. I wasn't drafted, but I didn't get to clerk [for Justice Douglas] either.'"[589]

Off went Irwin and Betty Lou to New York City on their first adventure. Neither had lived anywhere but their parent's home. Now, they found themselves flying 3,000 miles across the country.

"It took thirteen hours," my mom explained. "Irwin got us the cheapest ticket in the world."

"We stopped several places," my dad explained, "Detroit, Pittsburg, I don't know. Betty Lou came back for Jackie's wedding. I didn't come back. I didn't have any money. Her parents flew her in, but not me."[590]

Their new life in New York sounds so romantic. Living in Greenwich Village – New York City – the Big Apple. New York University School of Law provided the young couple a one-bedroom apartment at 33 Washington Square West, across the street from Washington Square Park.

Then, reality set in.

"The apartment was filthy," my mom said. "I didn't know what to do. I called my mother and cried on the phone. Mother told me, 'Betty Lou, roll up your sleeves, get a rag, and start cleaning.' So, I did."[591]

Nanny gets huge points for this advice. Nanny grew up in the Staadecker home with maids, cooks, and gardeners, and had a maid and a cook in her home in Magnolia. She never "rolled up her sleeves" in her life. She had a bell that she rang for the maid as she sat at the dining room table. She assessed my mom's situation some 3,000 miles away from home. She married a "poor boy" and Nanny knew they couldn't afford a maid. "This is your situation," she was telling her eldest daughter, "now do what you need to do."

The New York kitchen was big enough for the two of them to stand in, but that was about it. After growing up with a cook, my mom "didn't know how to boil water." As she learned to cook, she learned "Kosher."

"It wasn't hard to keep a Kosher kitchen," my mom said, "because I had never kept any kitchen before. I just learned this way."[592]

The freezer was tiny, not big enough to hold much. They found a Kosher butcher shop on the Lower East Side that delivered and with two sets of dishes – one for milk and one for meat – they figured it out.

My mom's first paying job was with the Institute of Math Science, now called the Courant Institute, at New York University. This Institute had the second computer ever built. It was called UNIVAC and it took up a whole room.

"I found the job," my mom said, "by going to the NYU hiring office and telling them, 'I would like a job.' I just had to walk across the park. I sat at a desk and my main job was to only let people with proper ID into the room that housed the computer. They paid me to sit there. It was boring, but I got to read a lot of books. The library was across the street."[593]

Betty Lou (Friedlander) Treiger, Courant Institute, NY, 1957/58 (Treiger Collection).

It was, in fact, a magical newlywed year in New York. They made close friends – other couples in the NYU LLM program, played tourist in New York City, went to Broadway shows, traveled to Washington, D.C. where my father's brother Ray and his wife Nancy lived, had a snowball fight in Washington Square Park, had their first Passover Seder away from their parents, and laid a solid foundation for their lives together.

Irwin Treiger and Betty Lou (Friedlander) Treiger, NY 1957/58 (Treiger Collection).

Some thirty years later, I, together with my new partner in life Shlomo Goldberg, walked the same streets of Greenwich Village. I studied at the same law school as my dad, explored the nooks and crannies of New York City, and lived in a tiny apartment off Washington Square Park – even smaller than my parent's. It was so small that we pulled out a sleeper sofa each night and folded it back up in the morning to have room to walk around.

During my foray in Greenwich Village, I thought of my parents living there in 1957 and '58. It's hard to imagine one's parents as young, but I felt their young spirit hovering about me and on the streets and through the craggy alleys of the Village. I often felt strangely close to

Betty Lou (Friedlander) Treiger and Irwin Treiger, Passover Seder, NY, 1958 (Treiger Collection).

that young couple that left Seattle, leaving behind their families to build a life together.

And build they did. Since the graduate program was only one year, the threat of the draft loomed over my father's head. There was only one other way to avoid the draft – have a baby. My mom became pregnant and they moved back to Seattle.

"Why didn't you stay and live in New York?" my nephew Avraham Treiger asked.

"We loved New York," my father said, "but it's not a great place to live, particularly for a struggling starting lawyer. Summer was really hot. We didn't have air conditioning."[594]

They found a small apartment near what is now University Village. They moved there because my mom's sister, Jackie, and her husband, Alvin Goldfarb, lived there.

"University Village wasn't there in those days," my mom said. "It was a garbage dump."

Well, the draft dodging baby enabler was born on January 3, 1959. His name: Louis Harold Treiger. His Hebrew name is Elazer Chayim after Chayim Leib Steinberg, my father's maternal grandfather. The name Louis is after Louis

Friedlander, my mother's paternal grandfather, who died on January 3, 1955, four years to the date before my brother's birth. His middle name, Harold, was for Claire (Treiger) Kaufman's son, known as Sonny. Claire was Sam Treiger (Papa Sam)'s sister, who moved to Philadelphia in the late 1920s. Sonny, a pilot in the US Air Force during WWII, was killed in a tragic accident, when his plane crashed into a mountain during a training exercise.

Even though my dad only met Sonny (Harold) one time, he was impacted by his cousin. Sonny was handsome and looked regal in his military uniform. My dad looked up to him as a hero, fighting for American freedom. After Sonny died in 1945, my father wrote a poem about him:

MY COUSIN – H.E. KAUFMAN (1923-1945)
Out of 2,000 he was at the top
Out of 2,000 he was the best
He worked all day and half the night
Never having rest.

His work was over,
He asked for more,
And then he died,
Not going to war.

There he was,
Looking down at ground,
There was a terrible crash,
And later his dead body was found.

But it was the will,
Of the Almighty God,
That's the way it had to be,
And onward his soldiers of victory plod.[595]

Perhaps my Brother Louis's birth, the first grandson on the Friedlander side, redeemed the couple with my mom's family. After his birth, my mom's grandmother, Belle (Singerman) Friedlander, who we called Gigi, paid for a baby nurse, allowing the tired parents to get some sleep during those first exhausting weeks. My mom paid this favor forward, springing for baby nurses for her great grandchildren – to the great appreciation of their parents.

Harold (Sonny) Kaufman (Treiger Collection).

Before Louis was born, while still in New York, my dad set about finding a legal job in Seattle. How do you find a job in Seattle's antisemitic legal community?

"There were only two law firms," my father said, "in all of Seattle that would hire a Jew. I wrote letters to three firms... One firm had no Jews, and I was pretty sure that they wouldn't offer me a job and I was right, they didn't. The other firm, which had a couple of Jews, had the Jewish partner write me back and say they didn't have any openings. But there was this other firm – Bogle, Bogle & Gates and a couple of days after I sent the letter, I got a phone call. 'One of our partners is going to be in Washington DC. Could you go down and meet him?'

Irwin Treiger with baby Louis (Treiger Collection).

Which I did. They paid for my ticket, and I went down to DC. I met Bob Graham for an hour or two. Two days later, I got a call, we want you to come work for us. I had a job when I got back to Seattle."[596]

Thus began a fifty-five year long legal career, with forty-one of those years at Bogle & Gates. There was no doubt that young Irwin was smart and driven, but how was he to build a reputation and a thriving law practice?

"Ambition," my father told a group of Jewish attorneys in 1997 as he accepted an honor from the Jewish Federation's Cardozo Society, "is only one part of the equation. Some hard work and diligence in pursuing one's ambitions help a bit.

I decided at the start of my career as a lawyer that I would devote my first couple of years to learning how to practice law, that is, how to apply the learning which four years of legal schooling had provided; and that I would then seek to reveal myself, to make myself known to the community – the professional community, the business community and, of course the Jewish community. I undertook a program of involvement, a program which I have attempted to continue to this very day.

To make the professional community aware of my existence, I spoke, and I spoke, and I spoke. I delivered papers on tax topics to the local bar, to the State bar, to the Estate Planning Councils of Seattle, Portland, Spokane, Yakima; to the Montana Tax Institute; to the CLU's; to the Trust officers; and on and on. And after I made the mark locally as a speaker on Tax topics, I moved on to the national scene – the ABA tax section, the Practicing law Institute, Ali-Aba, and others.

But I didn't regard this as enough. I began active participation in civic and charitable endeavors, something easy to do then and still easy to do in a community crying for able and interested participants.

Fortunately, both Betty Lou and I enjoy the involvement, enjoy the satisfaction which comes from participation and contribution. And how much more pleasant and rewarding when it carries with it the added dividend of enhancing one's reputation in the community."[597]

By January 10, 1961, when I entered the world, my family had moved to the to the East Side of Lake Washington, to Bellevue's Enatai neighborhood. My mom's sister, Jackie Goldfarb, also moved to Enatai with her family. Why they gave me the English name of "Karen" I don't know. When I asked, they said they liked the name. Had my parents only known that in the 2020s, "Karen" would carry a negative stigma of a pushy, privileged white woman who always gets her way – usually loudly asking for the manager (and sometimes with a gun) – they may have reconsidered their choice. My real legacy namesake is my father's maternal grandmother – Chaya Tsivia Steinberg. This strong, ambitious woman from Samke, Belarus, ensured a smooth transition for her family of seven when they immigrated to the United States in 1911. So, as a strong-willed Karen, I am proud to carry the Hebrew name of Chaya Tsivia.

Homes, Homes, More Homes

We moved from Enatai to the Woodridge neighborhood in Bellevue before I turned four years old. It was in this home where my baby brother, Kenneth Bruce, arrived on August 26, 1965. Ken was named Baruch Tzvi in Hebrew. Baruch after Uncle Bert Treiger and Tzvi after Papa Sam's grandfather, Tzvi Hirsch Treiger. The day that Kenneth was brought home from the hospital, I got the boot. I was whisked away by my grandmother, Rose Treiger. This was unjust – a new live toy had just been delivered and I was exiled, forbidden to play with the new living doll. So unfair. Just because I had chicken pox.

The south end of Mercer Island was our family's next destination. My parents built a new home in the Lakeview Highlands neighborhood at a time when the south end of the island was sleepy. I close my eyes and can see myself sitting on a wooden bench supported by two white brick pillars adorning the entrance to the neighborhood. I sat on that bench many a day waiting for the school bus to pick us to go across the floating bridge to the Seattle Hebrew Academy.

After the last nails were hammered and the brown paint slathered on the wood siding, my mom's station wagon and my dad's yellow Mustang pulled into the covered carport. Just to the right of the front door were wooden stairs heading up to four bedrooms and two bathrooms. I loved my bedroom. The yellow wallpaper with a flower design made for a cheery, yet calm decor. A yellow dresser and desk set fit in perfectly. In my pre-teen years, the white closet doors were the backdrop to a collage of Seventeen magazine photos which declared my love for Bobby Sherman and David Cassidy.

My brothers had rooms next to each other just down the hall, though I can't recall the color schemes. They were closer to the bathroom we shared, but I was right next to our parents, so I felt I got the better deal. The main floor had a huge living room with an adjacent den. To me, the den was the most important room in the house. It had a desk for my dad, where he sat each evening with his Tanqueray on the rocks; a couch where my mother sat with her gin and tonic; and some chairs for the rest of us. Most importantly, there was the record player, with its speakers built into the wall. Listening, I felt that its music arrived from heaven. The Beatles, the Carpenters (OK don't laugh), and Shlomo Carlebach magically entered our home, and I loved it. Hours of my life were spent in that den listening and singing along.

The kitchen had an adjacent eating area with a TV. It was here on Saturday and Sunday mornings, we three kids watched cartoons in our pajamas and were admonished to close all the doors and be quiet to allow our parents to sleep.

The basement was unfinished with gray cement floors. But it was there, atop those cement floors that I learned to play ping-pong. My dad was not athletic, but he was a ping-pong pro. The day I was able to beat him at ping-pong was a day I celebrated. I cherished our time together, bouncing the small white ball back and forth on the smooth green surface. Ping-pong and Rummikub are the only two games I can recall ever playing with my father. He was a busy man.

The backyard was a grassy space enclosed by eight foot tall blackberry bushes. We lost many balls (and one shoe) in that back yard – gobbled up by the thorny brush. The Seattle summer brought sunshine and the sunshine brought blackberries. We spent hours picking the juicy berries, dropping them into the empty coffee tins and dutifully delivering them to our mother in the kitchen. In August, the house was filled with the sweet smell of jelly simmering on the stove and berry crisps baking in the oven.

"Why did we move to Mercer Island?" I asked my mom.

"Well," my mom said, "the country clubs in Seattle wouldn't let in Jews, so we moved to the south end of Mercer Island that had a club that would let us in."[598]

I loved the club – the Mercer Island Country Club (MICC). It wasn't fancy like the Seattle Tennis Club, but it had a large, welcoming swimming pool and lots of tennis courts, locker rooms for changing, and a canteen to buy snacks. In the winter, bubble domes were erected over the pool and the tennis courts, so we enjoyed it all year round. My mom played tennis there with friends and I took swimming and tennis lessons as a young girl. Later, I joined the swim team and the tennis team. My summer days would begin at 8 a.m. with swim team and after drying off and downing a quick snack, I proceeded to tennis team. By the time I was back home, I was exhausted, sweaty, and happy.

We were allowed to walk by ourselves on a dirt path from the Country Club to the small shopping center which had a grocery store, a drug store, and a gas station. There was an occasional candy bar or bubble gum, but mostly I bought Archie comic books. We didn't need money, the owner of the drug store just put it on our "tab," which my parents paid at the end of each month. We just had to sign our names to the receipt. This is where, in my recollection, my younger brother got his nickname – Ken T. He used to buy comics and other things there, like I did. When asked to sign his name, he would sign Ken T. So, we started calling him Ken T., a nickname that has continued to this day.

My aunt's family followed us to Mercer Island, building a house just up the street. The uphill trek took about five minutes, and we were allowed to walk there by ourselves. Having cousins the same ages as us meant we always had someone to play with. We also had other neighbors who made life fun. One of our best buddies was a kid named Phillip Bacon – a great name for a friend of kids who keep Kosher. Another neighbor, Gary Mullen, taught me to ride a bike when I was six, and yet another was Jaimie Walker, the now famous local ceramic artist. It was with Jaimie's help that we built our first tree house.

When I was twelve, my family moved a mile south to a lakefront home – 12 Meadow Lane. Down a narrow, steep road we drove to reach an old, white farmhouse with a rolling lawn down to the shore of Lake Washington. It was a teen's dream. Lots of space to roam, a pool table left by the previous owners, our ping-pong table and pin ball machine purchased at a Seattle Hebrew Academy school auction. There were apple trees and plum trees that made August and September especially delicious. I periodically climbed high into the tall pine tree in front of the house. Settling onto a sturdy branch, I was invisible to all, yet I could see everyone. Gazing at the tall buildings in downtown Seattle and watching people biking and walking across the lake on the eastern side of the Seward Park loop, I became a "people watcher" at a young age.

The day a bright yellow seventeen foot Bayliner boat was delivered to our dock was one of the best days of my life. My twelve year old self couldn't stop smiling as my dad backed out of the dock and let the boat rip. The wind blew my hair and the speed sent happy shivers down my spine. Parking the boat after this first excursion didn't go as well; my dad crashed into the dock, scratching the new yellow hull. Not as easy as it looks. My parents hired Mr. Otis to come and give us kids lessons on boat safety.

A boat in one's backyard is a recipe for fun. I learned to ski when I was eight years old, and now at the age of twelve, there was no stopping me. My lifelong love affair with water skiing was solidified. At fourteen, I bought myself a slalom ski and learned to lean back and yell "hit it!" I still wait (not so) patiently through the winter and early spring for the rain drops to clear and Lake Washington to warm. Once the lake reaches a temperature that I can tolerate with a wet suit, I get up early and chase the

Karen Treiger skiing on Lake Washington (Treiger Collection).

glass to find a spot on the lake where the surface shines, reflecting the blue or white sky. Our boat is now on the Seattle side of the lake, not far from our home, but we often zip across the lake and ski down the western shore of Mercer Island, often passing our old home. As I fly across the wake, the early morning sun rises over the island, my endorphins surge, and the rest of the world fades away. I'm fourteen years old again.

Seattle's World Fair – 1962

I was a mere one year old when Seattle hosted its second world fair. The first one was in 1909, when Seattle's Census population was just under 250,000 – the Alaska Yukon Pacific Expo. I imagine that the Singermans, the Staadeckers, and the Friedlanders all attended that Expo. Seattle's second shot at a World Fair was called Century 21 Exposition. By the time of the 1962 World's Fair, Seattle's census population count was 557,087.[599]

The dual purpose of the fair, states Paula Becker and Alan Stein in *The Future Remembered: The 1962 Seattle World's Fair and It's Legacy*, was "to celebrate their city while stimulating its growth, and to create the enduring legacy of a permanent civic center, which became Seattle Center... Century 21 was the first exposition in 22 years to be held on American soil. It looked forward with bold audacity, literally reaching for the stars through emphasis on science, seeking to ease global tensions through emphasis on peaceful uses of space technology, and transforming 13 square blocks – 74 acres – of Seattle into what would become a treasured resource for the city, through the late 20th century and bravely on, into the real 21st."[600]

Seattle threw a party for the whole world and people showed up. Over 10,000,000 visitors entered the fairgrounds between their opening in April 1962 and their closing in October. The opening of the fair was covered by four television stations, with fifteen cameras all around the fairgrounds. All the important TV news figures of the day showed up, including Walter Cronkite, who rode the monorail to arrive at the fairgrounds. President Kennedy opened the fair with a telegraph key that was "encrusted with gold nuggets" – the same key President William Howard Taft had used to open Seattle's Alaska Yukon Exposition in 1909. President Kennedy didn't visit the fair in person, but rather via video hookup and after a short speech, stated: "Let the fair begin."[601]

So many of the buildings that Seattleites know and love were built for the 1962 World's Fair: The Opera House (previously a barn like structure called the Civic Auditorium built in 1928), the Science Center, the Center House, the Space Needle, the Fountain, the Rep, the Playhouse, and most important the Fun Forest.[602] I grew up going on all the Fun Forest rides and throwing darts at balloons in the hopes of taking home a stuffed animal.

Each state of the United States and countries from around the world had pavilions, exhibiting different aspects of science and technology. Some of the famous people who arrived at the fair included the Shah of Iran; Robert Moses of New York; John Glenn; Richard, Pat, and Julie Nixon; Bob Hope; Prince Phillip; the Rev. Billy Graham; Nat King Cole; Attorney General Robert Kennedy and his wife Ethel and two children; and Elvis Presley, who shot a movie at the fair.[603]

Two lesser-known Seattleites, Irwin Treiger and his friend and client Walter Schoenfeld, received the exclusive franchise for burgers, beer, and popcorn. There was one other investor, but no one remembers his name. Their restaurant, Camelot, opened and was the only place in the entire fairground that you could get a burger or a glass of beer, so I imagine they were very busy. Popcorn stands dotted the fairgrounds but were controlled by this young trio.

Victor Alhadeff, Walter Schoenfeld's nephew, was hired to help. Victor's memories spilled out as we discussed his long relationship with my dad.

"I was fifteen years old," Victor said. "Your dad and Uncle Walter, along with a few other Jewish men, had the exclusive rights to beer, burgers, and popcorn at the World's Fair. The World's Fair was a high-risk venture. That's your father's claim to fame in tax law... [He] got an IRS ruling to depreciate the Space Needle and all the construction at the Seattle Center in nine months. He was at the forefront of the tax law. Your dad's name should be on the Space Needle. All those guys would never have done it – it was too risky – who knows if it was going to last. There was a 70% tax bracket at the time. They got this huge write off so your dad was a *Macher* – Walter was also a big shot. They had made a name for themselves. That is why they got the exclusive rights to beer, burgers, and popcorn.

Camelot Taven at Seattle Worlds Fair, 1962 (Treiger Collection).

The fair opened February or March. My job was working the popcorn stand, helping in the burger restaurant – sweeping the floor, stuff like that. But I got to know your grandmother, Rose. All the purchases at the World's Fair were in cash. It was before credit cards. They had beer, the only alcohol, and they had hamburgers and french fries, and the only popcorn. Do you know how much cash accumulated every day? A lot! Paper bags full of money. Bags and bags of money.

Who had the money? Your grandmother, Rose. There was a closed room at the top of the center and all the money went to her. She didn't trust anybody, but the Jewish boys. Only let the Jewish boys in the cash room. I worked with her a couple hours a day. At the end of the day when I did my shift, I sat with her, and we counted the money. Sat side by side for nine months.

She was very demanding. Pennies were here; nickels, here; dimes, here. She was a brilliant woman and precise. I thought she was an old lady. She was probably fifty."[604]

My dad confirmed the IRS ruling regarding the Space Needle in a January 2007 interview with Max Kvidera for Seattle Business Monthly:

"He was also the tax attorney for the Space Needle Corp., a group of local business leaders who originally owned the Space Needle," wrote Kvidera. "When the Seattle icon was built in conjunction with the Seattle World's Fair in 1962, he wrestled with the idea of how to depreciate the structure as an investment. Treiger negotiated with the Internal Revenue Service that just might be the best depreciation deal in Seattle's history.

'We didn't know how well the World's Fair would do or how the Space Needle would do,' Treiger recalls. 'I decided there was a possibility that half of the economic value of the Space Needle would be lost after the fair ended. We met with the IRS and they agreed with us. It was an astounding result.'"[605]

I have no personal memories from the World's Fair since I was only one year old. However, it was a significant event in Seattle's history and in our family's history. It was my parents' first venture into a profitable endeavor not related to the law. However profitable it was, it was sure fun. My brother, Louis, tells me that our parents built their first Mercer Island home with the profits from the World's Fair. My mom confirmed this fact, recalling that they made $25,000 on the fair ($260,500 in today's dollars).

"Your father went to the fair almost every day after work," my mom told me. "I would drive over from Enatai whenever I could get a babysitter. I waited tables and did whatever I could to help out. It was really fun; we had a good time. I loved it."[606]

Betty Lou – A Powerhouse

My mom, Betty Lou, was the quintessential volunteer. She worked hard and got results. When we were children, she chaired an art show at our school, the Seattle Hebrew Academy, and she, together with Chani Genauer, initiated the annual fund-raising auction. She dove into work at the Seattle Jewish Federation, where she served on the Board of Women's Division for many years and rose to the position of first Vice President of Women's Division in Charge of Campaign. As the VP for Campaign, my mom launched a new format for the campaign and an innovative training program for volunteers.

"I have worked with Betty Lou for a number of years and have found her to be one of the most competent and capable people I know," said Bernice Rind, the Women's Division President in an article in the Jewish Transcript. "With her enthusiasm, dedication and rare qualities of leadership, she will undoubtedly make the 1973 Campaign the most successful in the history of the Women's Division."[607]

The Transcript article went on to profile the new VP for Campaign as a "native of Seattle who attended Queen Anne High School and the University of Washington, who is now married to Irwin Treiger and has three children: Louis, 14; Karen, 11; and Kenneth, 7. In spite of her great family responsibilities, Mrs. Treiger has been extremely active in Seattle area organizations. Her extensive involvement with the Seattle Hebrew Academy has included organizing the PTA Luncheon for two years, twice chairing the annual Art Show. She is also the past president of the Dr. Raymond Somers Orthopedic Guild. Mrs. Treiger has been on the Board of Directors of the Women's Division of the Federation since 1969. In this capacity she has been Vice President in charge of Publicity, chairwoman of M-Day for two years, and most recently was Assistant Chairwomen of the Women's Leadership Mission. 'When I saw how people in Israel live, it struck me that it is by mere accident of birth that I live in the United States, and that therefore I have not had to flee from persecution,' commented Mrs. Treiger. 'Because of this, I feel that it is not only my duty but my privilege to do what I can to make life a little easier.'"[608]

Anyone could have predicted that Betty Lou would do great things. After all, in 1948 she was the Donut Winner for the Magnolia District Camp Fire Girls. She sold the most donuts in the district and won a free week at Camp Sealth.

The year after this Transcript Article, my mom ascended to the pinnacle of female Jewish power. She became the President of the Federation's Women's Division. It was during her tenure that the Federation published the first Seattle Jewish Community Directory. This has morphed into what is called today: the Guide to Jewish Washington.

My mom also stepped outside the Jewish community, volunteering for the Children's Orthopedic Hospital and Medical Center, Cornish College of the Arts, Seattle Art Museum, and the Seattle Chamber Music Festival, where she served as President of the Board.

At a Federation Lion of Judah event at my parents' condominium after they moved to First Hill Plaza, my mother welcomed the guests. She mused about how it was that she ended up hosting the luncheon and launched into the pitch for donations:

"I certainly have no regrets," she said. "Federation is in my genes, both my grandfather and my father served as President of Federation, as did my husband. My personal mentor was the late Elsa Levinson, who, in many ways, should be considered the mother of Women's Division. And as I became more and more involved, it was my friend and now neighbor, Jo Jassney, who is here with us today, who talked me into taking the job of chairing Women's Division's Campaign, which led to the Presidency of Women's Division.

The longer I have been involved the more I realized that, in substance, needs don't change; they may take different forms, from opening the exit doors of the Soviet Union and resettling Russian Jews, to caring for the immigrant residents of Kiryat Malachi, a special project undertaken by Seattle's Federation several years ago; from providing housing and support for Russian immigrants who settled in Seattle to the current need to feed and support so many members of our community who find themselves jobless and unable to support their families."[609]

My parents trained us from a very young age to join in with their civic and Jewish Community endeavors. My brothers and I were among the kids who ran from table to table collecting the pledge cards and delivering them to the main table to be processed at Federation's annual Super Sunday. We were also sent out into the neighborhood to knock on doors, first with the blue and white JNF box and then later for the "March of Dimes" campaign supporting the Children's Orthopedic Hospital. I took great pleasure in gathering all the dimes and fitting them into the calendars that were provided with dime holders. There was something strangely satisfying to place all those dimes in the slots and then give them to my mom who delivered them to the hospital.

Children's Orthopedic was one of my mother's early non-Jewish charities. To support the work of the hospital she co-chaired a post-opening game cocktail party for the UW Huskies at the Edgewater Hotel. The cost to attend the no-host party was one dollar, with proceeds helping "sick children." The photo in the Bellevue American on September 15, 1966 shows my mom, Joan Leshgold, and Mrs. H. Shapiro sitting on a couch, holding martini glasses with perfectly teased hair towering on their heads and a football on the coffee table in front of them.[610]

My mom's energies were spread to many fortunate organizations over the years. The Cornish College of the Arts benefited from her wisdom and energy as she served on committees and the board for many years, chaired gala fundraising dinners, and was the founder of the Cornish Players Club, which she named "Give Your Heart to Art." She was active at the Seattle Art Museum as a Member of the Art Members Supporters and chaired an annual luncheon. One of her favorite organizations was the Seattle Chamber Music Festival, which she and my dad loved to attend. She served on the board and rose to be the President. She was also a secretary and member of ARCS, Achievement Rewards for College Scientists.

My parents shared a passion for community involvement. Though they played different roles, together they had a formidable impact. They worked as a team.

"One must recognize the teamwork of Betty Lou and Irwin together," explained Jim Tune, one of my dad's closest colleagues and friends. "It wasn't just Irwin; it was Betty Lou as well – the two of them together. Cornish – was a Treiger team. Symphony, Rotary Club, Rainier Club, Chamber. People respect people who are doers."[611]

My mom didn't restrict her energies and intellect to volunteer causes. When we lived on Mercer Island, she, together with my Aunt Jackie Goldfarb and their close friend Joan Vertleib bought a few houses and rented them out. I'll never forget the time that they learned that one of the houses was being used as a brothel. That didn't go over well with these three moms. They evicted the tenants, cleaned up the house, and sold it. They laughed about it for years. She also managed family-owned real estate that she and my father bought together. She operated them with a careful eye towards aesthetics and profit.

My mom loves to play bridge, exercise, and play craps at the Snoqualmie Casino. Her love and warmth extend naturally to her nine grandchildren. When the grandchildren were young, my parents lived in a waterfront house in Denny Blaine, just a few blocks from where my mother's grandparents, the Staadeckers, lived. During the wonderful summer months, we were there all the time, swimming, boating, and just hanging out. Most Sunday evenings were spent at their home, with a wonderful home cooked meal – cooked by my mom, not a maid. My mom took the kids to Children's Theater, clothes shopping, and out for ice cream. She shared with them things she loved to do. Her passion for life and her love of her children, grandchildren, and now great-grandchildren, serves as an example to me. I am grateful for the exceptional role model that she is.

Betty Lou (Friedlander) Treiger (Treiger Collection).

Irwin – How Did He Do It All?

Jim Tune came to Bogle & Gates as a summer intern and his initial exposure to the Treiger power couple was at one of the annual summer events in our home – a dinner for the summer associates. It was a full-on party with tons of good food, a bonfire on the beach, and plenty of liquor. My mom was the party planner; my dad was the bartender and schmoozer-in-chief.

"My earliest memory of your dad," Jim told me in a 2019 interview, "was when I was a summer intern at Bogle. He had a party for the summer associates. You lived in the white house – it had a fire pit. Your father introduced me to the Rubenstein – the drink – so that you know it's 2/3 brandy with port dripped on top. Sounds terrible, and actually it is terrible. But after a few of them...

It was called a Rubenstein because Sam [Rubenstein] invented the drink. Your dad infected all summer associates with a Rubenstein."[612]

During the final two weeks of my dad's life in October of 2013, as his body failed him, he didn't want to see anyone besides his family. But he allowed two non-family members to visit, one was Rabbi Moshe Kletenik and the second was Jim. To me, this shows the depth of this long friendship.

"I considered your dad my mentor," Jim said, "and I enjoyed his intelligence and sense of humor. His eccentricities... What did I admire? His keen intellect, remarkable sense of humor and he was fun to be around...

He didn't suffer fools very well. One had to have at least a sufficient amount of intelligence to get in his inner circle. He was so smart and he was so committed to the community. All those things make you admire a person...

Some people try to lead by commanding. But the best leaders demonstrate their own commitment to do things right and they incorporate people into that. He did that with the firm and the ABA tax section. You can't be a leader in a law firm unless people respect you for what you can do and your thought process – have to work as hard or harder than others."[613]

Boy, did my dad work hard. I had no idea until after he died how many organizations he was involved with. Why is it that we don't know the full picture of a person until after they die?

"He was listed in Best Lawyers in America (1983-2013)," my dad's obituary states.

"His professional activities included Washington State Bar Association (Chair of Tax Section and IRS Liaison Section), American Bar Association (Board of Governors, Chair, Section of Taxation, and Distinguished Service Award recipient), American Bar Foundation, American College of Tax Counsel, American Tax Policy Institute and American Law Institute. His many civic activities included the Greater Seattle Chamber of Commerce (Chair and Trustee), Jewish Federation of Greater Seattle (President and Co-Chair of General Assembly Host Committee), Corporate Council for the Arts

(Chair), Samis Foundation (Trustee), Seattle Symphony Foundation (President), The Seattle Foundation (Chair), UW School of Law Visiting Committee, Cornish College of the Arts (Co-Chair), Mayor's Symphony Panel (Chair), Seattle Baseball Park Commission (Chair), Rotary Club of Seattle (Trustee), Seattle Rotary Foundation (Chair), Seattle Rotary Service Foundation (Chair), Washington State Historical Society (Trustee), Seattle Junior Chamber of Commerce (Vice President), King County Multiple Sclerosis Society (Director), Seattle Hebrew Academy (President), The Jewish Transcript (President), American Israel Public Affairs Committee (Washington State Board Member), Northwest Foundation (President), Corporate Council for the Arts (President and Chair), Seattle Day Nursery Association (Director), and Puget Sound Regional Council (Tax Reform Task Force).

Irwin Treiger, date unknown (Treiger Collection).

In recognition of Irwin's receipt of the Benjamin Cardozo Outstanding Service Award, Governor Gary Locke proclaimed May 28, 1997 "Irwin Treiger Day."[614]

Irwin Treiger Day was proclaimed to coincide with my dad being honored by the Seattle Jewish Federation's Cardozo Society.

PROCLAMATION

WHEREAS, Irwin Treiger was born and raised in Seattle, Washington; and

WHEREAS, Irwin has been a prominent and active member of the Jewish and civic communities in Settle for many years, including serving as president of the Seattle Chamber of Commerce; and

WHEREAS, Irwin has been a trusted advisor and counselor to many political and business leaders; and

WHEREAS, His dedication and superior leadership as well respected by all those who know him; and

WHEREAS, Irwin is known for his cigars and 'holding court' in the courtyard of Two Union Square; and

WHEREAS, Irwin and his wife, Betty Lou, raised three children while maintaining their involvement in the community; and

WHEREAS, Irwin is being bestowed the Benjamin Cardozo Award Outstanding Service on this date;

NOW, THEREFORE, I Gary Locke, Governor of the state of Washington, do hereby proclaim May 28, 1997, as

IRWIN TREIGER DAY

in Washington state, and I urge all citizens to join me in this special observance.

Signed this 28th day of May, 1997
Gary Locke
Governor

How did my father have a successful law practice, work with all these organizations, AND show up for dinner? Family dinner was taken very seriously. The five of us sat at a round table. First course was often a green salad and then some kind of meat or chicken with some sides. We kids took turns setting the table, clearing the table and helping with dishes.

"Keeping Kosher was the best thing for our family," my mom told me. "Because your father couldn't eat meat out, he would come home every

Back Row: Karen, Louis, Ken. Front Row, Irwin and Betty Lou (Treiger Collection).

night for dinner. The other young associates stayed much later grabbing food from a nearby restaurant. We were lucky. He worked every night in his den, but he was always home for dinner."[615]

Since my father's legal work was confidential, the dinner opener was: "who did you have lunch with?" Here is where I became conversant with the names at the firm: Dick Sprague, Paul Steer, Don Bagley, Thad Alston, Jim Tune, Bob Kaplan. I don't know why this was so important that it got top billing each evening, but it clearly was. But at the time, they were the names of my dad's life outside the home – so they were the secret society that we only dreamed of.[616]

We kids were asked about school, sports, or the happenings of the day. We were expected to have something to say. But my dad's day was the central focus of the dinner conversation.

We also heard about Rotary and the Monday lunch at the Community Development Round Table, where fifty carefully picked leaders of Seattle's business, civic and governmental worlds met and, "talk[ed] about how to find the money, build the political support, and craft a convincing public message to turn cocktail-napkin sketches into blueprints. The new Mariners and Seahawks stadiums. The Nordstrom-Pacific Place retail complex. The Seattle Commons. The Washington State Convention & Trade Center expansion ... if it has at least an eight-digit budget, chances are it ha[d] been or [would] be discussed by the Monday Club."[617]

Beginning in 1979, a new topic was introduced at the dinner table – the SAMIS Foundation. The SAMIS Foundation was created by Sam Israel, an immigrant from the Island of Rhodes in Greece who started out as a shoemaker and amassed a fortune in real estate holdings in downtown Seattle and Soap Lake. Having no children, he wanted to do something meaningful with his wealth. According to his nephew, Eddie Hasson, Sam had a vision for a charitable foundation. He wanted to fund Hebrew schools in Seattle; a Jewish cemetery; assistance to orphans, widows, the poor, and victims of emergencies around the world. He also wanted to fund endeavors in Israel, such as the preservation of nature and archeology.[618]

My dad became his lawyer and one of the first trustees of the Foundation. But before Eddie introduced Sam to my dad, he plowed through three other lawyers. They wouldn't do what Sam wanted, so he fired them.[619]

"Treiger," writes Richard S. Hobbs in *Our Brother's Keeper: The Life of Sam Israel*, "was a highly regarded tax attorney with a national reputation for his expertise in trusts, estates, and foundations. He was known for his sharp wit and an exceptional ability to listen to his clients and find solutions for their legal needs... The two men 'hit it off very, very well,' in Eddie Hasson's words. From the start, Treiger knew the key to working for Sam. 'I didn't try to tell him what to do,' he said. Treiger prepared the paperwork to Sam's satisfaction, and the organizing documents for the nonprofit Samis Foundation were filed with the Office of the Secretary of State in Olympia on December 19, 1979."[620]

While Sam was alive, there were three trustees, my dad, Eddie Hasson, and Sam himself. Sam made the decisions in these early years and my dad and Eddie went along for the ride. In 1989, Sam had a stroke, and Al Maimon was appointed to serve in Sam's stead as a trustee. The three trustees managed the Foundation until Sam's death in 1994.[621]

Pursuant to the Foundation documents, after Sam's death the Foundation expanded to sixteen trustees. These were all picked by Sam and appointed to serve life terms. The Foundation morphed over the years and trustees began to be appointed for specific term of years.[622] In 2019, my brother Louis Treiger was appointed as a trustee and I feel that this appointment honors not only Louis for the hardworking lawyer and community leader that he is but also for our father whose legacy is carried on.

Legacy is a heavy word that is laden with emotion and sometimes trauma. Both my parents described their true legacy as their grandchildren. My father referred to them as his "dividends." All the hard work and the hopes for the future are bundled up in the dreams for the grandchildren. In my dad's first speech as Chairman of the Chamber of Commerce in 1993, he first thanked my mom "who ha[d] been [his] true partner in all [their] professional and civic efforts for thirty-six years." He then continued to thank all his children and their spouses who were in attendance.

SAMIS Trustees. Irwin is third row back - center (with a beard) (Courtesy of SAMIS Foundation), 2013.

"There is a selfish element in my work for the chamber," my dad said. "I am really working for my children and, more particularly, my grandchildren. You will see four of my five grandchildren pictured in the chamber's 1993-1994 annual report. These children are sixth generation Seattleites. Their forebears arrived here in the 1870's seeking economic opportunities. And they found them, as did the four succeeding generations who have lived and worked and thrived here. Will the sixth generation be able to follow? Will there be jobs for them here? Some of them may, of course, decide to move from Seattle, but if they do I want it to be by their choice, not economic necessity."[623]

As of 2024, five of Irwin and Betty Lou's nine dividends live in Seattle (Mordechai Treiger, Avraham Treiger, Shmuel Treiger Jack Golderg, and Olivia Owens Trieger). The hard work paid off.

Back row, left to right: Ken Treiger, Lauren Antonoff, Irwin Treiger, Betty Lou (Friedlander) Treiger, Shlomo Goldberg, Karen Treiger, Louis Treiger, Bayla Friedman Treiger. Middle row: Jack Goldberg, Elisheva Goldberg, Eitan Treiger, Mordechai Treiger, Avraham Treiger. Front Row: Olivia Owens Treiger, Shoshana Goldberg, Shmuel Treiger, Esther Goldberg (approx. 2010) (Treiger Collection).

Did They Ever Relax?

My parents weren't all work. They knew how to have fun. There were family summer vacations at Lake Chelan, Passover vacations at gorgeous resorts, trips to Israel, trips to attend the ABA Tax Section meetings (not all work), and my dad's infamous fishing trips with his friends from his law firm and others with Herman Sarkowsky and Pat Stusser.

"We did it [the Bogles trip] for 10 years." Jim Tune said. "Your dad brought a huge supply of cigars. We stopped at the border and bought a huge bottle of Tanqueray and vodka (for Bloody Mary's). The cooks always loved your dad the most – they were fascinated by his food issues – what he could eat or couldn't eat – fins and scales – they got quite used to accommodating what Irwin wanted. It always annoyed me that your father was better than me in fishing. He always caught a big one."[624]

My mom, in turn, went on an annual trip to Rancho La Puerta, a health spa just south of the U.S./Mexico border. One year, as a college student, I was invited to come along. It was a heavenly week among mountains, healthy food, yoga, aerobic classes, and really nice people. My favorite was the sunrise hike up the mountain. Reaching the top as the sun crested over the hills, I would release an audible sigh. The sense of awe I felt on those early mornings still inspires me during the early morning hours.

Parties were key – lots of parties. Some were small dinner parties with a highly curated guest list. There were slightly larger parties too, like the shindig with the summer associates. But there was one huge event – the biggest event of the year – the Treiger Labor Day party. It was held in the backyard of the waterfront home on Mercer Island, and it was an extravaganza. Hundreds of people came by car (with valet parking) and some by boat. There were hot dogs and hamburgers. There were games for the kids and booze for the adults. Everyone had a great time. Waking up early on Labor Day, I would head out to the expansive lawn, and with shovels and paper bags, my dad and I would spend the next hour picking up goose poop. One might think that was a terrible job, but it is a special memory of something I did with my father that I hold dear.

Then there was my dad's annual summer baseball trip to major league stadiums across the US. Oh, how he loved that trip. The group chose a different set of cities to visit each year and ultimately visited every major league stadium in the country. He talked about it for weeks after. From his youth, my dad loved baseball. He was the manager of the Garfield High School baseball team.

"From High School days," writes Sally Gene Mahoney in a 1986 profile in the Seattle Times, "baseball has been Treiger's 'love,' though he was always the scorekeeper and never played the game. His Mariners connection keeps that love alive."[625]

My dad was the first attorney for the Seattle Mariners baseball club. He represented the team for sixteen years. This fed his love for baseball and provided him with season's tickets and a coveted parking pass. Each season he would make a point of taking his grandchildren – one at a time – to a game. Through these outings, he built a relationship with the kids and shared his love of baseball with them. The capstone of his baseball romance was throwing out of the first pitch at a Mariner's game for his seventieth

Left to Right: Elisheva Goldberg, Jack Goldberg, Mordechai Treiger, Irwin Treiger, Shmuel Treiger, Mariner Moose, Shoshana Goldberg, Avraham Treiger, Ken Treiger, 2004 (Treiger Collection).

birthday. He practiced for weeks. He didn't want to embarrass himself by throwing the pitch and have it land half-way to home plate.

In the 1986 Seattle Times profile, Mahoney opens the piece in a way that perfectly captured my dad's essence: "When Irwin Treiger leans back in his swivel chair, smoke swirling from his ever-present cigar, there's an almost mischievous air about him that suggests 'I know something you don't know.' He probably does."[626]

His deeper knowledge and mischievous air came through in a conversation I had with the former Mayor of Seattle Norm Rice. My dad called him "Your Worship" and they often had lunch at the Rainier Club. Mayor Rice explained that my dad had a way of asking hard questions without ever directly confronting you. Mayor Rice described my dad as "brilliant."

"What about my dad was 'brilliant'?" I asked.

"He knew how to ask the questions and make you think. That's what made him brilliant. The more you talk, the more you expound, pretty soon you are laying out a story that is much broader than the specific thing... He made you feel comfortable sharing what was going on. He was a listener. He would challenge your assumptions – but never tell you that you are wrong. Maybe by the end you were challenging you own assumptions."[627]

His admiration went further. He admired my dad's understanding of human nature.

"He didn't like phonies," Mayor Rice told me. "If you spoke truth and you believed it, he believed you. I think there was an honesty that I really liked about him. In his quiet way, he would say, why do you think such and such? After each conversation, I ended up reassessing something. Subtle nudge. That's what a good friend is – asks why you did what you did."[628]

At the end of the day, Mayor Rice explained that "a good deep question was as good as a lecture."[629]

Toward the end of Mayor Rice's tenure, my dad was honored at a dinner given by the Seattle Jewish Federation's Cardozo Society on May 28, 1997. In his speech, my dad thanked the mayor for coming:

"My special thanks to my friend, his Worship, the Mayor," my dad stated right up at the top of the speech. "I know he has other things to do and that he took valuable time away from preparing his unemployment comp application to be with us."[630]

My father continued to describe the Seattle in which he grew up.

"The Seattle in which I was born," he stated, "was quite a different place from Norm Rice's vibrant city. In the 30s the cable cars still chugged up and down Yesler and Madison; the street cars still clanged their way to Alki, where we would often go for Sunday picnics, the ferries still plied Lake Washington; and Boeing had just moved out of the red barn. All told, it was a peaceful, but provincial environment, and a relatively closed society.

The majority of the Jewish community was even more provincial and parochial than its neighbors. Although some cracks had appeared, the ghetto still stood, albeit without walls, and united us in a way we shall never again experience. I was born in that ghetto, the approximately fifteen block band between King and Union Streets, with its five synagogues and one Temple; Its four Kosher bakers and six Kosher butchers; when Thursdays meant excursions to Block's poultry shop where my mother would select a live chicken for slaughter; when going to the grocery meant walking with my wagon to Weinrobe's or Neslon's on Cherry street, not driving to QFC.

As was usual with immigrant families such as mine, the central theme of life during my childhood was education. My mother, who immigrated to the U.S. when she was six, the valedictorian of her class at Franklin High, never went to college; straight from High School to work. My dad, who immigrated to the U.S. when he was fourteen, had to drop out of college after three years because the money simply ran out. But they, as their siblings, were determined that their kids would be educated, and they sacrificed greatly to attain that goal. And God forbid that we should ever bring home any grades but A's. Eight of the ten grandchildren of my mother's parents went to college, and among those eight, fifteen degrees were accumulated."[631]

That speech reveals an underlying truth about my dad and about all of us: at the end of the day, we are defined by our childhood. Both my parents, Betty Lou and Irwin, were and are defined by their childhoods. My dad's immigrant household, surrounded by the love of a large family and wrapped in Jewish tradition, led to his commitment to family, Jewish tradition, and Jewish community. His parents, owners of a mom & pop store in Seattle's central district, worked long hours and saw their children's future in education – demanding perfect grades in school. This inspired my dad to work hard, study hard and excel. My mom's Reform American Jewish household, living in far-away Magnolia, whose wealthy family owned a large, jewelry store in the center of downtown, left her with mixed messages about family (her parents divorced after she got married), but gave her a solid footing and provided strong examples of leadership. Though they both grew up in different worlds, they took what they saw as the good parts of their childhoods, incorporated them and left behind the pieces they didn't like.

There was much that was fate, but my parents made choices to be strong, successful citizens. Along this fifty-five year journey together, their support and love taught me the meaning of a true partnership and inspired me to have a family, become an attorney, and take leadership roles in the Jewish community. I've taken the parts I loved about my childhood and have fashioned a life, with some modifications, that reflects the values and personalities of my parents. I've learned so much from them, and I hope I make them proud.

Initially, I was terrified to research and write these stories about my parents. How to tell their story and express the nuances of their lives? How to express the impact they had and continue to have on my life? How to show how deeply I love and admire them both. As I worked on these stories, I'm not ashamed to admit that I cried more than a few times. I wish my father were still alive so I could talk to him, hug him, ask him for advice.

My first grandson, Theodor Irwin Goldberg, is named for my dad (Hebrew - Yisroel Aryeh). My daughter-in-law, Emma, asked me for some photos of my dad in order to frame one and put it up in Ted's room, so he will look at that picture and know for whom he is named. She chose a photo of my dad at the baseball stadium on the day that he threw out the first pitch. Couldn't be a better choice. Four more great-grandchildren followed Theodore Irwin and I'm sure that in the world beyond my dad is counting his dividends.

At a remembrance of my dad on the anniversary of his death in October of 2023, my brothers and I sponsored a *kiddush* (reception after services) at our Minyan Ohr Chadash, the synagogue that Louis and I attend. We placed a picture of my dad on the table.

Ted saw the picture and asked his father, Jack,

"Dada, is Grandpa Irwin dead?"

"Yes," Jack said, "Grandpa Irwin died before you were born."

"So where is Grandpa Irwin?" asked Ted.

"He is in heaven – with God," said Jack

"Can Grandpa Irwin see me?" Ted asked.

"Yes," said Jack, "he is always there watching you and is very proud of you."

silence

"Am I the new Grandpa Irwin?" asked Ted.

"Well, kind of," said Jack. "You're named for him and one of the reasons we named you after him is because we hope you will grow up to be like him. He was a great and very kind man."

"MAMA," screamed Ted, "I'M THE NEW GRANDPA IRWIN!"

My hope is that my children and my grandchildren learn about the families from which they come and derive strength and character from the lives that were lived. There is so much to learn, so much to mourn, and so much to celebrate. I hope that after I am dead, my children and grandchildren read these words and remember me and say – oh, she learned so much from her parents, her grandparents, and ancestors. She taught me so much. And her laugh was so loud, it made everyone else laugh along.

Irwin Treiger and Betty Lou (Friedlander) Treiger with dog Winston (Treiger Collection).

Keep laughing – it makes everything better.

I can think of no better way to end this chapter about my parents than the words of an ancient Indian poet with which my dad ended his Cardozo speech in May of 1997:

"The past is history;
The future, mystery;
And the present, a gift from G-d.
Thank you all for being here with us tonight."[632]

CHAPTER 8

ANTISEMITISM

The stories of these five families cannot be told without considering one of the oldest forms of hatred affecting Jews throughout history – antisemitism. How has antisemitism in the United States affected my family? In grappling with this question, I have had to confront how antisemitism affected and still affects my own life.

I've been particularly distressed by the surge in antisemitism around the world since the vicious October 7, 2023 attack by Hamas. Approximately 5,000 Hamas terrorists invaded Israel's southern border, murdered 1,200 innocent men, women, and children and kidnapped 240 people, including the elderly and infants.

I've lost sleep many a night over the attack itself, the war that ensued, and the loss of Israeli and Palestinian lives. I worry for my daughter and son-in-law who live in Israel and my many friends and other family there. In the United States, the Antidefamation League reported a 360% increase in antisemitic incidents since that attack.[633]

But what is antisemitism? And what was the source of it? Explaining it is no easy task.

"It's hard, if not impossible," states Professor Deborah Lipstadt in *Antisemitism Here and Now*, "to explain something that is essentially irrational, delusional, and absurd. . . The shape of the hatred may be adapted and massaged, the basic ideas or illusions that are at its core remain a constant. In ancient and medieval times it was religious in nature. Jews were hated because they refused to accept Christianity and later, Islam. In the 18th century, racial and political rationales were added to the religious one."[634]

Antisemitism and a bleak economic outlook pushed my ancestors to leave Europe and build a better life in North America. They dreamed and hoped that the *Goldene Medina* (the Golden Land – the U.S.) would be a haven for Jews.

Maybe it was a haven, but just not as perfect as they had dreamed.

• • •

"It's just the way it was," my mom, Betty Lou Treiger and my aunt, Jackie Goldfarb, said in unison when I asked them how antisemitism affected them growing up in Seattle. "We just didn't pay attention to it."

Their lives were shaped within a context of an antisemitism that had grown decade by decade from events in the eastern United States and had reached Washington State and fully developed in the 1920s.

According to historians of Seattle's early years, antisemitism wasn't a big factor in civic life before 1900.[635] It seems that in those early days, discrimination and fear were focused on Native American, Chinese, Black, and Japanese residents.[636] Jews could rise to high political office. In 1870, Edward Solomon was appointed Washington Territory's ninth (and only Jewish) territorial governor.[637] In 1875, Bailey Gatzert was elected the eighth (and only Jewish) mayor of Seattle.

Paul Singerman, who arrived in 1874, earlier than the rest of my family, didn't hide his Judaism and was welcomed into Seattle's small civic and business community. Paul became a high-ranking Mason and a leading Seattle merchant. Jenny, his wife, who came from Germany to marry him, moved to Seattle in 1879.

What then was the intensity of antisemitism in Seattle when most of my ancestors arrived in the Pacific Northwest between 1900 and 1913? Victor Staadecker arrived in Portland in 1900 and made his way to Seattle in 1905; Sam and Augusta Friedlander arrived in 1906; the Steinberg family arrived in 1909 – 1910; the Treiger family arrived in Portland in 1914.[638]

Seattle had approximately 240,000 citizens in 1910 and according to the American Jewish Yearbook of Statistics, there were approximately 4,500 Jews living in Seattle (1.9% of the population).[639]

By the second decade of the twentieth century antisemitism was squarely planted in the Pacific Northwest. In 1920, quotas were the norm at universities.[640] Jews were barred from membership in social clubs, and many businesses wouldn't hire a Jew.

At the University of Washington, quotas were the norm by 1920, restricting the number of Jews accepted. By the time my mom, dad, aunt and uncles enrolled, Jews were not welcome to join fraternities and sororities; their choices narrowed to the few Jewish ones.

My father, Irwin Treiger, graduated first in his class at the University of Washington Law School and graduated with a Masters in Law (LLM) in tax from New York University Law School. Yet, in 1959 he had just two choices of law firms in Seattle. The others wouldn't hire a Jew.[641]

The KKK had surged to social importance and political power. In 1922, Oregon elected Walter Pierce, a Klan member, as Governor.[642] In Washington State, thousands attended Klan rallies. When the Klan's Imperial Wizard, Hirm Wesley Evans, visited Seattle in 1924, he was hosted by Seattle's Chamber of Commerce.[643] This was the same Chamber of Commerce that had been founded in 1875 by Mayor Bailey Gatzert.

Nonetheless, my resilient ancestors found their way through the maze of gentile society and succeeded where they could. For example, Paul Singerman, Victor Staadecker, and Sam Friedlander all became high ranking Masons and all were members of the Chamber of Commerce that welcomed the Klan's Imperial Wizard.

The 1920s and 1930s also saw restrictive real estate covenants, and banks that would not lend to Jews who wished to purchase property outside a specific area. This was called red-lining. Jews were restricted from buying homes in most of Seattle. They were allowed to purchase homes in the central district and parts of Capitol Hill. This created as my father once said, "a ghetto without walls."

The Washington Athletic Club (WAC) also barred Jews from membership. When this policy was instituted, the WAC already had about forty Jewish members. They were allowed to remain, but no additional Jews were admitted. There was a disagreement among the Jewish members as to how to best react to this antisemitic policy: stay as members and work for change from within or resign and fight for the rights of all Jews to join?[644]

My great-grandparents, Belle and Louis Friedlander, were members of the WAC. I don't know how they reacted to this new policy, but I don't believe they resigned their membership. Once these restrictions were removed, my parents joined the WAC. I, too, joined the WAC when my law office moved across the street. I loved going there in the mornings and spent hours in the small Hogwarts-like library, when I was writing my first book about Shlomo's parents' survival though the Holocaust.

In 1923, the Staadeckers and the Friedlanders helped start the Glendale Golf & Country club in South Seattle. They opened the new club because Jews were not welcome in other clubs in Seattle. This club provided a place where Jews could gather for golf, cards, dinners, and parties.

"Daddy knew the antisemitism was there," Aunt Jackie said about her father, Jack Friedlander, "but it didn't seem to bother him. He loved the Glendale Country Club. All his friends were there."[645]

I had been sheltered from the antisemitism they dodged so casually. As I matured, what I learned put a new perspective on their resilience and willingness to find and cultivate support among their families. I wondered about their choice to avoid confronting the ugliness others were so willing to throw at them. To move forward was the choice, to find a way to keep their families secure was the priority.

When I asked my mom why we moved to the south end of Mercer Island when I was a child, she responded because none of the tennis and swim clubs in Seattle would let in Jews. There was a new swim and tennis club at the south end of Mercer Island (the Mercer Island Country Club) that let in Jews, so we moved there.

My Aunt Jackie and Uncle Alvin played tennis every Sunday at the same Mercer Island Country Club with a non-Jewish couple. After a few weeks of playing together, the woman of the couple remarked, "you know, you're really nice for Jews."

• • •

I grew up in Seattle in the 1960s and 1970s and encountered little overt antisemitism. I attended a Jewish day school for elementary and middle school and most of my family's social connections were in the Jewish community. My parents' close friends were all Jews, as were mine. This sheltered our family from much of the antisemitism that may have otherwise affected us.

My younger brother, Ken, however, experienced unfiltered antisemitism at his Eastside private school. Ken said in his middle and high school, there was a mean kid who drew swastikas and said "Heil Hitler" in his face. Ken got into fights with this kid, but as he said, "I usually lost those fights; I wasn't a good fighter."

In 2004, my son Jack was in eighth grade at the Seattle Hebrew Academy. Once a week, after school, Jack walked a few blocks to a local coffee shop to meet with a tutor. I would dutifully pick him up after the tutoring and take him home.

One day, I picked him up and he seemed shaken.

"What happened?" I asked.

"I was walking down the street," Jack said, "minding my own business, listening to my music. Then when I was about a block away from St. Joseph's school, I saw a group of kids. One of the boys broke away from the group and started down the street toward me. I didn't think anything of it until he gave me the finger. I stopped and asked why he did that. He said, 'because you're a Jew.'[646] So, I punched him in the face and he fell to the ground. I stepped over him and kept walking to the coffee shop."

Jack," I said, "you can't just hit people because they insult you. He could have had a knife or a gun and you could have been killed. You have to be careful."

Then, I paused and looked him in the eye and said, "And I'm really proud of you."

• • •

After passing the Washington State Bar exam in 1989, I joined a large Seattle law firm. During my first year, I was the associate on some litigation that involved a partnership dispute. It was a family business, and the two sides were arguing about how to dissolve the partnership and distribute the assets. Four attorneys, two from each side of the dispute, sat in the judge's chamber reviewing a motion. Earlier in the courtroom, there had been some heated exchanges between the parties to the dispute.

The lawyer for the other side said calmly to the judge:

"Judge, listen, this is how these people are. It's these people. You know – Jewish people. They scream and yell at each other, but it doesn't mean they can't get along. It's just the way these people are."

I had a split second to decide to stay quiet or open my mouth.

I opened my mouth.

"Excuse me," I interrupted, "I'm Jewish and the statement you made is terribly offensive. Being Jewish has nothing to do with the fact that these family members don't get along."

The judge then chimed in and shared:

"Well, I once saw David Ben Gurion in person, and he was also arguing with people."

Like that explained everything? I felt like I was in the twilight zone.

At that point, the partner I was working with deftly moved the conversation back to the motion we were discussing and that was the end of it. However, when I returned to my office, I called my father, Irwin Treiger, and told him the whole story. He was upset and promptly called a Jewish friend at the opposing law firm and had a "conversation" about what happened. For my father, "conversation" meant "a talking to" and usually a call to action. My father called me back and assured me that his friend would speak to the attorney who made the remarks and let him know that such statements "are unacceptable." My father would not allow such expressions of subtle antisemitism, and neither would I.

• • •

In the spring of 2024, my daughter Elisheva shared a book that her spouse Judah recommended, *Anti-Judaism* by David Nirenberg.[647] His 600-page work shows the history of anti-Jewish thought and action. He traces many old stereotypes and anti-Jewish tropes back to ancient Egypt. He then drops by the doorsteps of Islam and moves to a heavy focus on Christianity, especially Christian Europe. He finishes his tour in Nazi Germany.

He argues that negative ideas about Jews and Judaism became so embedded and encoded in western thought and culture that people saw and still see the world, in part, through the lens of Jews and Judaism, even when there are no Jews living in that place. These ideas, myths, and tropes shape the way people view themselves, their governments, and the world.

Dr. Nirenberg's argument that anti-Jewish ideas are embedded in western culture, provides a different perspective on this ancient hatred. However, Dr. Nirenberg's thesis is troubling. If, as a result of history, anti-Jewish ideas are now deeply embedded in the culture in which we live, can society and western culture change or are we doomed to live in a world with hatred of Jews forever more?

I don't have answers to these questions, but I do know that we find ourselves in a bewildering post-October 7th world. The negative focus on Israel and Jews worldwide has alarm bells ringing in Jewish communities everywhere.

• • •

My personal exploration of antisemitism in the United States has jolted me into a new awareness of challenges my ancestors and even my parents faced. The *Goldene Medina* (Golden Land) did indeed provide a haven from the persecution and harshness of Europe and allowed for opportunities that they never would have had. The children nurtured in these immigrant families received subtle and not so subtle messages about their place in society and their acceptance as Americans by the non-Jewish majority. These messages were passed down. So, when I see White Supremacists chanting "Jews will not replace us" and people screaming "go back to Poland" or "Hitler had it right," I am confronted with how to react. Fear? Anger? Resignation? Energized to fight back?

Can we change how people think and behave? I have no idea. I do know that hatred of Jews is a very old idea. But I also know that there are plenty of people in the world who are not Jew haters and who want to make the world a good place to live for all people. After this exploration of antisemitism, I'm left with a pit in my stomach, worry in my heart, but with hope for humanity. We make the world we want to live in.

These five families found their way through the antisemitism that surrounded them. They built a solid future for their families. They enriched their entire communities, Jewish and gentile. They leave us with the way they modeled their lives in spite of the discrimination they faced. In this, I find inspiration and hope.

• • •

The secret of life is enjoying the passage of time ...
Nobody knows how we got to the top of the hill
But since we're on our way down
We might as well enjoy the ride ...
And since we're only here for a while
Might as well show some style.
James Taylor, Secret O'Life.

A Letter To The Future

I write this letter to "the future." But what exactly is the future? Tomorrow, next year, 100 years? At some point all that will be left of me are these words and the fragments of DNA I leave in my children and grandchildren.

I filled in family trees, made maps, and wrote the stories of my Seattle ancestors. But what have I indeed done? Has this work made a difference for my dead ancestors? Have I kept the last nail out of their coffins? Will this writing leave a nail out of *my* coffin when that day arrives? Have I left, as Betty McDonald put it, a trail behind me like the shiny mark of a snail?

Maybe.

"Building a tree," writes Penny Walters, "and devising narratives, and maybe even producing a family history book means that we have left a mark in history, and theoretically, our lives won't be completely forgotten."[648]

The connecting tissue of the stories in this book are the city of Seattle, my parents, and me. Researching and writing each story has been a journey into my ancestors, my city, and myself, allowing me to feel part of the march of history and the building of one of America's great cities.

I learned that my family members were part of a retail and manufacturing transformation in Seattle, some in the downtown core, while others served the neighborhoods. Some turned their small retail store into a grand business operation, while others reflected Seattle's "mom and pop" establishments. All these businesses helped to build Seattle's retail landscape and developed our unique customer service culture.

Paul Singerman turned his tiny 1874 dry goods store into a "mercantile palace." It became a place where Seattle citizens would line up outside and wait their turn to enter – to see the first electric lights, to see the newest fall fashions, to see the "fire-proof" brick store built on 1st and Columbia and then the rebuilt store after the Great Fire. To walk into Toklas & Singerman was to experience a barrage of sights and sounds. The lights were on, the phone was ringing, the elevator was taking customers up and down, the clerks were there to welcome you and give you the best Nordstrom service – before Nordstrom existed.

I never had the pleasure of stepping into a Toklas & Singerman store, but I had many opportunities to enter the retail masterpiece built by Sam, Lou, Jack and Paul Friedlander at 5th and Pike. For this store too, people lined up outside to take their turn inside the remodeled space and marvel at its elegance. Just as I felt like a princess each time I walked in, I'm sure that others felt similarly royal. And there was Papa Jack, standing on the crack, welcoming each customer with his deep, gruff voice and his bigger-than-life personality. When you walked out of Friedlander's with an exquisitely wrapped package, you knew you had gotten away with a treasure, even if you had to pay more than $1.

Staadecker's Millinery factory's move to 5th avenue in 1909 catalyzed a northward shift of Seattle's downtown. When Friedlander & Sons relocated to the corner of 5th and Pike some twenty years later, it was just footsteps away from Staadecker's.

Staadecker's wasn't a retail outlet, but a manufacturing plant that occupied the entire building. The hats made there adorned the heads of women of the Pacific Northwest and beyond as they went to tea, to parties, to church, to synagogue, shopping, or to the theater. They made life more beautiful with their craft.

These three families, over the course of 100 years, brought something important to our city – an honest way of doing business that was elegant, customer- centered, warm, and welcoming.

While the Singermans, Friedlanders and Staadeckers achieved the elegance of style and grandeur of their business operations, the other side of my family brought something else to Seattle, the warmth and honesty of a small business. Sam and Rose Treiger's Thifty's 10 cent Store on 23rd and Jackson was a neighborhood store, the place you "run over to" or "stop by" on the way home. It had everything you might need, just at that moment. They knew their customers well and their honesty was legendary. This store wasn't fancy and there were no chandeliers or elevators, but when you walked in Papa Sam and Bobby treated you as if you were the most important person in the world.

Similarly, Steinberg & Sons began, after the peddling phase, as a tiny retail store on 6th and Jackson, again, a neighborhood store. The story of my great-grandmother walking down to the store to bring soup for lunch and giving two men sitting outside the store some of the soup, tells me all I need to know. Food is love and there was much love in this family. Though the Steinbergs opened a wholesale line, they continued to run retail stores throughout the Pacific Northwest and Alaska. Their customer-centered, honest business dealings helped them succeed and build strong relationships.

My parents, Betty Lou and Irwin, were not proprietors of a retail store or a wholesale empire. Rather my mother carried on the family tradition of volunteerism, serving a wide swath of Jewish and civic Seattle. She continues to be a daily inspiration to me and my brothers. My father, the son of two immigrants, became a leading citizen of Seattle using "only his poor mind," but adding a heavy dose of honesty and warmth. His success as a lawyer and volunteer speaks volumes about the fire that burned inside him to make a difference.

My father has been dead for twelve years and I still miss him every day. My heart aches at the idea that he didn't get to meet his great-grandchildren. But I do feel that the hole in my heart is mending. Getting to know him as a child and as an adult in new ways brings peace to my troubled soul and fills me with pride to be his daughter. My grief has moved in stages this past decade and I have come to feel his joyful presence as I move through life, rather than feelings of anger at his leaving me.

"Grief," the author and psychotherapist Francis Weller said a podcast interview with Anderson Cooper in October of 2024, "is the nit between us – to stay in relationship with them is to stay in the tender melancholy of their absence." Tears we shed in grief Weller said, "are holy tears -showing how much we loved." I especially loved his thought that "grief is a powerful solvent, it can soften the hardest places in us. It can loosen and open our hearts again."

This family history project has softened my grief and opened my heart. I have created a container for memories of my father that can hold my love and be shared and passed down through the generations.

My five families became part of what made Seattle the remarkable city it is today. My family history reveals that relationships and connections, personal and professional, shape not just the citizens of a city, but the city itself. As I look back 150 years, I see the generational passing of values and pride in the city that we call home.

"Mom," my son Jack said to me one day, "I really appreciate how you treat every person with warmth and as if they are the most important person in the word."

This was a tremendous compliment to receive from my adult son. As I contemplate this reflection, I see where it comes from – DNA passed along for generations that, nurtured by loving, warm parents, turned me into an archetype of my family. As I contemplate this fate, I realize that we are all perhaps some kind of mash up of our family members that came before us, the same substance reshaped in every generation.

The work on this book has humbled me as I contemplate my ancestors and the long reach of time. I'm awakened to the realization that each of my ancestors visited the world only briefly – 50, 60, maybe 80 years. The time we are granted is but a blip. These thoughts, however, do not defeat me. I'm empowered to make the most of my time on the world stage. We *should* see our lives as fleeting and as a gift of time to explore what brings meaning to us. Stories from the past come together to make our present time. Stories we create today build the foundation for the future.

Does it matter that people lived, loved and laughed? I believe it does. It matters because each of us matters. We each must reckon with what path to take in life and what our priorities and values are. We are compelled by human instinct to make a difference. And make a difference we do. Even if we don't receive a Nobel prize, we each impact the world through our labor, our families, our connections, our acts of kindness, our acts of generosity and compassion. The waves that emanate from each of us outward into the universe connect us to all others and reverberate onward.

"If nothing in the universe is different, even better, because I exist," writes Daniel Taylor in *The Healing Power of Stories*, "then I am hard pressed to justify my next breath. It is difficult for me to see why anything I am or do is meaningful unless I begin to understand my connectedness to others, to the past, and to the future. That connectedness is primarily the connectedness of story – of lives interwoven over time in a purposeful plot."[649]

Taylor believes that the stories we choose to tell and pass on to the next generation define us. I agree. I choose to tell stories about my parents, Irwin and Betty Lou Treiger, my grandparents, Rose and Sam Treiger and Jack and Elizabeth Friedlander. Others that I knew and have some memory of, include Anne Friedlander and Belle (Singerman) Friedlander. Telling stories about these ancestors allows me to recall my childhood in a deeper, more meaningful way. Then there are those who died before I was born - Lou Friedlander, Paul and Jenny Singerman, Victor and Ada Staadecker, Sam and Augusta Friedlander – they impacted me in in ways that I'm still discovering.

It's the stories that we tell ourselves and others that define who we are. What stories will we choose to tell our children? Why? What stories will they choose to tell in turn?

I chose to tell these stories and connect back in time to my ancestors and forward in time to my descendants. Through this telling, I learn that I matter, if for no other reason than I was born, given the name of my great-grandmother, Chaya Tsivia, provided a heritage, and blessed with a family. But there is much more. I learn that I, like each of my ancestors, am a flawed human who must constantly recalibrate my actions and often atone for my mistakes – big and small. None of the people whose lives I share with you were without flaws, but the good they did changed the world.

I'm so grateful to have a loving mother who, at 89 is going strong, two wonderful brothers and their families, four children who I adore, a daughter-in-law and two sons-in-law and five grandchildren (my dividends)[650] who I dream about each night and of whom I watch endless videos that their parents send. To my children, I say, you are spectacular humans and I hope that you learn from the stories I've shared and gain a tiny understanding of your place in the universe.

"What you leave behind," Pericles said, "is not what is engraved in stone monuments, but what is woven into the lives of others."

I hope that you weave these stories into your lives and share them with your own children. Allow them to be a pebble in the pond, whose impact starts small but grows as it gets further away from the center. Let's learn from the people who came before us and use our flawed humanity to make a difference today and in the future.

APPENDIX A

Here are some steps that you can take to get started:

- First, sketch a family tree going back as far as you can – see how much you know about each member of your family.
- Make a list of people to interview; contact them and record an interview (audio or video).
- Start with a Google search – you may be surprised.
- Go to the library (or its website) to search for books about the places your ancestors are from or for books that mention them. Make an appointment with a genealogy librarian – they will guide you.
- As you read, take notes and allow the relevant footnotes to guide your next research step.
- Use Ancestry (free at Seattle libraries); Family Search (The Church of Jesus Christ of Latter-Day Saints genealogy site); Genealogy Bank (separates searches into newspaper articles, obituaries, US Federal Census reports, and more); and JewishGen (if relevant).
- University Archives – if there are archives at your local university, it may be helpful. In my case, the University of Washington Jewish Archive was a fantastic resource.
- Newspaper Archives – you may have to subscribe to the digital version of the paper to get access – it's worth it.
- Timelines – of a city, county or world history – can be found on-line with a Google search. This will put your family's story into historical perspective.

- Old Photos. Look in the attic and basement of your parents or grandparents. Often there is a notation on the backside letting us know who is in the photo and the year and/or place. Other photos can be found through the university archives and local museums. I found amazing old photos in the University of Washington Special Collections and the Museum of History and Industry (Mohai). These photos can be ordered for use in a book or a presentation (licensing fee).
- Court records.
- Make a list of questions you wish you could ask your ancestors – this can be a directional guide.
- Go to places of interest if you can. Places where they lived, worked, and played. U.S. Federal Census reports provide addresses of homes people lived in. The library often has old phone books and business records that can give you exact addresses of businesses and residences. I was lucky that many of the locations of interest are here in Seattle. I didn't travel to Europe (except Samke) to see where the family originated. I drove to Portland, where the Treigers and Victor Staadecker got their start in the Pacific Northwest. Utilize Google maps to locate places, both local and overseas.
- Keep good notes and records of who you interview, what you read and where you find your information.
- Create a timeline of your family's milestones. Use a different color typeface for each family and put it all in one document. Using this method, it's easy to see what happens to each family in a certain time frame.
- Create a bibliography as you go.
- Be open to twists and turns along the road and enjoy the ride.

ENDNOTES

1. Walters, Penny, *The Psychology of Searching,* United Kingdom (2020), 23.
2. Two Jewish Houses of Prayer.
3. *See* Welcome to the Pioneer Association of the State of Washington! (wapioneers.com)
4. The exception in my family was Victor Staadecker who came to America and went into the Millinery business in Portland. To learn more about Jewish peddlers, see Diner, Hasia, *Roads Taken: The Great Jewish Migration to the New World and the Peddlers who Forged the Way*, Yale University Press (New Haven) 2015.
5. *See* Asaka, Megan, *Seattle from the Margins: Exclusion, Erasure, and the Making of a Pacific Coast City,* University of Washington Press, Seattle (2022).
6. Watt, Roberta Frye, *The Story of Seattle*, Seattle, Lowman and Hanford Company (1932).
7. Bagley, Clarence, *History of Seattle*, Vol. II, 317-318, The S.J. Clarke Publishing Company (Chicago) (1916).
8. Speidel, William, *Sons of the Profits or, There's No Business Like Grow Business! The Seattle Story, 1851-1901,* Nettle Creek Publishing Company (Seattle) (1967).
9. Sale, Roger, *Seattle Past to Present*, University of Washington Press (Seattle), (1976, 2019).
10. Asaka, *Seattle From the Margins.*
11. Raczki's current population is 2,100. *See* Wikipedia, Raczki Podlaskie Voivodeship.
12. Paul's birth is recorded differently in various sources. The Washington Death Index records Paul's birth year as 1845. Ancestry dates Paul's birth as 1847 (Treigonoff Family Tree) and as 1848 based on the 1880 census. Paul applied for U.S. Passports three times – each one lists a different birthdate: January 10, 1847; February 9, 1847; January 20, 1849. Charles Bagley in the History of Seattle used February 9, 1849. Bagley, *History of Seattle*, Vol. II, 317-318.
13. Bialystok is city in Poland, not the name of a character in Mel Brooks' *Springtime for Hitler.*
14. *Memorial Book of Suwalki, Poland,* JewishGen, (New York) (2020), 14.
15. *Id.* 37. 1853 saw a cholera epidemic that "slew masses of people." *Id.* 20.
16. *Id.* 14.

17. *Id.* 555-86; 609-10. Raczki's Jewish community was religiously observant, but because of its proximity to the Prussian border, it was influenced by the Haskala (Jewish Enlightenment) and the ideas of Moses Mendelssohn. The *Haskalah* sought to preserve the Jews as a separate, unique collective and worked for a cultural and moral renewal, especially a revival of the Hebrew language. It also advocated integration of the Jews into surrounding societies, encouraging the study of native vernacular and adoption of modern values, culture and appearance. Finally, the movement believed that these efforts would lead to economic productivity and upward mobility. *See* Wikipedia, Haskalah - Haskalah - Wikipedia
18. *Memorial Book of Suwalki, Poland,* 24.
19. "Pioneer Merchant of Seattle is Dead," *Seattle Daily Times*, August 28, 1915.
20. Memorial Book of Suwalki, Poland.Jewish Gen -- https://kehilalinks.jewishgen.org/Raczki/Emigration.html. *Memorial Book of Suwalki, Poland,* 17.
21. *Memorial Book of Suwalki, Poland,* 37. See also, Ancestry.com.
22. *Memorial Book of Suwalki, Poland.*
23. Jewish Museum of the American West - http://www.jmaw.org/toklas-jewish-washington/ In 1870, Santa Cruz had a US Census population of 8,743.
24. Interview with Jack Friedlander, Archives of the University of Washington (December 16, 1975), Paul was Jack's maternal grandfather.
25. Wikipedia, "First Transcontinental Railroad": First transcontinental railroad - Wikipedia
26. Bagley, *History of Seattle*, 317. The covered wagon story repeated in *A Family of Strangers: Building a Jewish Community in Washington State.* This book states, "[Paul] arrived [to Seattle] in 1874 via San Francisco, having crossed the country on his way to California by covered wagon." Cone, Molly, Droker, Howard, Williams Jacqueline, Eskenazi, Stuart, *A Family of Strangers,* 2nd edition, (Seattle) (2003) 19.
27. Friedlander Interview 6.
28. *See*, Diner, *Roads Taken.*
29. *Id.*, 13-83.
30. Born 1877.
31. Wikipedia, "Alice B. Toklas," Alice B. Toklas - Wikipedia
32. Jewish Museum of the American West.
33. Friedlander Interview 6. They married in San Francisco in January of 1879. "Matrimony Notice," *San Francisco Bulletin*, January 15, 1879. *See also, History of Seattle*, 318.
34. For all dollar conversions, I use the CPI Inflation Calculator. https://www.officialdata.org/us/inflation/1882?amount=10000
35. Bagley, *History of Seattle*, Vol. II, 698.
36. Jewish Museum of the American West, Ohaveth Shalom - Ohaveth Sholem: The First, Short-Lived Synagogue of Seattle – JMAW – Jewish Museum of the American West. Some of the founding Jews of Seattle included "Bailey and Babette Gatzert, the David Kaufmans, whose daughter, Sara Kaufman Rucker, was the first Jewish child born in Seattle and the Samuel Frauenthals. *Family of*

Strangers, 15. The Schwabachers had a hardware store and also opened a wholesale grocery in Seattle in 1869. Bailey Gatzert, who was elected Seattle's sixth Mayor in 1875 and married a Schwabacher, was put in charge of the operation and "made Schwabacher's the leading wholesaler in Seattle." *Family of Strangers*, 15-16.

37. Seattle Times Timeline. http://old.seattletimes.com/news/local/seattle_history/articles/timeline.html
38. Located at 4th and University. This became the University of Washington.
39. Horton's Seattle First National Bank.
40. *See* Asaka, *Seattle from the Margins*, 25.
41. Bagley. *History of Seattle*, 246.
42. Speidel, *Sons of the Profits*, 217.
43. *Id.*
44. *Id.* 57-80
45. Costello, Gilbert, S., *Manuscript History of Seattle's First Department Store, Embracing San Francisco Store, Toklas & Singerman, MacDougall & Southwick* (1924). Place of publication not identified; publisher not identified (located at Seattle Public Library).
46. *Pacific Coast Architectural Database*, University of Washington Libraries, Toklas, Singerman and Company, Store #1, Pioneer Square. PCAD - Toklas, Singerman and Company, Store #1, Pioneer Square, Seattle, WA (washington.edu)
47. Costello, *Manuscript History of Seattle's First Department Store.*
48. Jewish Museum of American West.
49. Costello, Manuscript.
50. Costello, Gilbert, S., Chronological History of the MacDougal & Southwick Company (1924). Though Costello doesn't mention Ferdinand Toklas coming up to Seattle with Paul, the article I found in the Jewish Museum of the American West indicates that 1876 Seattle City Directory lists Ferdinand Toklas as living in the New England Hotel.
51. Costello, Gilbert, S., Manuscript History of Seattle's First Department Store (quoting Post Intelligencer).
52. *San Francisco Bulletin*, January 15, 1879. My grandfather, Jack Friedlander, believed that Jenny was born in Breslau, Germany. *See* Jack Friedlander Interview, 1. But the marriage announcements states otherwise.
53. Wikipedia, "Kepno," Kępno - Wikipedia
54. Asaka, *Seattle on the Margins*, 164.
55. *Id.* Asaka notes that "[d]uring the 1920s, Yesler Hill had emerged as a center of commercial sex after a widespread crackdown on prostitution near the waterfront; the area then acquired the nickname Profanity Hill." *Id.*
56. Bagley, *History of Seattle* - Seattle and King County Milestones - HistoryLink.org
57. *Family of Strangers*, 19.
58. Sale, *Seattle Past to Present*, 35.
59. Costello Manuscript.
60. *Id.* The lease was signed December 9, 1879. *Id.*
61. PI, February 7, 1880.
62. Costello Manuscript.

63. Costello Chronology. Alaska Gold rush was 1897.
64. I only found one source that includes Auerbach in the company name. "Auerbach, Toklas and Singerman," writes *A Family of Strangers*, "opening in Seattle in 1875, became one of the state's first department store, the first firm in the city to use electric lighting (1866) and the first to install a telephone (1883)." Family of Strangers, 19. But the source cited by the Family of Strangers is the *Jewish Museum of the American West*, which does not actually call the firm "Auerbach, Toklas and Singerman." It merely mentions that these three were partners in the endeavor.
65. Costello, Manuscript.
66. *Id.* Another reason the store moved is that the Squire Opera House closed in September. Because of the lack of railroad terminus in Seattle, the greatest musical and theatrical talent found it too challenging to come to Seattle, and the theater couldn't survive.
67. *Id.*
68. Bageley, *History of Seattle*, Vol. 2, 686.
69. PI, September 20, 1882.
70. Costello Manuscript.
71. Costello Manuscript, quoting Weekly Pacific Tribune, April 10, 1878.
72. Costello Chronology.
73. Thomas Edison offered electric light bulbs for sale to American consumers in 1880.
74. Costello Manuscript.
75. *See* Sale, *Seattle Past to Present*, 37-49.
76. When Belle turned six, a new superintendent of public education was hired in Seattle – Frank J. Barnard. Between 1891 and 1900, Mr. Barnard oversaw construction of fifteen schools. As Seattle grew, enrollment in the school district went from 1,500 students in 1885 to 6,650 in 1893. Johnson Partnership, Seattle School District No. 1 History, General Historical and Building Context, Appendix 3, A3-1 (June 2015).
77. PI, August 19, 1894.
78. *See* Seattle Times, February 16, 1901; June 5, 1905, Tyee Yearbook, 1900.
79. *See* Seattle Public Schools, 1862-2000: Bailey Gatzert Elementary School, HistoryLink.org, Essay 10511, Posted September 7, 2013 (discusses Old South School).
80. Bagley, *History of Seattle*, 318. In a 1901 article about the Mason's Feast of the Pascal Lamb, held on the day before Good Friday, the officers of the Washington Chapter Rose Croix No. 1 were listed. Paul Singerman was mentioned as the "Almoner," who is responsible for the well-being of lodge members and their families. He remains in contact with members who are unwell, and also maintains a discreet presence in the lives of widows of former members, so that the lodge may readily assist them should they find themselves in any particular need. Of necessity, the Almoner must be well versed in local and national Masonic charities and the scope of their charitable work, so as to offer advice to those who might qualify for such assistance." Wikipedia, Masonic Lodge Officers - https://en.wikipedia.org/wiki/Masonic_lodge_officer#Almoner

81. Washington Jewish Historical Society, *The Jewish Experience in Washington State: A Chronology 1845-2005*,3rd edition (Seattle 2006), 9.
82. *Id.*, 10.
83. Costello Manuscript, quoting PI July 17, 1887.
84. Costello Manuscript.
85. Jewish Museum of the American West, citing Northwest Real Estate and Building Review, March-April 1891, vol. I, number 2, p. 5.
86. These hours were in accordance with a request by the Clerk's Protection Association.
87. Seattle PI, Advertisement, April 9, 1888.
88. Costello Manuscript. They had $150,000 ($5.1 million in today's dollars) worth of insurance to cover this loss. *Id.*
89. *Id.*
90. *Id.*
91. *Id.*
92. *Id.*
93. PI, *The Fire*, June 24, 1889, quoted by Costello Manuscript. The article indicates that Toklas, Singerman & Co. opened offices in the Longacre building on the corner of Third and Cherry streets. *Id.*
94. Costello Manuscript.
95. *See* Costello Manuscript, Getting on Their Feet.
96. *Alice B. Toklas Was Once a Seattleite*, The Seattle Times, March 9, 1967.
97. Brown, Rebecca, "Alice B. Toklas Lived in Seattle Before She Met Gertrude Stein," *The Stranger*, September 9, 2015.
98. The PI reported their attendance at a luncheon at the home of J.F. Eshelman at 922 Washington street in October of 1892. PI, October 2, 1892.
99. *Alice B. Toklas Was Once a Seattleite*, The Seattle Times, March 9, 1967.
100. Friedlander Interview, 7.
101. November 11, 1889.
102. *Family of Strangers* at 103-04.
103. *Id.*, 105.
104. *Id.*, 83.
105. Friedlander Interview, 22.
106. As an adult, Belle donated the everlasting light that currently graces the main sanctuary. Interview with Betty Lou Treiger (2022).
107. *Id.*
108. PI, March 26, 1889.
109. Seattle Daily Times, September 27, 1903, p. 43.
110. This was the exact hour that, one year before, the flames reached the Toklas and Singerman store.
111. Costello Manuscript, citing PI, June 7, 1890.
112. Jewish Museum of the American West, citing Northwest Real Estate and building Review, March-April 1891, volume 1, number 2, p.5.
113. Costello Manuscript, citing Northwest Real Estate Review.

114. Speidel, *Sons of The Profits*, 229.
115. Id. 238.
116. Id.
117. Costello manuscript, citing *Northwest Real Estate Review.*
118. Costello Manuscript, citing PI, July 16, 1891.
119. Just a few months before the Alaska Gold Rush began, a Courthouse Note in the PI, shed light on why Hyman Auerbach fell out of the picture.

"In the matter *Hyman Auerbach vs. Ferdinand Toklas*," notes the PI, "in a suit to recover the sum of $10,000 [$378,000 in today's dollars] wherein an attachment has been issued, plaintiff's attorneys have applied for a writ of garnishment against the Puget Sound National Bank in a hunt for funds. I.D. McCutheon has withdrawn from plaintiff's case and Messrs. White, Mondray and Felton appear." PI, February 1, 1897, Courthouse Notes. It must have been a doozy of a fight. I would love to know how Jenny felt about a legal battle between her brother and her husband's business partner. That couldn't have been easy. Sometimes, the only ones that win are the lawyers.

120. Speidel, *Sons of the Profits*, 306.
121. Asaka, *Seattle From the Margins*, 82-83.
122. Speidel, *Sons of the Profits*, 306-07.
123. Tyee Yearbook (1900) University of Washington Archive. Here is a link to the sheet music: https://digitalcollections.lib.washington.edu/digital/collection/sm/id/288/rec/27
124. Seattle Times, February 16, 1901. Louis is also noted in the PI as playing as part of Hadley's string quartet in December of 1903, at an Elks Memorial Service for Reverend W.D. Simonds. *See* PI December 7, 1903.
125. Society Page, PI January 20, 1901. For more on Whist see https://en.wikipedia.org/wiki/Whist
126. In preparation for the big move to the Lumber Exchange Building, Paul and Isidore held a "Removal Sale." "To the public," began their ad in the Seattle Times on December of 1902, "[o]ur removal sale will continue during the month of December. Undoubtedly our stores will be crowded tomorrow as it has been for the past five weeks. The people of Seattle appreciate genuine reductions. You are not in danger in our store of buying a 'gold brick.' Our goods are all marked in plain figures and our sale is conducted on a 'one price' principal. We repeat we have no damaged goods, bankrupt stock, nor do we do business under assumed names." Seattle Times, December 5, 1902.
127. Sherrard, Jean, Seattle Now &Then: *The Lumber Exchange Building 1904*, March 30, 2019, citing the Seattle Daily Times.
128. Id.
129. Seattle Times, September 28, 1902.
130. Id.
131. The Seattle Sunday Times, September 27, 1903.
132. Jack Friedlander Interview.
133. Id.
134. See "Pioneer Merchant of Seattle is Dead," Seattle Daily Times, August 28, 1915.

135. Seattle Times, November 22, 1903.
136. Seattle Times, May 5, 1904.
137. The Seattle Daily Times, May 5, 1904.
138. Lincoln Hotel, Downtown Seattle. PCAD. PCAD - Lincoln Hotel, Downtown, Seattle, WA (washington.edu)
139. It was at this time that Paul changed the name of his firm from Toklas, Singerman & Co. to Singerman and Sons and made Isidore and Louis partners.
140. *See* Deed, dated May 31, 1904, File No. 299202, King County. Clinton C. Filson (1850-1919) moved to Washington in 1890. He opened a series of general stores, moving his operation to the downtown corridor in 1897. His company became well known for high quality outdoor gear such as clothing, boots, sleeping bags and blankets that could withstand harsh weather – perfect for prospectors heading to Alaska. After his death in 1919, his wife, Winifred, took over as President. The business remained in the family until 1970. *See* Poyner, Fred IV, "C.C. Filson Company", HistoryLink.org Essay 11150, posted November 25, 2015.
141. Seattle Times, July 8, 1904
142. Landmark Preservation Board Report on Designation: Gaslight Inn/Singerman House -1727 15th Avenue, 5.
143. Seattle Daily Times, May 1, 1905.
144. Seattle Times, May 5, 1907. The Millers didn't live in the house – they rented it out. One of the families they rented to from 1910 to 1915 was Nathan Eckstein and his wife Mina (nee Schwabacher). The Ecksteins moved out in 1915 and in 1918 became a single room boarding house until it was purchased by Steven Bennett who turned into an Inn and did the work to give the home Landmark status with the city of Seattle.
145. Landmark Preservation Report.
146. The Seattle Sunday Times, July 14, 1907, p. 21.
147. "Isidore R. Singerman, the eldest son of Paul Singerman, the well-known merchant returned to this city Tuesday night from an extended tour of the continent, bringing with him his bride, formerly Miss Gertrude Stern of New York City. Mr. Singerman was united in marriage with Miss Stern in Delmonico's in New York City on November 10, and at the same time and place her sister Miss Grace Stern was joined in marriage to Arthur Miller, a prominent New York merchant. The sisters are nieces of Henry B. Harris the well-known theatrical manager and granddaughter of William Harris, secretary of the Theatrical Trust." Seattle Times, November 27, 1908. Gertrude was known for painting miniatures. See "Numbers Visit Contest Exhibit," Seattle Daily Times, Oct. 17, 1915 ("Mrs. Gertrude Singerman of Seattle has three delicately executed miniatures. 'Emily,' 'Youth' and 'An Old-Fashioned Girl.' Mrs. Singerman is a serious student of art and possesses the faculty of subtle delineation which gives life to her faces."); "Miniatures by Local Artist Exhibited on Fine Arts Walls," Seattle Daily Times, Oct. 29, 1916 ("Being a zealous student [Mrs. Singerman's] work grows constantly more interesting and her 'Portrait of Mrs. A.' is truly lovely."). Gertrude died March 6, 1956 in Seattle.
148. For more on the life of Anne Friedlander, *see* chapter 4.

149. Alaska-Yukon-Pacific Exposition Collection, 1906-1910, Archives West. www.swest.orbiscascade.org
150. Seattle Times, May 10, 1910.
151. Ancestry.com.
152. Seattle Times, July 11, 1913.
153. The 1915 Seattle Directory lists Paul's address as 709 15th.
154. The Seattle Times, August 8, 1915.
155. "Pioneer Merchant of Seattle is Dead," The Seattle Times, August 28, 1915.
156. Seattle Times, August 3, 1915.
157. Seattle Times, October, 29, 1915.
158. Seattle Times, September 8, 1915.
159. Seattle Times, November 19, 1915.
160. Seattle Times, Dec. 6, 1923.
161. Seattle Times, Dec. 27, 1923.
162. Friedlander Interview.
163. *Id.*
164. *Id.*
165. Jack Friedlander and Paul Friedlander, both deceased.
166. Betty Lou (Friedlander) Treiger, Jackie (Friedlander) Goldfarb, Paul Friedlander Jr. and John L. Friedlander
167. Louis Treiger, Karen Treiger, Ken Treiger, Susan (Goldfarb) Wolfe, Steven Goldfarb, David Goldfarb, Laura (Friedlander) Mattita, Benjamin Friedlander, Sam Friedlander.
168. Mordechai Treiger, Avraham Treiger, Shmuel Treiger, Olivia Owens Treiger, Eitan Treiger, Elisheva Goldberg, Jack Goldberg, Shoshana Goldberg, Esther Goldberg, Jack Wolfe, Sam Wolfe, Jake Mattita, and Marlee Mattita.
169. Theodore Irwin Goldberg, Caroline Goldberg, Samuel Isseroff, Evelyn Isseroff and Eden Isseroff.
170. Theodore and Caroline.
171. Nanny's date of death was September 19, 1972.
172. Which included a ballet titled "A Legend of Egypt." Seattle Times, June 15, 1919.
173. *Juedischen Gemeinden in Baden*, 198-200.
174. Interview with William Staadecker, Jewish Archives Project, November 6, 1981.
175. Letter Elizabeth Mirels to Ken Treiger and Lauren Antonoff, February 13, 2008.
176. Rabbi Zacharias Staadecker served as the Rabbi of Merchingen for 27 years. Remarkably, someone messaged us through ancestry with information about the marriage of Barbara's parents. It seems that Barbara's parents, Abraham Rosenfeld and Elise Thalheimer, were married on May 4,1840 in Merchinger. The Rabbi officiating at their wedding was Zacharias Staadecker. Marriage Protocol of Merchingen Jewish Community. See Treigenoff Family Tree, Ancestry.com.
177. William Staadecker Interview.
178. *Id.* There is a fascinating twist to Uncle Abraham and Aunt Mina's legacy. One of their granddaughters became a Countess – Countess Rosie Waldeck. An article in the Jewish Transcript noted a visit by a Countess visiting her Uncle Victor

Staadecker. *Distinguished Guest Seattle Visitor,* Seattle Jewish Transcript, January 13, 1939, Social and Personal Page. One of Abraham and Mina's daughters, Rose, married three times. Her third husband was Count Waldeck of Hungary. This third marriage to the Count was a marriage of convenience. In Nazi Germany Jews became stateless, with no citizenship or passport. The Count married her as a favor. After the marriage, Rosie received Hungarian citizenship and a passport, allowing her to escape. Interview with Ernest Latham Jr. February 15, 2021. Rosie was a journalist and an author of two memoirs and several novels. Victor Staadecker also helped to bring Abraham and Mina's other daughter, Ella, to Seattle, to live. *See* Seattle Daily Times, May 23, 1937. For more information about the Countess, see my blog, soyouwanttourteaholocaust.wordpress.com and search "countess." There is a series of blog posts on the Countess, written in 2021.

179. The Talmud is the central text of Rabbinic Judaism and the primary source of Jewish religious law and Jewish theology. Until the advent of modernity, in nearly all Jewish communities, the Talmud was the centerpiece of Jewish cultural life and is foundational to "all Jewish thought and aspirations", serving also as "the guide for the daily life" of Jews. Wikipedia, the Talmud. Talmud - Wikipedia
180. William Staadecker Interview.
181. Population statistics for New York City: http://physics.bu.edu/~redner/projects/population/cities/newyork.html
182. Little Germany, Wikipedia: https://en.wikipedia.org/wiki/Little_Germany,_Manhattan; See also: https://www.researchgate.net/publication/305770017_German_Immigrants_in_New_York_City_1840-1920
183. Silverman, Janette, *Stories They Never Told Us*, Relativa Tree (United States, 2024).
184. William Staadecker Interview.
185. *Id.* Uncle William did not know the name of the relatives in Idaho.
186. *Id.* Ignatz Lowengart was born in 1862 and before moving to Portland, lived in San Francisco. There, in 1896, he married Leah Gerst and worked for the W.P. Fuller Company. By 1900 he had moved to Portland and he and Leah had a daughter named Ruth.
187. See Holmes, Tao, Tao, *When Going Out Without a Hat was Ground for Scandal*, Atlas Obscura, March 21, 2016.
188. The Sunday Oregonian, page 9, January 7, 1900 - https://oregonnews.uoregon.edu/lccn/sn83045782/1900-01-07/ed-1/seq-9/ocr/
189. *See* US Census Report 1900.
190. Wikipedia, History of Portland. https://en.wikipedia.org/wiki/History_of_Portland,_Oregon#:~:text=Early%2020th%20century,-Portland%20in%201910&text=This%20event%20increased%20recognition%20of,1900%20to%20207%2C214%20in%201910.
191. A 1907 article in the Illustrated Milliner shared that Lowenart & Co. "occupies probably more floor space than any millinery jobbing house of New York city, does an astonishingly large business." The Illustrated Milliner, July 1907, Vol. III, #7, p. 34. By 1915, Lowengart & Co. was housed in a seven story concrete building on Broadway and Burnside with lots of windows and employed between 150 – 250 employees.

192. 1900 US Census Report.
193. Eisenberg, Ellen, "Jews in Oregon," Oregon Encyclopedia, Oregon Historical Society. https://www.oregonencyclopedia.org/articles/jews-in-oregon/
194. *Id.*
195. Because most of them had spent a few years in New York, like Victor.
196. Eisenberg, Ellen, "Jews in Oregon."
197. *Id.*
198. *Id.* This stands in stark contrast to the experience of the second wave of Jewish immigrants from Eastern Europe, of which my great-grandfather, Yisroel (Israel) Aryeh Treiger was a part. *See* chapter 5.
199. Sylvia Epstein, Interview with Jewish Historical society, November 29, 1973.
200. Seattle Times, May 1, 1904, Society Page. They married on August 7, 1904. *Id.* The Wolff family remained close to the Seattle Staadeckers, with frequent visits. Their daughter Sylvia was one of my grandmother Elizabeth's closest friends.
201. Wikipedia, "Timeline of Seattle," Timeline of Seattle - Wikipedia
202. *See* Kueter, Vince, "Seattle Through the Years," The Seattle Times, Nov. 13, 2001.
203. The east side of Western Avenue, between Spring and Madison Streets.
204. This building is a Seattle Landmark. It was home to the National Grocery Company until 1930 and was later occupied by small manufacturing and distributing firms and has been used as an office building since the late 1960's. *See* Wikipedia, "National Building," National Building - Wikipedia
205. William Staadecker Interview. These early years of Staadecker & Co. were not without scandal among the employees. On October 20, 1906, the Seattle Daily Times reported that, "Miss Linda Stewart, a young woman who ... has been employed by Staadecker and Company, wholesale milliners at 1012 Western Ave has been placed under arrest pending the hearing of a search warrant complaint sworn by Miss Clair Cunningham, a stenographer in the Bailey Building Office, who alleges that diamonds, pearls, emeralds and other valuable jewelry and together with articles of wearing apparel had been stolen from a trunk belonging to herself and sister who roomed in the house occupied by Miss Stewarts' mother." *See "Arrest Girl on Suspicion of Theft: Officer Takes Milliner's Employee into Custody After Two Young Women Friends Miss Valuable Jewelry and Monday,"* Seattle Times, October 20, 1906, Front Page.
206. William Staadecker Interview.
207. I asked my Aunt and my mom if they ever heard any such rumors about their grandparents. They both said "no."
208. *See* King County birth records; see FamilySearch.org
209. Jewish Transcript, Social Page, November 7, 1924.
210. *See* Jewish Transcript, May 28, 1926.
211. William Staadecker Interview. I cannot tell what level of religious observance they had in their home, but the Jewish Transcript Social Page, dated April 6, 1928 notes the Staadeckers "entertained with a Seder dinner at their home on Wednesday evening."
212. Epstein Interview.

213. National Council of Jewish Woman Yearbook 1927-1928, University of Washington Archive Collection, 3, https://www.jstor.org/stable/community.29379976. Just before this section of the Forward, Mrs. Sternberger writes: "Jewish womanhood, through the National Council of Jewish Women, has been enabled to meet one great test and challenge after another. The Jewish woman has been taught the privileges and responsibilities of the ballot. She has been enabled to participate in great national and world movements. She was competent to care for the hundreds of thousands of Jewish immigrants who have streamed into America for these thirty-five years. She was found prepared to lift European Jewish womanhood from the depths of confusion and despair after the World War. She is the companion and teacher of the Jewish women in Rural America. She is the priestess leading many to the alter of Judaism and carrying its spirit into the home. She has fused differing minds into a unity of aspiration and purpose." *Id.*
214. *Id.* at 13.
215. *Id.*
216. *Id.*
217. Only five years after this yearbook was published, Jack Friedlander and Elizabeth Staadecker, children of two women on this Social Committee, married. Twelve years before the publication of the NCJW yearbook, the Seattle Times reported on an NCJW Charity Ball and Cotillion. The event was held at Broadway Hall on February 13, 1914. "Decorations will consist of American Flags," the Seattle Times reported, "red white and blue bunting, palms and greens. . . Music will be furnished by Dewey's orchestra ... The following will participate in the second and third figures: ... Miss Gertrude Staadecker." Seattle Times, Society Page, February 13, 1914. Gertrude, Victor's half sister, was featured in this concert only eight years after her arrival in Seattle.
218. Seattle Jewish Transcript, Social Page, April 6, 1928. *See also*, Seattle Jewish Transcript, November 16, 1928 (noting Ada's involvement in NCJW events to raise money for a scholarship fund).
219. William Staadecker Interview.
220. *Id.*
221. "A Seattle Magician Who Takes Payroll Dollars from Hats," Seattle Times, March 16, 1930.Victor brought his brother, Sam to Seattle in 1906.
222. *Id.*
223. *Id.*
224. William Staadecker Interview. Uncle William recalled that they would park their car in middle of the wooden street. *Id.*
225. "Wholesale Milliners Plan Big Building," Seattle Times, May 9, 1909.
226. William Staadecker Interview.

227. Mimi Lee married a man named Berman and Uncle William describes being "invited every year for two or three weeks" to their summer home in Pend Orielles in Eastern Washington. They would "swim, boat, and have nothing but fun." William Staadecker Interview. In her 60's Mimi became a well known photographer and as Uncle William states, "'[s]he's really a superb photographer. I have many of her photographs. She just did the photograph of Ansel Adams in the book he published. ... She's just amazing. She's absolutely a celebrity today. I grew up with her. We are very close friends." *Id.* The Smithsonian has a collection of Mimi's photographs of famous people: https://www.aaa.si.edu/collections/photographs-artists-taken-mimi-jacobs-photographer-9285
228. Letter from William Staadecker to Betty Lou Treiger, July 19, 1978.
229. Lee, Mimi, Garfield High School, Composition #4 (May 2, 1929) at 1.
230. *Id.*
231. *Id.* 1-2. It's hard to imagine Nanny, who went by Elizabeth, as a little girl being called Beth. Even my mom never knew she went by Beth as a child. She was skeptical until I showed her Mimi's essay. "I guess she did," my mother conceded.
232. *Id.* at 1.
233. *Id.* at 2.
234. *Id.*
235. *Id.*
236. *Id.* at 3.
237. *Id.* at 2-3.
238. *Id.* at 3.
239. *Id.*
240. "Seattle Magician," Seattle Times, March 16, 1930.
241. *Id.*
242. *Id.*
243. *See e.g.*, Seattle Jewish Transcript note that "Mr. Victor Staadecker returned last week from a two week trip to the East." Seattle Jewish Transcript, Society Page, May 24, 1928.
244. William Staadecker Interview.
245. Grosvenor Glenn, *From Coast to Coast, The Illustrated Milliner*, January 1915.
246. *Id.*
247. "Aigrettes May be Sold Openly," Seattle Times, July 28, 1909.
248. *Id.*
249. *Id.*
250. "Plume Thieves Again Abroad in this City – Upwards of $2,000 in Ostrich and Birds of Paradise Feathers taken from Fifth Avenue Store," Seattle Times, July 30, 1912.
251. *Id.*
252. "Masons to Put on Unusual Work," Seattle Times, June 11, 1908
253. In reporting on Victor's 70th birthday celebration, the Seattle Jewish Transcript described Victor as "one of Seattle's pioneers and a leading figure in civic and philanthropic affairs of the city." Seattle Jewish Transcript, Social Page, January 6, 1939.
254. Where he served as President.

255. A Jewish Fraternal Association. A chapter was established in Seattle in 1883. See The Jewish Experience in Washington State, 9.
256. A golf club, established in 1922. The Jews built this club because the antisemitism of the day excluded Jews from membership at golf clubs.
257. Established in 1928, to raise money for Seattle's Jewish organization. Victor was a member of the Executive Committee, which was "composed of representatives from each Congregation in the city and also of Bnai Brith. The most prominent Jewish men in the community have fallen wholeheartedly in line with the Community Chest." "All Local Jewry Back Community Chest: Most Prominent Jews of Seattle Gladly Serving on Executive Committee for United Campaign for National Jewish Charity," Seattle Jewish Transcript, March 9, 1928.
258. Seattle Times, October 30, 1921.
259. Seattle Jewish Transcript, May 27, 1924.
260. Seattle Jewish Transcript, May 21, 1926, Society Page mentions that Ada and Victor will be home to welcome guests in honor of William Bonnar's confirmation (260 39th). It is unclear why Elizabeth, his twin sister, was not mentioned. She may have been at Annie Wright School in Tacoma for some time (boarding school) and perhaps she missed too many classes to be confirmed. I do not know.
261. Seattle Times, November 20, 1921.
262. Id.
263. Brazier, "Brechts Acquire Famous Old Home," Seattle Times, April 12, 1971.
264. William Staadecker Interview.
265. Id.
266. Id.
267. Seattle Jewish Transcript, Social Page, November 23, 1933.
268. "Wedding Joins Two Prominent Families Here," Seattle Daily Times , December 28, 1933.
269. Seattle Jewish Transcript, Society Page, December 29, 1933.
270. Id.
271. Id.
272. Id.
273. From the 1850 opera Lohengrin by German composer Richard Wagner, commonly known as "Here comes the bride." *See* Wikipedia, "Bridal Chorus."
274. Seattle Jewish Transcript, Society Page, December 29, 1933.
275. The case, known affectionately in Washington State, as *Friedlander I* – was in 1961, the year of my birth.
276. Interview with Jackie Goldfarb.
277. My mom, Betty Lou married Irwin Treiger and my Aunt Jackie married Alvin Goldfarb. Irwin died in 2013 and Alvin died in 2016.
278. William Staadecker Interview.

279. Emil Sick was the founder of Seattle's Rainier Brewery and the Seattle Rainiers baseball team. Sick was born in Tacoma in 1894, raised in Canada and moved his family to Seattle in 1933. "When, the Sick family moved to Seattle in 1933," Historylink.org explains, "they occupied the spacioius Victor Staadecker residence in the upscale Denny Blaine neighborhood." Cipalla, Rita, "Sick, Emil George (1894-1964), HistoryLink.Org Essay 22867, Posted 1/02.24.
280. "Brechts Acquire Famous Old Home," Seattle Times, April 12, 1971. Emil Sicks sold the house in 1964 to someone who rented the home to the Canadian Consulate-General, who purchased it in 1967. In 1932, Victor, Ada and William moved to an apartment on 1223 Spring Street. Sometime later, they moved to Magnolia to be near their daughter, Elizabeth (Nanny).
281. "1223 Spring Street," HistoryLink.
282. *Id.*
283. "Yale's Limit on Jewish Enrollment Lasted Until the 1960's," New York Times, April 3, 1986.
284. *Id.*
285. "It would take about a year for the full effect of The Depression to hit Seattle and King County. Virtually every sector of the economy was hit. Exports through the Port of Seattle dropped, leaving maritime and dock workers unemployed. Construction, which had boomed in the 1920s, slowed dramatically. Wood products industries reduced production. Manufacturers lost orders and lay off workers or cut back their hours. Coal mining, which had been a foundation of the Puget Sound economy for decades, ended." Wilma, David, *The Great Depression*, History Link, March 6, 2020.
286. Interview with Joel Staadecker Jr.
287. William Staadecker Interview.
288. *Id.*
289. *See* Description of Staadecker & Company written by Irwin Treiger for Seattle Jewish Historical Society.
290. William Staadecker Interview.
291. Treiger, Irwin, Description of Staadecker & Co. for Seattle Jewish Historical Society.
292. William Staadecker Interview.
293. Treiger, Irwin, Description for Seattle Jewish Historical Society. *See also*, Berg, Clara, Best's Apparel (Seattle), History Link, March 8, 2022. Nordstrom was a shoe store before the merger with Bests.
294. William Staadecker Interview. Regarding decrease in hat wearing, *see* "History of Hats for Women, fashion-history-of-womens-hats," March 19, 2012; Holmes, Tao Tao, "When Going out Without a Hat was Grounds for Scandal," Atlas Obscura, March 21, 2016.
295. Angelos, Constantine, "William Staadecker; Jeweler Always Wanted to Be an Actor," Seattle Times, March 5, 1990.
296. Seattle Times, March 5, 1990.
297. Betty Lou Treiger Interview.
298. They lived at: 2536 40th Avenue West.

299. Betty Lou Treiger Interview.
300. Seattle Jewish Transcript, September 24, 1937.
301. *See* Seattle Jewish Transcript, May 25, 1964. In 1940, Victor Jr.'s family lived at 5411 E. 38th Street, Seattle. *See* 1940 Census Report
302. Victor Keating Staadecker III was known in the family by his nickname "Happy." According to my Aunt, he had developmental delays and needed care during his life.
303. Commander Victor Bonnar Staadecker, San Francisco Chronicle, January 16, 1973.
304. 1906 was the year that their father Joel died in Merchigen.
305. After Emmanuel's wife died, he moved to Seattle until his death in 1940.
306. Settled in Aberdeen, WA.
307. Of Sophie's other three children, Max came to the U.S., Hilda died before the Holocaust, and Robert was killed in battle during WWI. Staadecker Family Tree packet, Treiger Archive.
308. *See* Yad Vashem website of names of Victims of the Shoah. Betty's daughter Selma and her husband left after Hitler's rise to power and settled in Aberdeen.
309. The Talmud in Brachot 7b, states the following: Regarding the basic assumption that these homiletic interpretations of names are allusions to one's future, the Gemara asks: **From where do we** derive **that the name affects** one's life? **Rabbi Eliezer said** that **the verse says: "Go, see the works of the Lord, who has made desolations [*shamot*] upon the earth"** (Psalms 46:9). **Do not read** the word as ***shamot*, rather** as ***shemot*, names.** The names given to people are, therefore, "the works of the Lord upon the earth." Sefaria, Brachot 7b.

    Hakoisev, Rav Yaakov ben Rav Shlomo Ibn Chaviv, who was born in Spain around 1440, clarifies that parents' naming of a child is not related to receiving a prophetic vision, but "G-d inspired them to select a particular name that has significance unbeknown to the parents. Many years later, the aptness of the name may become apparent to all." Hakoisev.
310. MacDonald, Betty, *The Plague and I*, University of Washington Press (Seattle) (2016), 41-44.
311. *Id.* at 37.
312. Interview with Jackie (Friedlander) Goldfarb.
313. 15th Avenue NE and 150th Street.
314. Stiles, Victoria, NW Public Health, "King County: Tuberculosis and the Firland Sanatorium."
315. *Id.*
316. See Fircrest Website: https://www.dshs.wa.gov/dda/consumers-and-families/fircrest-residential-habilitation-center

317. In 1947, 48,833 people died in the United States of TB. Lewis, Sara, "Tuberculosis in the United States, 1947," April 1, 1949. In 2021, an estimated 1.6 million people died worldwide from TB. *See* Nolen, Stephanie, "Ending TB in Reach, But It's Still Top Killer," New York Times, Nov. 7, 2023. Sadly, 40% of the people with TB go undiagnosed and untreated. *Id.* "[N]ew medications – the first to come to market since the 1970's – can be taken as just a couple of pills each day, rather than as handfuls of tablets and painful injections, the way TB treatments have been delivered in the past." *Id.*
318. Bynum, Helen, *Spitting Blood: The History of Tuberculosis*, Oxford University Press, (Oxford) (2012), Xvi; xviii.
319. Goldfarb Interview.
320. Bynum, *Spitting Blood,* xxiii.
321. McDonald, *The Plague and I,* 98.
322. Mann, Thomas, *Magic Mountain*, Verlag & Knopf (Germany 1924) (English ed., 1927).
323. Firland Sanatorium, Wikipedia. Firland Sanatorium - Wikipedia
324. Mann, *Magic Mountain*, 122.
325. *Id.* at 218.
326. *Id.* at 643-644.
327. Firland, Wikipedia.
328. *Id.*
329. Betty Lou Treiger Interview.
330. Susan Schwartz, Corrine's daughter from a previous marriage.
331. The first case is known as *Friedlander I.* This 1961, Washington Supreme Court case settled the divorce case between Papa Jack and my grandmother, Elizabeth, who we called Nanny. The case turned on whether Papa Jack's interest in Friedlander & Sons was separate or community property. If it was community, he would have to split it with Nanny. If separate, it was all his. The court said – Jack – it's all yours. Nanny got screwed. *See Friedlander V. Friedlander*, 58 Wn.2d 288, 362 P.2d 352 (1961)

     After airing his dirty laundry in the court record for all to see in 1961, Papa Jack didn't want to do that again. So, before he married Polly, with whom he had been having an affair for five years while married to Nanny, he insisted on a prenup which stated each party would keep their separate property in the event of divorce. But when the divorce came, Polly contested the prenup. The court, In *Friedlander II*, threw out the prenup because the terms had not been sufficiently explained to Polly to allow her to make a sound decision. "The prospective spouse," the court states, "must sign the agreement freely and voluntarily on independent advice with full knowledge of her rights... It is clear that defendant did not have such advice prior to signing the agreement." *Friedlander v. Friedlander,* 80 Wn.2d 293, 494 P.2d 208 (1972).
332. Born April 15, 1865.
333. Born March 1866.
334. U.S. Census Report 1930, Seattle, WA.
335. Hanford, C. H., ed., *Seattle and Environs: 1852-1924*, Vol. III, 331.
336. U.S. Census Report 1920, Seattle, WA.

337. U.S. Census Report 1930, Seattle, WA.
338. See Jack Friedlander Interview, 4.
339. Id., 2. Papa Jack explained that Friedlander is a German name and his family is from Russia, implying that Friedlander couldn't have been their name in the old country. *Id.*
340. Id, 4-5.
341. Id. at 4.
342. US Census in 1880 was 89,000 and by 1890 it jumped to 133,000. US. Census Report, 1880.
343. Wolf, Rabbi Horace J., *History of the Jews of Rochester*, Published in Rochester Historical Society Publication Fund Series, Vol. II, 1923.
344. Jack Friedlander Interview, 6.
345. Hanford, *Seattle and Environs*, 331.
346. Jack Friedlander Interview, 2.
347. Id., 3.
348. Id. 2-3.
349. Jack Friedlander Interview. There is a cleaned-up version of this story that was reported by the Washington State Jewish Historical Society during their exhibit called *Who's Minding the Store*?: "Sam walked into [Harrison's pawn shop] to catch up with his old acquaintance. After some polite banter, Sam inquired about this $890. Harrison told him, 'Sam, I have invested it in the shop and I haven't made it back yet.' Sam promptly took off his coat, hung it on the peg behind the door and said, 'Well, my friend Harrison, you just got yourself a partner.'" Washington State Jewish Historical Society, "Who's Minding the Store: Celebrating 150 Years of Jewish Business & Commerce," "Friedlander & Sons," (2009).
350. The 1900 Seattle Census shows 80,671, up from 42,837 in 1890. History Link: 1900 Census.
351. History: Klondike Gold Rush. Klondike Gold Rush (history.com)
352. WSJHS Friedlander & Sons.
353. Klondike Gold Rush, 3
354. WSJHS, Friedlander & Sons.
355. Hanford, Seattle and Environ, Vol. III, 331.
356. Id. Sam's obituary in the Seattle Times, dated December 9, 1943 confirmed the arrival date of 1906.
357. The narrative in the WSJHS write up states that in 1912 Sam bought out Harrison's interest and renamed the store, S. Friedlander Jeweler. So, take your pick. Papa Jack's version is of course, more colorful.
358. I have a source that indicates Louis Friedlander attended the University of Washington. However, in his obituary in the Seattle Times, it states he attended Ohio State University. Seattle Daily Times, January 4, 1955.
359. Paul Middents, "Seattle's First Watchmakers 1869 -1889: In Bringing Time to the Public in the Pacific Northwest," Dec. 6, 2015.
360. Id.
361. Id.
362. Email correspondence from Rob Ketcherside, December 13, 2022.

363. *Id. See also,* Ketcherside, Rob, "Time Travel to Pike's Forest of Street Clocks," BA-KGROUND, Time Travel to Pike's Forest of Street Clocks - background
364. Named for Louis Friedlander.
365. My brother was never mugged either; however, his college roommate was mugged.
366. Volunteer Park was originally purchased by the city of Seattle in 1876 and designed as a city park by the Olmsted brothers in 1887, named Lakeview Park. It was later renamed City Park and in 1901 finally named Volunteer Park in honor of the volunteer soldiers in the Spanish-American War. *See* Volunteer Park, Historylink Volunteer Park (Seattle) - HistoryLink.org
367. Jack Friedlander Interview.
368. Seattle Public Schools, 1862 – 2000, Lowell Elementary School, HistoryLink.org, Posted 9/09/2013. Seattle Public Schools, 1862-2000: Lowell Elementary School - HistoryLink.org
369. Dorpat, Paul, Broadway High School, Seattle's First Dedicated high school, opens in 1902, HistoryLink.org Essay 3204, Posted 4/15/2001. Broadway High School, Seattle's first dedicated high school, opens in 1902. - HistoryLink.org
370. Hill Military Academy, Wikipedia, Hill Military Academy - Wikipedia
371. Thanks to Harry Stern for letting me know of this plaque.
372. It was during this year, 1916, that Anne played in a piano recital at the Sorrento Hotel: "Mrs. Sara Andrews Thorton will present her pupil Mrs. Anne Friedlander Singerman in a dramatic recital, at the Sorrento Hotel, on Wednesday evening May 24th at 8:15." Seattle Sunday Times, May 21, 1916. She and Louis must not have been completely estranged because the article notes, "musical accompaniment by Mr. Louis Singerman." *Id.*
373. They married sometime between 1937 and 1943. *See* Seattle Times, December 9, 1943 (obituary for Sam Friedlander names his daughter, Anne Fink) (Obituary contains a photo of Sam).
374. Seattle Jewish Transcript, Social Page, January 23, 1925.
375. Seattle Jewish Transcript, Social Page, July 1, 1924.
376. See *Louis Friedlander, Jeweler, Dies*, Seattle Times, January 4, 1955. *See also*, Family Search, Augusta Friedlander, NY Passenger Arrival (Hamburg to NY) Sep. 1, 1922.
377. Hanford, *Seattle and Environs*, 332. A Mystic Shrine is a "secret fraternal association." To join you must already be a Master Mason. Only once you reach this lofty goal are you are eligible to become a Shriner. "In the 32nd Degree," states the website for the Scottish Rite of Freemasonry, "the Scottish Rite Mason vows to serve as a 'True Soldier' who seeks truth and knowledge, demands freedom of voice, vote, and opinion for all people, combats spiritual tyranny with reason and truth, encourages men to be self-reliant and independent, and performs zealously his duties to God, his country, his family, his brethren, and himself." Scottish Rite of Freemasonry. https://scottishrite.org/blog/about/media-publications/journal/article/why-the-scottish-rite/
378. *Id.*
379. Jack Friedlander Interview, 14.
380. Seattle Times, "S. Friedlander, Early Jeweler, Dies in Calif.," December 9, 1943.

381. "Friedlander Plays Host to 10,000 Visitors to Enlarged Establishment," Seattle Times, October 6, 1954.
382. Id.
383. "Friedlander's to Leave Downtown," Seattle Times, January 26, 1995
384. Seattle Times, July 1, 1994.
385. Marjorie died April 7, 2004. Seattle Times, May 9, 2004. Their son Paul Jr. has no children and John Louis has three, Laura, Benjamin and Sam. *See* Friedlander Family Tree.
386. More on the wedding in the Staadecker chapter.
387. Goldfarb Interview.
388. Id.
389. Trieger, Ray, Interview by Karen Treiger, March 25, 2018.
390. My older brother, Louis, mispronounced the Yiddish name for grandmother – Bubbi.
391. Ray Treiger Interview.
392. Id.
393. Shim's legal name was Mark Elyn, but we called him Shim, a shortened version of his Hebrew name *Avraham Shimshon*.
394. Elyn, Shim, Interview by Karen Treiger, January 24, 2018.
395. Ray Treiger Interview. The "son" was Martin Selig, who as an adult became a well-known real estate developer.
396. Treiger, Irwin, Book of Original Poems (1977). He wrote this poem at approximately age 11.
397. Age 14.
398. Note spelling change from poem.
399. Treiger, Irwin, *My Ambition*, Vol. 10, Number 4, May 28, 1948, page 2.
400. The Jewish Sabbath, which is from Friday at sundown until Saturday at sundown.
401. Ray Treiger, Interview.
402. A Succah is a temporary dwelling built outdoors in which Jews eat (and sometimes sleep) during the holiday of Sukkot. *See* Sukkah, Wikipedia, Sukkah - Wikipedia
403. Elyn Interview.
404. Census Report, Seattle, 1940.
405. Treiger, Irwin, Interview by Avraham Treiger, 2011.
406. Synagogue. He attended Bikur Cholim, where he sat in the very back row and gave candy to the kids.
407. Ray Treiger Interview.
408. Irwin Treiger Interview.
409. Demydivka, Wikipedia https://en.wikipedia.org/wiki/Demydivka; Yahad in Unum; JewishGen https://www.jewishgen.org/Ukraine/GEO_town.asp?id=442; https://www.jewishgen.org/Communities/community.php?usbgn=-1037610
410. Irwin Treiger Interview.
411. Id.
412. Id.

413. Schmaltz was seen as a delicacy. Ray Treiger Interview; Irwin Treiger Interview.
414. Lowenstein, Steven, *The Jews of Oregon: 1850-1950*, Portland, Jewish Historical Society of Oregon (1987), 74.
415. Irwin Treiger Interview. Joseph and Mary Shank are listed in the 1920 Portland Census as owning a metal manufacturing business. Joseph and Mary were born in the United States (Minnesota and North Dakota respectively), but their parents were born in Russia. In 1920, they were both 36 years old and had two sons, Edward A. (age 13) and Roland M (age 12). 1920 U. S. Census.
416. History of Portland, Oregon. Wikipedia. History of Portland, Oregon - Wikipedia
417. It was the great success of the Portland World Fair that led to Seattle's own world fair in 1909.
418. Lowenstein, *Jews of Oregon*, 78.
419. Id., 96.
420. Id.
421. Olsen, Polina, *Stories from Jewish Portland*, Charleston, The History Press (2011), 41-42.
422. Id., 56.
423. Leeches are worms that "have been used for clinical bloodletting for at least 2,500 years. *See* "Leech," Wikipedia. Bloodletting is the "withdrawal of blood to prevent or cure illness and disease." It is no longer a common medical practice. *See* "Bloodletting," Wikipedia.
424. Olsen, Stories Over Jewish, Portland, 53.
425. Lowenstein, *Jews of Oregon,* 108.
426. Irwin Treiger Interview.
427. Id.
428. Lowenstein, *Jews of Oregon,* 130.
429. Id.
430. 1920 Population Census, Portland, OR, Sheet 14B.
431. "Ambitious Russian Youth Knocks and Finds Opportunity: Lad Who Entered Primary Classes in Portland School is Forging Ahead," Oregon Journal, March 11, 1917.
432. Yes, this was the name of the school, I couldn't believe it, but it was named after Josiah Failing, a Portland Mayor.
433. Ambitious Russian Youth Knocks & Finds Opportunity, *Oregon Journal*, March 11, 1917.
434. Id.
435. Id.
436. The Neighborhood House was "the social anchor of the neighborhood, and it sought to meet every need that was not being addressed somewhere else." Lowenstein, *Jews of Oregon*, 138. It was located at 2nd and Wood street and had clubs, classes, health services and athletic events, as well the Hebrew School." *Id.*
437. Id., 118.

438. *Id.* 120. During his Junior year at Reed, Bert was appointed to a position on the faculty of the University of Oregon to teach Hebrew language through the University's Extension program. Oregonian, October 8, 1922. Bert was not only the principal of the Hebrew School, but was also a member of Bnai Brith and President of the Zionist Organization of Portland. Oregonian, Sept. 19, 1925.
439. Lena was related to one of my favorite cousins, Shim Elyn, whose paternal grandmother was a Farber.
440. Oregonian, October 11, 1930.
441. *Family of Strangers*, 293.
442. *Id.* 225-26.
443. *Id.* 229.
444. According to Jonathan Sarna in his book *American Judaism*, the women of the Conservative Movement revolutionized American Jewish women's knowledge of ritual and traditions and thereby revived and preserved Judaism in the United States after the Holocaust. The future of American Jewry, Rose B. Goldstein, the wife of a Conservative rabbi stated in 1938, "is directly conditioned on the education of its womanhood." Throughout the 1940s Conservative sisterhoods initiated workshops and classes to "promote Sabbath observance and other Jewish home rituals." They published a book in 1941 called *The Jewish Home Beautiful* to inspire women and give them "background information, photos, songs, recipes, and decorating suggestions. *The Jewish Home Beautiful* proved wildly popular among women of every Jewish religious movement." Sarna, Jonathan, D., *American Judaism: A History*, Yale University Press (Hew Haven) (2nd ed.)(2019), 269.

    There was a feeling that after the destruction of European Jewry, these women were "spared for a sacred task – to preserve Judaism and its cultural, social, and moral values." *Id.*, 271. Through the 1950's the Conservative movement introduced innovations: men and women sitting together in synagogue; women being called to the Torah for an Aliya; and girls celebrating their bat mitzva. I imagine that by the time Lena took over as Executive Director of the League of Women of the United Synagogue in 1962, she felt great satisfaction in helping change the role of women in the Conservative Movement and for the six years she worked as the Executive Director played a major role in shaping the future roles of women in the Conservative Movement. Lena remarried and moved to Israel, dying in 1972.
445. Interview with Betty Lou Treiger.
446. Irwin Treiger Interview.
447. The High School of Commerce was eventually renamed Grover Cleveland High School.
448. "Commerce Graduates 39," Oregonian, June 16, 1921.
449. Irwin Treiger Interview.
450. "Spelling Contest Today: Pupils to Vie with Portland Business Men: Several Children Born in Foreign Countries will Be Put to Test in Unique Match," Oregonian, May 5, 1921.
451. Dated June 25, 1922
452. Dated July 9, 1922
453. Irwin Treiger Interview.

454. Sam was 27 years old and Rose was 22. There is a remarkable article in the Seattle Times, published one month before the wedding, which reported on a car accident:

"J.P. McAvoy, Kirkland lumberman, was in Seattle General Hospital today in a critical condition with a possible skull fracture, received yesterday in a collision between the automobile in which he was riding and one driven by Mrs. M.F. Solomon, 2718 E. Fir St. Mr. McAvoy was riding in the machine of Sam S. Treiger, 2765 E. Washington Street. Mr. Treiger and another passenger, Jacob Ottren of Kirkland were cut and bruised." Seattle Times, May 22, 1928. I really wonder what my grandfather was doing in his car with a Kirklan lumbermen. My father, in an interview, told the story of his father's car accident just before the wedding a bit differently: "My father had a car when he was up here on a trip to court my mother, his car barreled down Yesler Street and the car turned over – totally destroyed the car. No one was hurt, but that was the last time my father had a car until 1946." Irwin Treiger Interview.

455. Judd, Ron, *Studying Seattle's Roaring '20s History Might Help Us Get Through This Next Decade*, Seattle Times, Pacific NW Magazine, January 10, 2020. Prohibition began in Washington State in 1916 and nationally in 1920.
456. Pre-cursor to the Seattle Center.
457. Judd, Ron, *Studying Seattle's Roaring '20s History might Help Us Get Through This Next Decade*, The Seattle Times, Jan. 10, 2020.
458. *Id.*
459. *Family of Strangers*, 146.
460. *Id.*
461. *Id.*
462. *Id.* 137-38.
463. *Id.* 138-40.
464. *Id.* 144.
465. *See Id.* 140 & photo at 149.
466. *Id.* 142.
467. *Id.*
468. *Id.* 148-49.
469. *Studying Seattle's Roaring '20s history might help us get through this next decade.* For more on Redlining in Seattle, see Honig, Dough, *Redlining in Seattle*, HistoryLink.org Essay 21296, Posted October 29, 2021.
470. *Id.*
471. Recipe – one package of wide egg noodles – boil the noodles, then mix with one egg and two Tablespoons of oil, salt and pepper. Put in pan and cook for 30 minutes at 350 degrees. Delicious.
472. *Family of Strangers*, 145.
473. The killing fields with the bones of the Demydivka Jews was located by an organization called Yachad in Unum. The place of massacre was marked and it can be visited or seen on Yachad in Unums website map. *See* Yachan In Un. https://yiu.ngo/en

474. My father wrote a poem as a child so all would remember his birthdate: "Remember, remember, the 10th of September."
475. 3rd Day of Av, 5691.
476. Bert and Lena moved to New York in 1930; Claire and family moved to Philadelphia; Henry was living with Clair in Philadelphia attending Pharmacology school; and Sandry married Hannah Wallen of Philadelphia in 1933 and they settled in Philly. *See* Seattle Jewish Transcript, December 8, 1933.
477. Married Kaufman and moved to Philadelphia.
478. Sandry Treiger moved to Philadelphia and married Hannah Wallen in 1933. He died in Philly in 1960.
479. *See* Jewish Transcript, September 13, 1933.
480. Irwin Treiger Interview.
481. Ray Treiger Interview.
482. *Id.*
483. *Id.*
484. *Id.*
485. Public Schools: 1862-2000: Horace Mann School, History Link, Essay 10553 (2013), https://www.historylink.org/File/10553
486. Jewish Transcript, September 29, 1933.
487. Seattle PI, October 5, 1946. When I was a teenager rummaging around the storage rooms of our home, I found a stack of poems written by my dad that had been typed by my grandmother. I took the poems and retyped them on thick paper and found a place in Belltown that would bind them into a book: *Book of Original Poems*, By Irwin L. Treiger. We gave it to my dad in 1977 as a Chanukah gift. It's one of a kind.
488. *See* Seattle Public Schools, 1862-2000: Washington Middle School. Historylink.org. Seattle Public Schools, 1862-2000: Washington Middle School - HistoryLink.org
489. Treiger, Irwin, *My Ambition*, 1948, 1.
490. Ray Treiger Interview.
491. Irwin Treiger Interview.
492. Seattle PI, "Hadassah Meet to Open," April 30, 1958.
493. It read to Rose Treiger: "For your selfless devotion to the high ideals of Hadassah, and for your zealous service to the Jewish people in Israel and the United States, this Service Award is gratefully bestowed as a mark of our esteem and hope for even greater achievements in the future."
494. *Family of Strangers*, 145.
495. Irwin Treiger Interview.
496. *Naches* is a Yiddish word, loosely translated as pride.
497. *See* Seattle High Schools Announce Top Students, Seattle Daily Times, May 27, 1951.
498. There were 200 entries.
499. "Five Win History Contest Award: Group Now Faces State Finals in U.S. Meet," PI (1950 or 1951).
500. "Treiger Receives Bond From Judge As History Award," Seattle PI, Feb. 16, 1951. *See also Hearst History Winner Named*, San Antonio Light, January 21, 1951.

501. Ray Treiger Interview.
502. "Three Firms, Transit Driver, Hit by Robbers Overnight," Seattle Daily Times, January 14, 1950, p.2.
503. *Bandits Assault Store Owner*, Seattle PI, April 8, 1960.
504. *Id.*
505. *Storeowner Slugged by Robber*, Seattle Daily Times, January 16, 1964.
506. *Id.*
507. Irwin Treiger, Interview.
508. Treiger, Irwin, Letter to Henry Shuster, March 19, 2010.
509. Interview with Shim (Mark) Elyn, (2018).
510. *Id.*
511. *Id.*
512. Twersky, Reva, "In the Footsteps of my Grandmother," Chapter I, 2.
513. *Id.*
514. *Id.*
515. Interview with Sam Steinberg & Reuben Steinberg by the Seattle Jewish Archive Project, June 8, 1972. When Sam and Chayim Leib arrived in New York in 1910, they were processed through Ellis Island. Ellis Island, which opened in 1892, was a very busy hub of immigrant processing. Ellis Island was located 1.5 miles west of the southern tip of Manhattan. Chayim Leib and Sam entered the U.S. through this portal.
516. *Id.*
517. *Id.*
518. Interview with Shim Elyn.
519. Interview with Riva Steinberg, Shamke, Nizkor, Vol. II, No. 2, Washington State Jewish Historical Society, July 1986.
520. Elyn Interview, *Chayim* is Hebrew for life.
521. Interview Irwin Treiger, Sheldon Steinberg and Shim Elyn, by Avraham Treiger (2011).
522. Interview of Irwin Treiger by Shoshana Goldberg and Avraham Treiger (2011).
523. Interview with Riva Steinberg, Nizkor.
524. Pale of Settlement, Wikipedia.
525. Elyn Interview.
526. Riva Steinberg Interview.
527. *Id.*
528. Elyn Interview.
529. *Id.*
530. *Id.*
531. Riva Steinberg Interview.
532. *Id.*
533. *Id.*
534. Elyn Interview.
535. Irwin Treiger Interview.
536. Elyn Interview.
537. *Id.*

538. Id.
539. Id.
540. Id.
541. Id.
542. Id.
543. See e.g., Numbers, 1:10.
544. Elyn Interview.
545. Bagley, *History of Seattle*, 558.
546. Id.
547. Sam Steinberg and Reuben Steinberg Interview. See also, summary of Steinberg on-line file in the University of Washington Special Collections.
548. Interview with Treiger, Steinberg & Elyn.
549. Sam Steinberg and Reuben Steinberg Interview.
550. Id.
551. Id.
552. Id.
553. Id.
554. See Summary of Steinberg file in on-line University of Washington Special Collections.
555. Interview with Steve Steinberg, June 12, 2023.
556. Id.
557. Id.
558. Id.
559. Elyn Interview.
560. See Eals, Clay, "Bikur Cholim Synagogue Now the Langston Hughes Performing Arts Center," Seattle Here and Now, September 26, 2019.
561. Interview with Treiger, Steinberg & Elyn.
562. Elyn Interview.
563. Id.
564. Twersky, Reva, "In the Footsteps of My Grandmother."
565. Elyn Interview.
566. Id.
567. In 1929, the Jewish Transcript notes a club for single young women in the Orthodox Jewish community called the Queen Esther Club. One gathering on February 10, 1925, "Miss Sylvia Lascowitz gave the story of Queen Esther which was both interesting and educational. Miss Freda Block gave two recitations which were entertaining. Miss Rose Steinberg talked on current events of the day and spoke of the Jewish emigration." Seattle Jewish Transcript, February 10, 1925.
568. "Religious School Closes," Seattle Jewish Transcript, June 3, 1924.
569. See Treiger Family chapter for more on Sam and Rose Treiger.
570. Seattle Daily Times, September 17, 1980.
571. Seattle Daily Times, May 7, 1968.
572. Seattle Daily Times, March 18, 1982.
573. The prayer for the dead is said daily for 11 months after death.
574. Interview with David Twersky, November 20, 2023.

575. Seattle Daily Times, July 22, 1973.
576. Seattle Daily Times, June 3, 1962.
577. Seattle PI, December 12, 1989.
578. Jack Friedlander Interview.
579. *Id.*
580. *Id.*
581. Betty Lou Treiger Interview.
582. Jack Friedlander Interview.
583. *Id.*
584. *Id.*
585. Music director at Temple and future father-in-law of Betty Lou's sister Jackie.
586. Interview with Irwin and Betty Lou Treiger, by Avraham Treiger (2011).
587. Seattle Times, Society Page, August 18, 1957.
588. "Mrs. Degree" is getting married before graduating college.
589. Kvidera, Max, *The Tax Man Cometh*, Seattle Business Monthly, January 2007, p. 50.
590. Betty Lou and Irwin Treiger Interview.
591. *Id.*
592. *Id.*
593. *Id.*
594. *Id.*
595. Treiger, Irwin, *Book of Original Poems*, (unpublished).
596. Irwin Treiger Interview.
597. Treiger, Irwin, speech given to Jewish Federation of Great Seattle Cardozo Society, May 28, 1997.
598. Betty Lou Treiger Interview.
599. Becker, Paula, Stein, Alan, & The History Link Staff, "The Future Remembered: The 1962 Seattle World's Fair and It's Legacy," Seattle, Seattle Center Foundation (2011), 8.
600. *Id.*
601. *Id.* at 76-77.
602. The Fun Forest is sadly no longer part of the Seattle Center complex.
603. "The Future Remembered," at 94-95; 154-61; 171-74.
604. Interview with Victor Alhadeff, (2019)
605. Kvidera, "The Tax Man Cometh."
606. Betty Lou Treiger Interview.
607. "Resourceful Leader to Call Signals in Women's Division," Seattle Jewish Transcript, 1973.
608. *Id.*
609. Treiger, Betty Lou, Speech at Jewish Federation of Greater Seattle Lion of Judah Luncheon.
610. Bellevue American, September 15, 1966.
611. Interview with James F. Tune, (2019).
612. *Id.*
613. *Id.*

614. *See* Obituary in Seattle Times, October 21, 2013; *See also*, Barlety, Nancy, Irwin Treiger 79, tax lawyer and civic leader, Seattle Times, October 21, 2013.
615. Betty Lou Treiger Interview.
616. Bogle & Gates dissolved in 1991 and after the dissolution Irwin went to work for Dorsey Whitney, but after a few years, joined Stoel Rives and practiced there until he died in 2013.
617. Worth, Mark, "Who Really Runs Seattle?" Seattle Weekly, November 12, 1998.
618. Hobbs, Richard, S., *Our Brother's Keeper: The Life of Sam Israel*, Seattle, The Samis Foundation (2021) at 107.
619. *Id.* at 106-07.
620. *Id.* at 107.
621. *Id.* at 179-80.
622. *Id.* at 189.
623. Treiger Speech/Chamber of Commerce Annual Meeting September 24, 1993.
624. Tune Interview.
625. Mahoney, Sally Gene, *Profile: Treiger, Tax Lawyer in a Changing Profession*, The Seattle Times, August 5, 1986.
626. *Id.*
627. Interview with Norman Rice by Karen Treiger (2019).
628. *Id.*
629. *Id.*
630. Treiger, Cardozo Society Speech.
631. *Id.*
632. *Id.*
633. Antidefamation League (ADL), Press Release, "U.S. Antisemetic Incidents Skyrocketed 360% in Aftermath of attack in Israel, according to Latest ADL Data," January 9, 2024; updated January 17, 2024.
634. Lipstadt, Deborah E., *Antisemitism: Here and Now*. New York: Schocken Books, 2019.
635. Cone, et. al, *Family of Strangers*, 252.
636. *Id.*, 17.
637. Washington State Jewish Historical Society, *The Jewish Experience in Washington State: A Chronology 1845-2005*, 3rd edition (Seattle 2006).
638. Sam Treiger moved to Seattle in 1928 when he married my grandmother, Rose Steinberg.
639. Jacobs, Joseph, "Jewish Population of the United States," Memoir of the Bureau of Jewish Statistics of the American Jewish Committee, in the *American Jewish Yearbook*, 1911, 336, 339, 377. In 1911 in the entire United States there were approximately 2.4 million Jews, which amounted to 2.5% of the population. *Id.*
640. Dinnerstein, *Anti-Semitism in America*, 84-86. "The action taken by Harvard [to impose quotas]," Dinnerstein writes, "inspired other institutions. Columbia, Princeton, Yale, Duke, Rutgers, Barnard, Adelphi, Cornell, Johns Hopkins, Northwestern, Pann State, Ohio State, Washington and Lee, and Universities of Cincinnati, Illinois, Kansas, Minnesota, Texas, Virginia and Washington." *Id.*, 85-86.
641. Irwin Treiger Interview. He got a job at Bogle & Gates and rose to be managing partner.

642. Egan, *A Fever in the Heartland: The Ku Klux Klan's Plot to Take Over America, and the Woman Who Stopped Them* (New York: Viking Press, 2023), 131.
643. *Id.* 175-76.
644. *See Family of Strangers*, 256. Those clubs that steadfastly refused to admit Jews finally changed their policy when in 1972 Governor Daniel Evans signed a law into effect denying Class H liquor licenses and discounted liquor to private clubs that excluded minorities from memberships. This ended the discriminatory practice rather quickly. *Id*, 257.
645. Goldfarb Interview, *See* Seattle Times, October 21, 1923 (announcing the formation of Washington Golf & Country Club – the original name of the club). Glendale moved to Bellevue in 1955 and still exists as a Golf Club that is open to all who wish to join. The person who purchased the golf club in south Seattle in 1955 retained the property as a golf club, renaming it Glen Acres Gold Club. *See* Early History of Glen Acres Golf & Country Club, Seattle, WA.
646. Jack had a Kippah on his head, identifying him as a Jew.
647. Nirenberg, David. *Anti-Judaism: The Western Tradition.* New York: W. W. Norton Press, 2014.
648. Walters, *Psychology of Searching*, 132.
649. Taylor, Daniel, *The Healing Power of Stories: Creating Yourself Through the Stories of Your Life*, Double Day, New York, (1966), 21.
650. At this writing, my son, Jack, and daughter-in-law, Emma are expecting a baby in February of 2025 and my daughter, Shoshana and son-in-law Micha are expecting a baby in June. So (may they be born at a good time), my dividend count may increase to seven in 2025.

ABOUT THE AUTHOR

Karen Treiger is a 5th generation Seattlite, who attended Mercer Island High School, University of Washington, Barnard College and NYU Law School, where she served as the Editor in Chief of the NYU Law Review. She practiced law in Seattle, but left her law practice in 2015 to write a book about her in-law's Sam and Esther Goldberg's remarkable survival in Poland during World War II under Nazi rule. The book, *My Soul is Filled with Joy: A Holocaust Story* was published in 2018 and won the PNWA Nancy Pearl Book Award for Best Memoir and the Bronze Medal in World History from the Independent Publisher's Association. Karen's new book is about her Seattle family's unique history and contribution to Seattle's business and Jewish communities. Karen is an active volunteer with her synagogue, Minyan Ohr Chadash and with Limmud Seattle. She is married to Dr. Sheldon Goldberg and has four children and is thrilled to have five grandchildren.

www.ingramcontent.com/pod-product-compliance
Lightning Source LLC
LaVergne TN
LVHW090003070725
815367LV00004B/14
* 9 7 8 1 6 8 4 9 2 4 0 0 4 *